FATHERS, FAMILIES AND RELATIONSHIPS
Researching everyday lives

Edited by Esther Dermott and Caroline Gatrell

First published in Great Britain in 2019 by

Policy Press
University of Bristol
1-9 Old Park Hill
Bristol
BS2 8BB
UK
t: +44 (0)117 954 5940
pp-info@bristol.ac.uk
www.policypress.co.uk

North America office:
Policy Press
c/o The University of Chicago Press
1427 East 60th Street
Chicago, IL 60637, USA
t: +1 773 702 7700
f: +1 773-702-9756
sales@press.uchicago.edu
www.press.uchicago.edu

British Library Cataloguing in Publication Data
A catalogue record for this book is available from the British Library

Library of Congress Cataloging-in-Publication Data
A catalog record for this book has been requested

ISBN 978-1-4473-3150-6 paperback
ISBN 978-1-4473-3147-6 hardcover
ISBN 978-1-4473-3151-3 ePub
ISBN 978-1-4473-3152-0 Mobi
ISBN 978-1-4473-3148-3 ePdf

Cover design by Hayes Design
Front cover image: 'rise and shine' by Giles Penny, MRBS, RWA, copyright 2017
Printed and bound in Great Britain by CPI Group (UK) Ltd, Croydon, CR0 4YY

For:

Lance Dermott (ED)

Max Mizrahi Simon (CG)

Contents

List of figures, tables and boxes

Figure

Tables

Boxes

Notes on contributors

Maria Letizia Bosoni is Assistant Professor at the Catholic University of Milan, Italy, and a member of both the Family Studies and Research University Centre (Catholic University). Her research interests are work–family reconciliation and fatherhood. Publications include 'Between change and continuity: fathers and work–family balance in Italy' (with Elisabetta Crespi and Isabella Ruspini) in *Balancing work and family in a changing society: The fathers' perspective* (edited by E. Crespi and I. Ruspini, Palgrave Macmillan, 2016), and, with Sarah Baker, 'The intergenerational transmission of fatherhood: a comparative study of the UK and Italy' in the journal *Families, Relationships and Societies* (2015).

Simon Burnett currently works for KPMG and has previously worked in the private, public and third sectors. He has expertise in working with financial services organisations in human resources transformation, people risk and culture. He has led and delivered change programmes, developed behavioural, financial and diversity analytics, and improved business processes, policies and benchmarking capabilities. He published a single-authored, research-based book, *The happiness agenda: A modern obsession* (Palgrave Macmillan, 2012), analysing how organisations and governments increase happiness and wellbeing at work. He has also co-authored multiple peer-reviewed articles and book chapters on wellbeing, flexible working practices, engagement and gender.

Rita Chawla-Duggan is a Lecturer in Education at the University of Bath. After graduating and practising as a teacher, she trained in educational ethnography and completed a PhD in childhood ethnography, researching social influences on children's learning in India. She has conducted ethnographic research with children in England, Japan, Ghana and India. Her recent research investigates the use of visual methods, early childhood development, and social influences on young children's learning, especially fathering. She is currently leading an international project funded by the British Academy/Leverhulme Foundation on paternal engagement in home learning environments, using digital visual methods.

Kristian Daneback is Professor of Social Work at the University of Gothenburg, Sweden. His research interest is how new technologies influence various social phenomena and aspects of everyday life.

Research topics so far have focused on sexuality and the internet, parenting and the internet, and cyberbullying. Another, methodological, focus is on how technology can be used for data collection. Professor Daneback is also Associate Editor of the journal *Cyberpsychology: Journal of Psychosocial Research on Cyberspace*.

Esther Dermott is Professor of Sociology at the University of Bristol. Her expertise is in families, parenting, intimacy, poverty and gender, and she has published widely on these topics. She has a longstanding research interest in fatherhood, using both quantitative and qualitative methods, and publications include *Intimate fatherhood* (Routledge, 2008) and a special issue of the journal *Families, Relationships and Societies* (2015, edited with Tina Miller). She is Co-Editor of *The Sociology of Children and Families* Policy Press book series, Co-Editor of Open Space on *Families, Relationships and Societies*, and a board member of the European Sociological Association Research Network on Families and Relationships.

Caroline Gatrell is Professor of Organization Studies at University of Liverpool Management School. Her research centres on family, work and health. From a socio-cultural perspective, she examines how working parents (both fathers and mothers) manage boundaries between paid work and everyday lives. In so doing, she explores interconnections between gender, bodies and employment, including theorising on masculinity and work, as well as development of the concepts 'maternal body work' and 'pregnant presenteeism'. Her work is published in leading journals, including *Human Relations; Sociological Review; Gender, Work and Organization*; and *Families, Relationships and Societies*. She is Co-Editor in Chief of the *International Journal of Management Reviews*.

Jonathan Ives is a Senior Lecturer in Biomedical Ethics and Law, and Deputy Director of the Centre for Ethics in Medicine at Bristol Medical School, where he is also Co-Director of Postgraduate Research. His research interests focus primarily on methodology in bioethics and the ethics and sociology of fatherhood, families and reproduction, but he also publishes (inter alia) in research ethics, end-of-life ethics, mental health and a range of other topics in medical ethics. He is a section editor (Methodology in Bioethics) for *BMC Medical Ethics* and associate editor for *Health Care Analysis*. He sits on the Royal College of General Practitioners Ethics Committee, and is Co-Editor of *Empirical bioethics: Practical and theoretical perspectives* (Cambridge University Press, 2017).

Carmen Lau-Clayton is a Reader in Family and Cultural Dynamics and a Senior Lecturer in Child and Family Welfare Studies at Leeds Trinity University. She is also the Programme Leader for the Working with Children, Young People and Families undergraduate degree programme.

Sara Mazzucchelli is Assistant Professor at the Centre for Family Studies and Research, Catholic University of Milan, Italy. She is interested in the transition to motherhood and the relationship with employers, as well as leave (maternity, paternity, parental) and interconnections with parental employment, early childhood services, and policies linking work, family and gender. She is currently part of an interdisciplinary research group (psychologists and sociologists) focused on delivering training activities and action research for companies and workers. She has recently published (with Giovanna Rossi) a special issue on the Italian family in the *Journal of Comparative Family Studies.*

Tina Miller is Professor of Sociology at Oxford Brookes University. Her qualitative longitudinal research interests span family lives, transitions and unfolding experiences of managing caring and paid work. The ways in which gender and structural features shape daily experiences of these practises are also ongoing research concerns. Her work has attracted international attention and she regularly advises policy makers, non-governmental organisations and the media. Her publications include *Making sense of motherhood: A narrative approach* (Cambridge University Press, 2005) and *Making sense of fatherhood: Gender, caring and work* (Cambridge University Press, 2011), and her third monograph, *Making sense of parenthood: Caring, gender and family lives*, was published in 2017 by Cambridge University Press.

Susan Milner, a member of the Oxford Network of European Fatherhood Research, is Reader in European Politics at the University of Bath. With Professor Abigail Gregory (University of Salford) she conducted research, funded by the French family-benefits agency, on fathers' access to and use of work-family measures in French and British workplace organisations; this research was reported in *Community, Work & Family, Men & Masculinities* and the *Journal of Families, Societies and Relationships*. With Dr Rita Chawla-Duggan, she evaluated a local authority initiative to involve fathers in children's education, and conducted a follow-up project using visual technologies to investigate the home learning environment. She is currently researching the provision of 'father-friendly' benefits in private-sector work organisations.

Lars Plantin is Professor of Social Work at the Malmö University, Sweden. His main area of expertise is family sociology with a special focus on fatherhood. Together with Kristian Daneback, he was responsible for the research project Parenthood and Internet: New Arenas and Information Pathways on Modern Parenthood. He has also published articles and books on themes such as reproductive health, HIV, migration, and work and family life.

Jon Symonds is a Lecturer in the School for Policy Studies at the University of Bristol. His research interests include fatherhood, parenting and social work, with a particular emphasis on applying conversation analysis to understand and improve professional practice. He has used this approach in previous research investigating GP appointments, calls to GP surgeries and social work assessments of disabled adults. He completed his doctoral research in 2015, which investigated how family support workers spoke about fathers in initial telephone calls.

Allan Westerling is Associate Professor in Social Psychology at Centre for Childhood, Youth and Family Life Research, Department of People and Technology, Roskilde University. His research interests include family life, social psychology of everyday life, research methods and early childhood education. He is Co-Editor of *Doing good parenthood: Ideals and practices of parental involvement* (Palgrave Macmillan, 2017). He has been a member of the scientific committee of the European Society on Family Relations since 2011 and the President-Elect since 2016.

Therése Wissö is a Senior Lecturer at the Department of Social Work, Gothenburg University. Her overall research interest is family life and parenthood. Ongoing research projects are on fathering, young parenthood and foster parenthood. Recent publications include 'Fathers and parental support in everyday family life: on informal support in Sweden beyond the auspices of the welfare state' in a special issue of *Families, Relationships and Societies* (2015). She is currently working on research projects concerning young fathers and parents with children in foster care.

Acknowledgements

This book has its origins in ONEFaR (Oxford Network of European Fatherhood Researchers) initially convened through a British Academy dissemination event held by Professor Tina Miller and then through a research grant from the Swedish Riksbankens Jubileumsfond held by Professor Lars Plantin. It was discussions between members that lead to the idea for this book and funded events to develop our ideas. We would also like to acknowledge our colleagues at Policy Press, in particular Shannon Kneis, Helen Davis and Jess Mitchell for patience and advice in getting the book to completion.

Introduction

Caroline Gatrell and Esther Dermott

Fathers, and their parenting, have never had such a high profile. Questions are raised continually by politicians and policy makers, and in the press and media regarding what it means to be a father, and how fathers are managing parenthood in the context of changing demographics and cultural expectations (Working Families, 2017). Both everyday fathering and the situations of celebrity fathers are increasingly a central focus within news and features. Recent debates have included whether fatherhood is less challenging among the privileged (following comments by the UK's Prince William that he finds fathering hard) to what the nature of paternal–child relationships should be post-separation or divorce (for example, in the recent case of actor Brad Pitt), alongside more prosaic attempts to document the everyday experiences and reflections of fathers in mainstream lifestyle columns and blogs that receive large volumes of traffic.

Over the past 30 years, there has been an extraordinary growth in research on fathers, fatherhood and fathering (Featherstone, 2009; Özbilgin et al, 2011, Mazzuccelli and Bosoni, 2011; Miller and Dermott, 2015). Studies of everyday lives, attitudes and practices among men with children have become a site of intense investigation across a range of disciplines including psychology, sociology, social policy, geography, law and history as well as more applied areas such as social work and health (Gatrell et al, 2012). Central questions addressed in this research include: What constitutes 'a father' and 'fathering'?; How has fatherhood changed over time? To what extent do men's experiences of paternity vary depending on age, ethnicity, class and other significant social characteristics and across countries? More recently, within the burgeoning field of fatherhood research itself, new questions have been raised over the emphasis that should be placed on studying the practices of individual men who identify as fathers, parental practices that are defined as 'doing' fathering, and broader cultural representations of fatherhood (Dermott and Miller, 2015).

The range of research questions posed by academics exploring fatherhood has, in turn, led to the adoption of a wide range of methods. This tendency is perhaps exacerbated by the fact that research on fatherhood, although often centred in the social sciences, has no one single disciplinary base. Fatherhood researchers, as a group, then tend

1

to have adopted a pragmatic approach to methodology using qualitative, quantitative, and mixed-method research designs as appropriate to the question in hand. Perhaps it is precisely because of the focus on methods as a tool rather than as something to be written about in terms of epistemological questions that writing about how research on fathers is, and can be, conducted has not previously emerged. Academic publications have of course documented their methods and, at times, reflected on questions of reflexivity and positionality in conducting qualitative research on or with fathers, it is safer, as more men are entering the field (see McKee and O'Brien, 1982 for an early example).

Thus far, perhaps surprisingly given the increased social and scholarly focus on fathering (Gregory and Milner, 2009), few texts have been devoted specifically to exploring and detailing research methods for investigating fathers' everyday lives and experiences. *Fathers, families and relationships: Researching everyday lives* seeks to address this omission. The collection emerged from discussions within the Oxford Network of European Fatherhood Researchers (ONEFaR), a small group of fatherhood researchers from across Europe that previously worked together on the special issue of the journal *Families, Relationships and Societies* edited by Esther Dermott and Tina Miller and published in 2015, and as editors we are grateful for the contributions made by our colleagues to this endeavour. The purpose of this edited collection is therefore twofold: to highlight recent wide-ranging substantive research on fatherhood, and to explore how researching fatherhood can shed light on particular methods and methodological approaches.

First, each of the chapters discusses how different research questions and methods can contribute to better understanding of contemporary fathers, fatherhood and fathering. Given the enhanced methodological diversity and increased sophistication of methods across the social sciences, embracing qualitative and quantitative approaches, traditional (such as interviewing) and contemporary approaches (such as netnography and visual methods), general 'handbooks' offering basic introductions to social research have, increasingly, limited use for advanced researchers and students. This collection addresses a demand for exemplars of how research on fathers and fathering has been carried out in practice, and in recent research projects. The chapters in this book aim to make more transparent the range and perspectives of research methods employed. As such, we hope that it will be adopted by those beginning to research fathers as a guide both to pertinent research questions and the methods they could consider adopting themselves, as well as those who are more experienced but are interested in new approaches that could complement their existing knowledge. While we therefore adopt a paradigmatically mixed-methods approach to research, we do not necessitate that those who read the book follow suit.

Second, the book seeks explicitly to link detailed concerns about conducting individual projects to wider methodological debates concerning the value of different forms and sources of data, the negotiation of research relationships, and the impact of research findings on participants, policy makers, employers and a wider public. In so doing, it features 10 chapters in which leading fatherhood scholars share their research strategies and experiences in qualitative, longitudinal and quantitative methods within European and Scandinavian research teams. The chapters illustrate a mix of methods and methodologies embracing qualitative and quantitative approaches, 'one-off' projects and longitudinal studies, and visual and oral methods. It further reflects on debates around ethics, the role of the researcher and impact of research on the researcher, as well as research participants.

Below, we give a brief synthesis regarding how fatherhood research has developed in the late 20th and early 21st century. We then offer a broad overview of the research methods addressed in this edited collection and questions regarding the direction of future research agendas for fatherhood research.

Fatherhood research in the late 20th and early 21st century

As early as 1986, Charles Lewis identified a potential shift regarding enhanced paternal involvement with children's lives, depending on the hours worked by female partners. He observed a correlation, among heterosexual couples, between maternal employment status and paternal engagement with childcare, observing how the men in his study who 'arranged their work to fit in with their wives' employment … stood out as taking a highly involved role' (Lewis, 1986, p 107). In 1993, Michael Kimmel questioned the myth of 'organization man'. He looked beyond the requirement for fathers to share childcare (if mothers were working) and reflected on what he saw as an increased tendency for fathers within marriage to desire closer relationships with children. Beck and Beck Gernsheim linked observations regarding 'involved' or 'intimate' fathering to a shift in masculine priorities (see also Dermott and Miller, 2015, p 183), while in *The normal chaos of love* (1995) they argued that 'Parsonian' models, whereby fathers might previously have aligned themselves with breadwinner identities (leaving to mothers the responsibility for nurturing parent–child relationships [see Gatrell, 2005]) were outdated.

The reasons posited for such shifts in masculine priorities and identities were twofold.

First, Beck and Beck Gernsheim argued that changes in labour market practices concerning the erosion of linear careers and job security, combined with fears about relationship breakdown (prompted by high divorce rates), had led to men's re-evaluation of personal priorities. *The normal chaos of love* anticipated that demographic trends towards increasing precarity within jobs and marriages would prompt fathers to seek closer engagement in children's lives. While marriage and jobs might prove unstable and unreliable, relationships with children offered potentially a lifelong reward and might therefore be a more inviting prospect for personal paternal investment. Thus while 'Parsonian' breadwinner fathers in long-term adult relationships might previously have been content to allow maternal mediation of father–child relationships (Ribbens, 1994), late modern fathers were increasingly likely to seek direct and intense relationships with children. Second, Beck and Beck Gernsheim (1995) argued that heightened divorce rates combined with growing paternal emphasis on the value of father–child relationships meant that separated men were likely to seek to retain an active role in children's lives. This foreshadowed Smart and Neale's (1999) research on divorce and work by Collier (2012) on the rise in campaigning groups such as Fathers 4 Justice. While some separated or post-divorce fathers may lose contact with children, others fight hard to maintain and grow paternal-child relationships (Dermott, 2013; Phillip, 2013, 2014; Gatrell et al, 2015; Haux et al, 2015). In keeping with Beck and Beck-Gernsheims' predictions, it does appear that a modification of millennial paternal priorities has occurred, with fathers becoming 'more visible figures on the parenting landscape as contemporary ideas of fatherhood ... [have] shifted' (Dermott and Miller, 2015, p 183; see also Westerling, 2015). At the turn of the millennium, as theoretical explorations of fathering, paternal identities and work–life balance have unfolded, empirical research on fathers has developed apace. Reflecting on the rich array of work on fathers published from the 1990s onwards, we have observed three key developments demonstrated in research on fathering practices.

First, while fathers might in theory seek more involvement in children's lives with the motivation to do fatherhood 'well' (Ives, 2015), the achievement of such engagement remains in practice challenging. As both Dermott (2008) and Miller (2010) have observed, where heterosexual couples might intend, pre-parenthood, to share childcare, social and labour market practices (at least in neoliberal economies) tend to see employed men back at work shortly following the birth with mothers continuing, post-maternity leave to take the lead as primary careers. Even in locations with strong gender equality regimes, where paternal–child engagement is resourced, couples may still 'fall back' into gendered behaviours (O'Brien and Shemilt, 2003; Miller, 2011; Wissö and Plantin, 2015), with fathers prioritising work identities, as the pressures to earn income and meet employer demands regarding availability are raised (see also Kvande, 2005; Ellingsaeter and Leira, 2006; Lammi-Taskula, 2006). Where employed fathers do seek to persist in prioritising children and childcare – and despite social policies apparently intended to enhance work–life balance among 'parents' – fathers' work–family requirements are often unmet; especially in comparison with maternal needs, fathers may be treated as invisible (or at best, as secondary parents) within organisational contexts (Holter, 2007; Tracy and Rivera, 2010; Özbilgin et al, 2011; Milner and Gregory, 2015).

Second, where fathers succeed in prioritising relationships with children through the ring-fencing of 'quality time', both in marriage/ co-habitation and post-divorce, this may not be matched by a similar commitment to undertaking the relatively unrewarding domestic chores associated with running a household. While some fathers may 'cherry pick' and nurture rewarding relationships with children, it is often mothers who are left to pick up the more thankless tasks of cleaning, laundering and tidying (Gatrell, 2007; Neale and Smart, 2001).

Finally, we note how, although fatherhood research continues to grow and flourish, coverage is patchy, with a lack of focus on groups other than middle-class employed men. In a special issue of *Families, Relationships and Societies* edited by Dermott and Miller (2015), a need for further research on fathers who are young (Shirani, 2015), poorly resourced, of differing racial and cultural backgrounds and not in relationships with children's mothers, was noted (Dermott and Miller, 2015). Reflecting on how paternal identities and practices may be changing (and how more research on fathers, perhaps especially in relation to marginalised groups, is called for) led us, as editors of this collection, to reflect on how fatherhood is being researched, and on relationships between research methods employed in individual studies and wider methodological debates around the appropriateness (or otherwise) of different approaches, traditional and contemporary, qualitative and quantitative.

The chapters in this edited collection reflect on, and begin to address, some of these issues and omissions. Regarding the quantitative/ qualitative debate, the collection offers perspectives on 'the bigger picture' (Chapter Eleven), weighing up the relative merits of using new, digital resources versus existing collections of 'administrative' data to gain a broader picture of fatherhood practices than might be offered through qualitative work. In Chapter Ten, Allan Westerling reflects on the challenges of mixing methods, building a qualitative study on the basis of a quantitative research project, while in Chapter Three Bosoni and Mazzuccelli explore the benefits and problems located in drawing down data from extant and longitudinal surveys. In relation to longitudinal research, Tina Miller in Chapter Two offers a reflexive account of undertaking qualitative research exploring fatherhood and fathers' experiences over an extended time period. On the ethics of fatherhood research, Carmen Lau-Clayton and Jonathan Ives each offer a differing approach, the former examining strategies for managing ethical risks in research interviews with young fathers (Chapter Eight), and the latter considering the ethics and philosophy of researching fatherhoods from a personal perspective (Chapter One).

The remainder of chapters in the collection focus on how different research perspectives and methods might facilitate new or different ways of understanding how men interpret and practise fathering. Drawing on their own and others' research, authors examine how such interpretations may affect paternal practices and what the impact on fathering might be of social constraints (for example, employment or lack thereof, flexible working practices, and the importance of place). Thus, Lars Plantin and Kristian Daneback (Chapter Four) offer methodological reflections on researching fatherhood on the internet; Therése Wissö recounts her experience of adopting an ethnographic approach to researching fatherhood and place (Chapter Five); Simon Burnett and Caroline Gatrell analyse the impact, benefits and challenges of conducting interviews and focus groups with fathers through audio-only teleconferencing (Chapter Six); Susan Milner and Rita Chawla-Duggan consider how using visual technologies facilitates the exploration of children's perspectives on fathers (Chapter Seven); and Jon Symonds explains the use of conversation analysis for exploring how child welfare services engage (or fail to engage) fathers (Chapter Nine).

As a collection, the chapters in this edited volume combine to offer two perspectives on fatherhood research. The first, we believe, assists in developing research practice and perspective as the authors, drawing from their own experiences, reflect on the complexities of how fatherhood research might be conducted so as to better understand the situation of contemporary paternity. We hope that these reflections will offer new insights for advanced researchers and students of fatherhood and fathering practices, taking debate beyond what might be found in generalist or introductory handbooks. Additionally, the collection links the conducting of individual projects with broader methodological concerns around ethics and scope in relation to fatherhood research. Authors reflect on the ethical principles and practices involved in researching fathers, recounting how they considered the wellbeing of participants and, in some cases, of the research teams themselves. As such, we anticipate that the book will be of value to students who are interested in exploring how particular methods operate in practice, even if they are researching a different subject. The future research agenda regarding fatherhood research is likely to be one of enhanced growth and significance across the social sciences. We anticipate that, in this collection, we offer some unique and interdisciplinary insights into fatherhood research across Europe and Scandinavia that will facilitate imaginative and thoughtful research in the future.

References

Beck, U. and Beck-Gernsheim, E. (1995) *The normal chaos of love*, Chichester: John Wiley & Sons.

Collier, R.S. (2012) 'Law and the remaking of fatherhood in late modernity: reflections of family policy in England and Wales 1997–2010', in M. Oechsle, U. Mueller and S. Hess (eds) *Fatherhood in late modernity: Cultural images, social practices, structural frames*, Leverkusen/Farmington Hills: Barbara Budrich Publishers, pp 295-316.

Dermott, E. (2008) *Intimate fatherhood: A sociological analysis*, Abingdon: Routledge.

Dermott, E. (2013) *Fragile fathering: Negotiating intimacy and risk in parenting practice*, London: British Academy.

Dermott, E. and Miller, T. (2015) 'More than the sum of its parts? Contemporary fatherhood policy, practice and discourse', *Families, Relationships and Societies*, 4(2): 183-195.

Ellingsaeter, A. and Leira, A. (2006) *Politicising parenthood in Scandinavia: Gender relations in welfare states*, Bristol: Policy Press.

Featherstone, B. (2009) *Contemporary fathering: Theory, policy and practice*, Bristol: Policy Press.

Gatrell, C. (2005) *Hard labour: The sociology of parenthood*, Maidenhead: Open University Press.

Gatrell, C. (2007) 'Whose child is it anyway? The negotiation of paternal entitlements within marriage', *The Sociological Review*, 55(2): 353-373.

Gatrell, C., Burnett, S.B., Cooper C.L. and Sparrow P. (2012) 'Work-life balance and parenthood: a comparative and transdisciplinary review and analysis', *International Journal of Management Reviews*, 15(3): 300-316.

Gatrell, C.J., Burnett, S., Cooper, C.L.C and Sparrow, P. (2015) 'The price of love: The prioritisation of child care and income earning among UK fathers', *Families, Relationships and Society*, 4(2): 225-238.

Gregory, A. and Milner, S. (2009) Work-life balance – a matter of choice?', *Gender, Work and Organization*, 16: 1-13.

Haux, T., Platt, L. and Rosenberg, R. (2015) *Parenting and post-separation contact: What are the links?*, London: CASE LSE.

Holter, O. (2007) 'Men's work and family reconciliation in Europe', *Men and Masculinities*, 9(4): 425-456.

Ives, J. (2015) 'Theorising the "deliberative father": compromise, progress and striving to do fatherhood well', *Families, Relationships and Societies*, 4(2): 281-294.

Kimmel, M. (1993) 'The new organization man', *Harvard Business Review*, November, pp 50-63.

Kvande, E. (2005) 'Embodying male workers as fathers in a flexible working Life', in D. Morgan, B. Brandth and E. Kvande (eds) *Gender, bodies and work*, Aldershot: Ashgate, pp 137-162.

Lammi-Taskula, J. (2006) 'Nordic men on parental leave: Can the welfare state change gender relations', in A. L. Ellingsæter and A. Leira (eds) *Politicising parenthood in Scandinavia: Gender relations in welfare states*, Bristol: Policy Press, pp 79-99.

Lewis, C., (1986) *Becoming a father*, Milton Keynes: Open University Press.

Mazzucchelli, S. and Bosoni, M.L. (2011) 'Priorità di carriera e scelte di coppia. Un'analisi sociologica della letteratura internazionale' ('Priority career and couple choices. A sociological analysis of the international literature'), *LA FAMIGLIA*, 42 (September): 63-80.

McKee, L. and O'Brien, M. (eds) (1982) *Father figure*, London: Tavistock.

Miller, T. (2010) *Making sense of fatherhood: Gender, caring and work*, Cambridge: Cambridge University Press.

Miller, T. (2011) 'Falling back into gender? Men's narratives and practices around first-time fatherhood' *Sociology*, 45(6): 1094-1109.

Miller, T. and Dermott, E. (2015) 'Contemporary fatherhood: continuity, change and future', *Families, Relationships and Societies*, 4(2): 179-181.

Milner, S. and Gregory, A. (2015) 'Fathers, care and family policy in France: an unfinished revolution?' *Families, Relationships and Societies,* 4(2): 197-208.

Neale, B and Smart, C. (2001) 'Caring, earning and changing: Parenthood and employment after divorce?', in A. Carling, S. Duncan and R. Edwards (eds) *Analysing families: Morality and rationality in policy and practice*, Oxford: Routledge, pp 183-198.

O'Brien, M. and Shemilt, I. (2003) *Working fathers: Earning and caring*, London: Equal Opportunities Commission, available at www.workingbalance.co.uk/pdf/ueareport.pdf.

Özbilgin, M.T., Beauregard, T.A., Tatli, A. and Bell, M.P. (2011) 'Work-life, diversity and intersectionality: a critical review and research agenda', *International Journal of Management Reviews*, 13(2): 177-198.

Philip, G. (2013) 'Relationality and moral reasoning in accounts of fathering after separation or divorce: care, gender and working at "fairness"', *Families, Relationships and Societies*, 2(3): 409-424.

Philip, G. (2014) 'Fathering after separation or divorce: navigating domestic, public and moral spaces', *Families, Relationships and Societies*, 3(2): 219-233.

Ribbens, J. (1994) *Mothers and their children: A feminist sociology of childrearing*, London: Sage Publications.

Shirani, F. (2015) '"I'm bringing back a dead art": continuity and change in the lives of young fathers', *Families, Relationships and Societies*, 4(2): 253-266.

Smart, C. and Neale, B. (1999) *Family fragments?*, Cambridge: Polity Press.

Tracy, S.J. and Rivera, K.D. (2010) 'Endorsing equity and applauding stay-at-home moms: how male voices on work–life reveal aversive sexism and flickers of transformation', *Management Communication Quarterly*, 24: 3-43.

Westerling, A. (2015) 'Reflexive fatherhood in everyday life: the case of Denmark', *Families, Relationships and Societies*, 4(2): 209-223.

Wissö, T. and Plantin, L. (2015) 'Fathers and parental support in everyday family life: informal support in Sweden beyond the auspices of the welfare state', *Families, Relationships and Societies*, 4(2): 267-280.

Working Families (2017) *The modern families index, 2017*, Cambridge: Working Families, available at http://workingfamilies.org.uk/wp-content/uploads/2017/01/Modern-Families-Index_Full-Report.pdf.

ONE

Framing fatherhood: the ethics and philosophy of researching fatherhoods

Jonathan Ives

Introduction

This chapter presents a reflection on some of the interconnected philosophical, ethical and methodological challenges that have arisen in my own research on fatherhood and in response to my engagement with fatherhood research. In it, I draw on my personal and interdisciplinary perspective as a bioethicist conducting fatherhood research that combines philosophical, legal, sociological, empirical (qualitative) and ethical questions and methods. The themes that I have chosen to focus on represent topics that I have come to think of as important and interesting in the context of my own research, and which I hope will be of relevance, interest and import to most contemporary fatherhood research.

Framing fatherhood research for funding

It should be no surprise that, in a book about fatherhood research, I shall not be arguing that fatherhood research is a poor use of resources. However, neither is it clear to me that fatherhood research ought to be a priority where resource is scarce. On a global scale, and from a broadly utilitarian perspective, this should be obvious. When we compare the urgency of humanitarian need across the globe, the massive benefit that would be gained from increasing access to clean water, basic medicines, food and decent housing, it is not hard to see that the comparatively very minor problems associated with fatherhood in economically advantaged countries must be a pretty low priority. However, unless we accept the requirements of moral sainthood (Wolf, 1982) and redirect all our resource in ways that maximise global welfare, we can still think that it is justifiable to direct resource to research that addresses contemporary issues and problems in our own society – and research that supports parenting, parents and children seems to be *prima facie* justifiable. However, even compared with other forms of parenting research, fathers may come out relatively far down the list, and fatherhood researchers (certainly in my experience) often seem to struggle to make the case that research into fatherhood ought to be supported or prioritised.

The case for research funding may be easier to make if the proposed research addresses a clear area of need and/or addresses issues in vulnerable populations. If there is resistance to fatherhood research, then, it is potentially influenced by the idea that fathers, as men, are already relatively advantaged, both socially and economically – and research that benefits an already advantaged group may be less important than research that benefits a more disadvantaged group. This depends, however, on who the putative beneficiaries of fatherhood research are.

In my experience, particularly of attempting to attract research funding related to fathers, health and health services, I have found that the only justificatory narrative that has been effective is one that views fatherhood research as a means of benefiting groups other than fathers themselves, on the assumption that by researching and understanding fathers we can enable them to better fulfil their role in supporting others. This narrative can be framed, broadly, in two ways. One is in terms of fathers failing to do the minimum and therefore failing their families and society (the so-called 'feckless father' or the 'deadbeat dad' – see Westwood, 1996). The other is in terms of fathers being in a position to prevent or fix various problems. Either way, I have been increasingly troubled by the thought that this kind of framing implies something about the value of fathers as subjects of research. It implies that fatherhood is valued as a function – a means to achieving an end – but fathers as people are not important in their own right.

The failing father

This narrative addresses the putative problem of fathers who fail to perform economically or pastorally. Fathers who fail to perform economically are those fathers who do not contribute to the functioning of the family as an economic unit – in terms of financial provision or undertaking domestic labour. A father who does not contribute economically to the raising of his children creates a problem for the welfare state, which must pick up the bill. By engaging in research that understands and enables fathers to better fulfil their economic role, the state benefits.

A father who fails pastorally is unable or unwilling to provide the emotional and psychological support that generally typifies a 'healthy' father–child relationship and, it is argued, leads to optimal outcomes for children. Research that links sub-optimal child development to uninvolved fathers or negative father–child relationships, or that shows positive outcomes flowing from father engagement (for a good overview, see Sarkadi et al, 2008; Lamb, 2010) can be used to suggest that fathers who fail in their role create a problem for their children and for the state. By engaging in research that understands and enables fathers to better fulfil their pastoral role, the state and society benefits in terms of well-adjusted children and adults, and children benefit from having healthy paternal relationships that allow them to develop to their full potential.

The fixer father

This narrative frames fathers as able to prevent or 'fix' certain problems that contribute to negative outcomes for mothers and children. For example the Fatherhood Institute, a UK-based organisation that lobbies for father-friendly practices, produced a report in 2008 that presented the case for greater father involvement and engagement in the perinatal period, citing studies that show the impact fathers can have on, *inter alia*, mother and infant health behaviours, impact and recovery from post-natal depression, and breastfeeding success (Burgess, 2008). With regard to post-natal depression, the report outlines the deleterious effect on mothers and infants, and says of fathers:

> The father's functioning as a support person is key, since depressed new mothers receive more support from their partner than from any other individual, including medical staff. Can intervening with these men prove fruitful? Few interventions have been rigorously evaluated, and sample sizes are small. However, indications are positive. (p 10)

It then goes on to say: 'Fathers' own depression is also an issue for concern, not least because of its potential to exacerbate maternal depression' (p 11), and then later asks: 'When, and how, can fathers' behaviour 'buffer' the negative effects of mothers' depression on their babies?' (p 13).

This kind of narrative, which focuses on the father as someone who can fix a problem for others, can be used to justify fatherhood research. It also, however, suggests that the primary reason we are interested in, for example, the mental health of fathers is because of its outcomes for mothers and children.

My own experience of applying for funding for fatherhood research reinforces the unsurprising truth that, as with any other research area, there is no magic formula. Neither of these narratives guarantees success, but anecdotal experience suggests that because they frame the need for fatherhood research in terms of goods that go beyond those that accrue to fathers themselves, they have more chance of attracting funding. Sometimes, of course a different approach might be tried. For example, I have been involved in a bid for funding to explore fathers' roles in birthplace decision making. This project arose through discussion with health service providers, and the justificatory narrative that was developed placed fathers as neither failing in their role nor fixing a problem, but as a barrier to good decision making. Anecdotal experience suggested that fathers-to-be tend to be risk averse when it comes to birthplace decisions, favouring the perceived safety of a hospital setting to the home. This attitude, so said the narrative, influences birthplace decisions, leading to women choosing a hospital setting when it was not indicated – putatively leading to sub-optimal birth outcomes and higher costs. I was sceptical about this narrative, as I felt that it seemed to judge fathers, take a problematic normative position that assumed a risk-averse approach was wrong, and *a priori* reduced what is likely to be a very complex process to a simple 'us and them' problem. As well as not being comfortable with it intellectually, I was concerned that framing fathers as a barrier to good outcomes for mothers and children took a position that could be perceived as 'anti-father' and would be politically risky. This turned out to be the case, and the minimal feedback we received made a point of being critical of this framing. Despite the fact that this 'barrier' narrative was focused on goods for others, rather than for fathers themselves, it seemed to go too far by framing fathers themselves as the problem – which may be an interesting gender-political statement in itself. All of these narratives – father as failure, as fixer and as barrier – nonetheless are part of a wider 'problem' narrative, and this remains, to my mind, most likely fundable rationale for fatherhood research. This does, however, raise a series of interesting ethical questions.

What these 'problem' rationales have in common are that they premise the need for fatherhood research on fathers as a means of achieving some other good, and rarely on the needs of fathers themselves. In other words, fathers are the subject of research because they are instruments that achieve other ends, not because they are ends in themselves. This is also reflected, for example, in the justifications offered in policies to engage fathers in maternity care. The UK's Royal College of midwives provide the following rationale:

> *Since fathers are important influences on mother's health choices and experiences before, during and after the birth*, it benefits the whole family when maternity professionals make fathers feel welcomed and involved and prepare them for their role at the birth and afterwards. (RCM, 2011, p 12, emphasis added)

This raises an interesting ethical question insofar as this rationale for fatherhood research (and engagement with fathers in general) appears, at first blush, to be in tension with a key and relatively uncontroversial ethical principle that permeates western ethics – most famously grounded in Kantian ethics (Kant, 2012) – that persons should not be used as means to the end of another, but treated and valued as ends in themselves. This is an ethical principle that grounds, for example, contemporary notions of autonomy, justifies the requirement for informed consent, and undergirds the wrongness of exploitative practise. The potential risk with framing fatherhood research in terms of 'problems' that can be solved using fathers is that it reinforces the idea that fathers are not important in themselves, and only instrumentally valuable – like a tool. This is a question I have struggled with personally, across the research with fathers I have done and attempted to do. Thinking again of the proposed study on birthplace decision making mentioned earlier, one of my main concerns when the rationale was being constructed is how we tell participant fathers what the research is about, and why we are doing the research, without telling them that we are talking to them because we think fathers are a problem. Is it permissible to say to participant fathers, or allow the implication, that we only want to speak to fathers because we want to change their behaviour so that others will benefit? There are a few things to say in response to this, which draws on some moral philosophy and principles of research ethics.

First, a great deal of research uses people, to some extent, as a means to an end. While sometimes research participants benefit directly from participation in research, very often they take part because they are happy to contribute to some social good. So, fatherhood is not a special case here. Furthermore, the essential 'wrongness' in using a person or a group as a means to an end lies in the fact that in using them we fail to acknowledge them as autonomous moral agents and treat them instead as things to manipulate. The putative wrong in 'using fathers' in this way depends on the ends of the research being contrary to the ends of the fathers themselves, or the presence of deception or coercion. Some of my own research might shed light on whether fathers' ends are contrary to those of research that seeks to achieve benefits of mothers and children. My study on transitioning fathers (Ives, 2014), suggests that some fathers at least are content to see themselves as supporters, whose primary role is to look after the interest of their children and partners. If it is the case that the 'problem' rationale for fatherhood research is compatible and consistent with men's own views about their role as fathers, some of the sting seems to be taken out of the criticism. Further, so long as the purpose and reason for the research is clear, so that fathers can freely consent to participate in research that they feel is of value (or not, as the case may be), there is no deception or coercion that might lead to them being improperly 'used'. An example from my doctoral work springs to mind here. During recruitment for focus groups with fathers for research exploring the basis of paternal responsibilities and rights, I was contacted by a man who angrily demanded that I had better not (I paraphrase) 'be one of those men who does research on fatherhood to support the anti-men feminist agenda', because if I was, he would use all his 'influence' in fathers' groups to make sure that I never got a single participant for my study. Speculation about his motives and threats of sabotage aside, this highlights the fact that potential participants may be cognisant or wary of research having an agenda, and the importance of such agendas being made explicit so that participants can make an informed decision about whether or not they wish to 'participate to support', 'participate to challenge', or just 'participate'.

A second, more concise and utilitarian, argument can be made. Even if there is some sense in which fathers are used in the way described here, and even if there is a risk that this sends a negative message about how and why we value fathers, the goods that might accrue for mothers and children, for fathers themselves, and even for society, are likely to outweigh the potential harms. If we need to use the problem narrative to get research done, doing so is arguably justified because if it were not for their instrumental value, fathers would not likely be researched at all. Even if the problem rationale is not good or desirable in itself, it is arguably a justifiable means to an end.

Framing 'fatherhood'

It may seem trite to say that researching fatherhood requires us to know what a father is, but the question of how we define fatherhood, and the answer we give, can have significant ramifications, not only for the data obtained and the resulting analysis, but also for the fatherhood research agenda. 'Fatherhood' is not a homogenous practice, and 'fathers' are not a homogenous group of practitioners. In fact, if we interrogate the question for a moment, it begins to get remarkably unclear how 'father' ought to be defined. My doctoral work, which examined concepts of fatherhood in terms of rights and responsibilities, sought to explore and define necessary and sufficient conditions for fatherhood. This ended up supporting a fragmentation thesis of fatherhood, with different kinds of fathers having different sets of rights and responsibilities (Ives, 2007; Ives et al, 2008; Draper and Ives, 2009). This work highlighted various ways to theorise fatherhood, each of which stipulates different necessary and sufficient conditions for fatherhood, and has different implications for who the 'subject' of fatherhood research ought to be. Accounts of fatherhood found in the philosophical literature can be broadly categorised in the following way:

- **genetic-proprietary:** the father is the man from whom the child is genetically derived, and is a father in light having provided the genetic material from which the child grew (Hall, 1999);
- **genetic-causal:** the father is the man from whom the child is genetically derived, and is father because he provided the genetic material that caused the child to exist (Callahan, 1996; Nelson, 2000);
- **causal-intentional:** the father is the man who intended to create the child, and is father by virtue of that intention to father (Hill, 1991);
- **causal-responsibility:** the father is the man whose voluntary actions led to the foreseeable creation of a child (Fuscaldo, 2006);
- **custodial-welfare:** the father is the man who has day-to-day care of the child (derived from Locke, 2003; Kaebnick, 2004);
- **sweat-equity:** the father is the man who puts in the work of caring for the child (derived from Moody-Adams, 1991; Laquer, 1996; Narayan, 1999).

Each of these accounts has its advantages and disadvantages, and none, at least to my mind, seems to be able to provide a complete account of fatherhood (Ives, 2007). Each account can generally accommodate some important feature, but fails to accommodate others. For example, a genetic account might explain why a man should be responsible for financial maintenance regardless of his relationship with the child's mother, but the same account cannot explain why sperm donors do not have that same responsibility and excludes the possibility of fatherhood by adoption. A causal account can explain why a one-night stand leads to paternal responsibilities, whereas a sperm donation does not, but it also seems to implicate others as fathers (for example, fertility doctors or the hotelier who provided the honeymoon bed). An intentional account can explain why a man can become a father by adoption and using donor sperm, but it also means that there can be no paternal accountability from accidental conception. What is clear, however, is that even in relation to one single child we might be justified in calling a variety of men 'father' depending on our chosen account of fatherhood. It is important, therefore, that the ambiguity of the term is recognised in fatherhood research, and that it is clear how fatherhood is defined and for what reason. This might simply be considered the same as having clear inclusion and exclusion criteria – but it seems more than simply a point about methodological rigour. The inclusion and exclusion criteria we choose make a statement about what we believe fatherhood is, and what kind of experience and relationships are important, making a political, philosophical and ethical statement that could have implications beyond the immediate research objectives, as well as influencing the narrative used to justify the research, for example, fatherhood as a biological or genetic fact, as a social or economic performance, or as gendered practice. I now consider each of these narratives in turn.

Fatherhood as a biological or genetic fact

One way in which we might frame fatherhood is in terms of a genetic relationship. Researching fathers, then, would involve research with men who have passed on their genes. The implication of framing of fatherhood in this way is that the category 'father' might include men who have never seen, or been involved in raising, a child, such as sperm donors or 'absent fathers'. This might be exactly what is needed and intended, but it is always worth considering that in framing 'fatherhood' in this way we are making a statement about who does not count as a father (such as 'adoptive fathers').

Fatherhood as a social or economic performance

Another way we might frame fatherhood is as social and/or economic performance. Researching this kind of fatherhood would involve researching people who perform a social fathering role, or perform the economic work associated with fatherhood. The implication of this kind of framing is that it excludes people who are not performing a social or economic role (however that is defined) and includes adoptive fathers, but it might also allow for the possibility of a single child having 'multiple fathers'. Further, it does not link 'father' to gender or sex – allowing in theory the possibility that women might participate in fatherhood research. This is not as counterintuitive as it might first appear, as illustrated through reflection on a problem that arose in one of my own studies. While recruiting men transitioning to first-time fatherhood, a woman whose partner was pregnant with their first child asked if she could participate in the project. This sparked a lively debate within the project steering group, with the decision ultimately being made that the project was set up to explore men's experience and so she was ineligible given the original terms set out in the project. I was, and remain, unsatisfied with this decision. By *a priori* defining fatherhood in a way that was tied to gender, rather than simply in terms of role performance, the study could not (or would not) access a perspective that could have provided a great deal of insight. This is particularly striking, given that the key findings of the project were connected to the role a father played in relation to his pregnant partner, leading me to conclude that a

> valuable continuation of this work would be a repeat of this study with the female partners of pregnant women. This would allow an exploration of whether the findings reported here are a reflection of a specifically male experience or the experience of being the partner of a pregnant woman. (Ives, 2014, p 1014)

In defining fatherhood in a particular, gendered way, I excluded the possibility of obtaining insights into accounts and perspectives that could have shed new light on, or challenged, dominant understandings of male gender as central the experience of fatherhood.

Fatherhood as gendered practice

The final way of framing fatherhood considered here is as gendered or embodied practice. This sees a father as someone very distinct from a mother, and ties the practice of fatherhood to the body of the practitioner. This might, at first glance, mean that fatherhood is seen as parenting through a male body, and therefore research with fathers will only involve men. It will quickly become complicated, however, if we are interested in, for example, transgender parents, and seems to close the door on questions about whether men can mother (Doucet, 2006) or, as asked earlier, whether women can 'father'.

The point to take from this brief (and certainly incomplete) discussion is that the assumptions we make at the start of a research project about what a father is and how fatherhood is practised will dictate both how we articulate and justify our research aims and who we include/exclude as research participants, and we need to be careful to align our *a priori* definitions of fatherhood with our research aims. If, for example, our rationale for fatherhood research is based on achieving better birthing outcomes for mothers, we should be defining fatherhood for the purpose of this research, in terms of 'the partner of the pregnant women' – and this has nothing to with gender or genetic relatedness to the child. It would seem odd to make the research so specific as to only focus on the support that men can give, because this does not speak to the broad agenda of bringing benefit to labouring women. Alternatively, that kind of research perhaps should not be considered fatherhood research at all – allowing us to preserve (if we feel it is important) a gendered conception of fatherhood. However we decide to respond to this issue – and there may be various justifiable responses – it is something that demands consideration.

Framing the conversation

It is widely understood, or perhaps assumed, that fathers are difficult to research because they are challenging to recruit and, once recruited, are not forthcoming about their thoughts and feelings. This is certainly tied to assumptions about the way that fathers practise hegemonic masculinity: that they are reluctant to talk about their emotions and feelings, and that they tend to present themselves as conforming to dominant masculine discourse. My experience of conducting research with fathers bears out these concerns in some respects, but challenges them in others.

The two issues that strike me as particularly worth focusing on are, first, access and recruitment, which are obvious prerequisites to having a conversation, and second, having the conversation itself.

Recruitment and access

One way I have come to think of the challenges in recruiting fathers is in terms of being either 'logistical' or 'motivational'. The challenges here are arguably no different from those we would come across researching any social group that is large and diverse, and there is nothing, to my mind, particularly unique about how they can or should be met when recruiting fathers. Nonetheless, it is always worth considering how we might respond to these challenges in the context of a specific research population.

Logistical challenges

Logistical challenges are perhaps in theory the easiest to address, because they tend to centre on institutional and structural issues that can be overcome to some extent with enough thought. Accessing fathers can be straightforward if all that is required is a convenience sample of men who have children. Men who have children can be recruited through schools or almost any other public or private institution. However, this convenience approach has risks. It is rarely the case that just 'any old father' will do, and often a specific kind of father is needed, or a sample comprising wide demographic variation. Accessing specific groups of fathers directly can be problematic, because it is relatively rare that fathers *qua* fathers will gather in a group, or interact with a public service, that can be targeted for recruitment; but targeted strategies may involve, for example, accessing fathers through specific interest groups (as in a recent study of mine with fathers of autistic children – Burrel at el, 2017), recruiting fathers who partners are undergoing in vitro fertilisation (IVF) through IVF clinics (for example, Ives et al, 2008), recruiting separated fathers through fathers support groups (Ives et al, 2008), recruiting transitioning first-time fathers through maternity units and community midwives (Ives, 2014). Even then, however, such strategies will only be successful in accessing those fathers who already engage with specific groups or services – which makes the sample less heterogeneous in important ways. Additionally, in all the studies of mine mentioned there is a clear demographic skew in favour of white, well-educated men, which seems to be a feature of much fatherhood research that does not exclusively target minority groups.

Assuming that an appropriate population of fathers can be accessed, another significant logistical barrier is time and timing, which is linked to location. Parents and parents-to-be are busy people, and participation in research can be difficult if only for the reason that time is a scarce and valuable resource, taken up with both paid work and family 'work'. This problem cannot be removed, but the best way to respond to it is to be as flexible with timing as possible, and make clear in recruitment material that interviews can be held at any time to suit the participant. In my own research, I have conducted interviews early in the morning before work, late at night, or during the day, on weekends and weekdays. This is linked to location because the time available to participants will be linked to the time and ease of travel to the interview location. For this reason, similar flexibility is essential with regard to location. Arranging interviews close to a place of work, for example, will be helpful, as well as being willing to interview in participants' homes. I have conducted interviews in my own home, on occasion, as participants were travelling past and it was more convenient for them to drop in. Overall, the key to mitigating the logistical barriers of time and location is to be flexible and responsive, and to reinforce this at every stage of the recruitment process. This level of flexibility is not possible, of course, in the absence of conversations with potential participants that allow you to understand their logistical barriers and co-develop solutions. This is a demanding and time-consuming process but, in my experience, essential to successful recruitment of fathers.

Motivational challenges

If we think of logistical barriers as issues that must be overcome in order to convert interest in participation to actual participation, motivational challenges are barriers to expressing that interest in the first place. These are arguably harder to overcome, because, by definition, they have to be anticipated and managed prior to having any conversations with individual potential participants, and so strategies have to be aimed at 'fathers in general'.

One point I find myself making repeatedly when talking about fathers is that they are not a homogenous group, and their motivation to participate in research (or in anything) will be as varied as there are varied people. Anecdotal evidence, and my own experience, suggests that men take part in fatherhood research for a variety of different reasons, including curiosity, a desire to help, a desire to learn, having an opportunity to talk, as a potential for catharsis, and for inducements that may be offered – but this is not an exhaustive list.

One key observation is that any strategy to motivate men to take part in research must be multifaceted and/or directed to the kind of father needed – without excluding anyone. One good (or perhaps bad) illustration springs to mind. In an effort to encourage fathers to attend special 'dads and kids' sessions, many playgroups I have come across advertise free bacon and/or sausage sandwiches. In fact, in the years I have been researching fathers, and paying attention to how fathers are encouraged to engage and communicate, I have noticed a general assumption that the way to attract fathers is to offer them food – usually bacon or sausages. On a personal level, and as a father myself,

I have always found mildly offensive the putative assumption that I will only be motivated to spend time with my children if such time is accompanied by a bit of pig. That aside, and also to my annoyance, I have also noticed that, to some extent, it seems to work – on myself and others. It is not so much a matter of thinking 'give a father some pork or else he will not spend time with his children', but rather 'if we want a father to spend time with his children at our event we need to offer something to entice him to us rather than do something else'.[1] Putting aside any personal indignation at the thought I can be anyone's for a bacon sandwich, there is a different kind of problem here. Assuming that this offer of food will be a motivational factor (even if nothing more than a nudge), it will only motivate fathers who eat bacon/sausages. It would be entirely ineffective on, for example, vegetarian, Muslim or Jewish fathers (who may, of course, take part regardless). The point is that while not every motivational strategy will attract all fathers, it is quite possible that a single motivational strategy might put some people off or be entirely ineffective for some groups of fathers. Hence, unless there is reason to exclude certain groups, a multifaceted and inclusive approach is going to be needed. While we all might be aware of, and accept, the motivational pull of free lunch, we still need to think carefully about what kind of lunch we offer.

It is also important to briefly note the essential, but in practice often blurry, ethical distinction between encouragement (a motivational strategy) and a coercive strategy. While a motivational strategy seeks to give men reason to think it desirable and worthwhile to take part, a coercive strategy seeks to make it difficult for men to not take part. A motivational strategy might to be emphasise, in recruitment literature, that the research is important and will help others. A coercive strategy might be to state or imply that not taking part will make the potential participant a bad father or bad person. Both strategies mentioned rely on a potential participant's ethical sensibility, but with different emphasis. A more difficult issue, perhaps, is financial inducement, compensation or payment. Depending on the time commitment involved, some kind of financial compensation might well be appropriate, albeit often it will not function as compensation for lost earnings but as an inducement without which a potential participant might not think participation worth their time. My view is that there is nothing wrong with offering a financial incentive or inducement, and calling it such, because to do so acknowledges the value of participants' time. In my longitudinal study of transitioning fathers, participants (taking part in up to 10 interviews) were offered £100 pounds in supermarket vouchers of their choice. Settling on an amount was difficult, which had to be sufficient to make it worthwhile (motivational), but not so much as to be impossible to refuse (coercive). One worry I had was that transitioning fathers may be concerned about money (financial concerns are something that few new parents can avoid), and so I had to consider whether offering this financial incentive was taking advantage of men's vulnerability at that time. Another way of looking at it, however, was that through this research I was in a position to provide participants with a small amount of extra resource, which while unlikely to make the difference between solvency and insolvency would nonetheless be appreciated (£100 buys a lot of nappies, for example). The option of offering more was available, but my concern was that the more I offered the more likely I was to recruit men whose sole motivation was financial and who had no other interest in the study. This, I felt, could result in poor-quality data and high risk of attrition. I wanted men to *also* be taking part because they had an interest in the research and thought it valuable in itself – if only for the very practical reason that such men would be more likely to stay the distance. This would not have been such a concern if participation involved a one-off interview, but for a longitudinal study requiring commitment over a period of around nine months it seemed important. This strategy worked, but it did nonetheless result in a sample of men who seemed relatively financially secure and committed to fatherhood – which, of course, affected the conclusions that could be drawn.

Having the conversation

The question of how to have conversations with fathers is both an ethical and practical one. In the final section of this chapter, I outline one of the main challenges I experienced when interviewing fathers for my transitions study (Ives, 2014), and then draw on the work of Oakley (1981) to think about my response.

The fathers I interviewed were excited and optimistic, but also nervous and uncertain. They had few opportunities to talk about their impending fatherhood openly, and similarly few opportunities to express concern or ignorance, or to ask questions of other men. While the majority of participants were happy and willing to talk about intimate aspects of their lives, they were also cautious, guarded and reluctant to talk about thoughts and feelings that they feared might be judged or reflect on them badly. This reflected one of the central themes to come out the data, which was that participants were reluctant to make the pregnancy and process of transitioning to parenthood 'about them'. As I reflected at the time:

> Generally, the men in this study appeared to be attuned to the moral risk of expressing disquiet or discomfort about their own situation. They felt that their own problems could not be compared to the experience of their partners and that complaining would be inappropriately self-centred. (Ives, 2014, p 1011)

This reflects a relatively brutal experience of my own, when after giving a talk with a colleague that asked questions about the ethical imperative for men to be involved in antenatal care and labour (which referred in part to difficulties men can experience in response to birth) I was heavily criticised in the media for focusing on the challenges for men. A typical response (I paraphrase, and put it slightly more diplomatically than the colourful way it was often put to me) was to ask the rhetorical question: 'So, I suppose you think it's easy for women, do you?' This reflection almost brings us back full circle to the research agendas discussed at the start of the chapter. The charge put to me was essentially: 'How dare you focus on fathers when they have it so easy.' The aim of the talk, and of the article that was subsequently published (Draper and Ives, 2013), was to explore ethical justifications for men's involvement and then look at the problems that can flow when each justification seems to specify a particular role, consider the frustration and role ambiguity this can lead to, and then to highlight how these problems were only really manifest in a medical setting, suggesting finally that the medicalisation of the transition to fatherhood, just like the medicalisation of pregnancy, was not an unambiguously positive thing. In the media, however, the subtlety was lost, and was reduced to a so-called male expert bleating about how tough it is for fathers.

Given that one of the aims of my study was to explore the frustrations and dissatisfactions that were part of becoming a father, and considering my own experience of being exposed to criticism for talking about it, I felt it was important to create a space for participants to talk freely without fear of criticism or judgement. I found, during these multiple interview encounters, that the more I shared my own stories about being a father, the more participants shared, and this reciprocity both built trust and showed that this was a safe space. I began to think about it in terms of ensuring that participants felt they had permission to talk about anything, and with a few participants the only way I could do this was to show that I was also willing to put myself out there and take the 'risk' of talking about my experiences, thoughts and feelings – making it possible to establish 'a trust and mutual understanding that made possible intimate disclosures' (Ives, 2014, p 1014).

This experience is similar to that described by Oakley (1981) when reflecting on her research with expectant mothers. Oakley highlights the problems of using, with mothers, the dominant (masculine) approach to interviewing, characterised as one that maintains a one-way flow of information from participant to interviewer and encourages the deflection of participants' questions rather than engagement. Oakley found, in a series of interviews with expectant mothers, that they often 'talked back' to her, asking questions, seeking advice, and generally wanting to hear her own thoughts. This, noted Oakley, runs contrary to the dominant interviewing paradigm, described by her as 'masculine', which saw an interview encounter as a unilateral flow of information, and in which the interviewee had to maintain absolute neutrality to avoid corrupting or biasing the data. Of the many examples Oakley uses to illustrate this paradigm, she feels that the following, from Goode and Hatt (1952), is the most detailed:

> What is the interviewer to do, however, if the respondent really wants information? Suppose the interviewee does answer the question but then asks for the opinions of the interviewer. Should he give his honest opinion, or an opinion which he thinks the interviewee wants? In most cases, the rule remains that he is there to obtain information and to focus on the respondent, not himself. Usually, a few simple phrases will shift the emphasis back to the respondent. Some which have been fairly successful are 'I guess I haven't really thought enough about it to give a good answer right now', 'Well, right now, your opinions are more important than mine' and 'If you really want to know what I think, I'll be honest and tell you in a moment, after we've finished the interview'. Sometimes the diversion can be accomplished by a head shaking gesture which suggests 'That's a hard one!' while continuing with the interview. In short, the interviewer must avoid the temptation to express his own views, even if given the opportunity. (p 198)

Oakley found this response unacceptable for three reasons, which I think can usefully be described as ethical, ideological and pragmatic in the following ways:

- **Ethical:** it is unreasonable adopt a 'purely exploitative' attitude toward participants.

- **Ideological:** her role was to create a new sociology for women, not to preserve sociological interviewing norms, and if this demanded movement towards an interviewing practice that was more co-productive and enabled women's voices to be better heard, this was justified.
- **Pragmatic:** refusing to engage in reciprocal dialogue, or answer participants' questions, was detrimental to developing the rapport necessary to gather good data and maintain participation.

Oakely's response is essentially the one that I adopted in my interviews with fathers, and to my mind it worked well. The risk is, of course, that when interviewers enter this two-way conversation and start to talk about their own experiences, there is always the possibility that they will influence the data or create expectations that the participant feels obliged to meet, or that the interview is turned on its head and becomes an advice session. The latter risk can and arguably ought to be avoided, as at that point the interview loses sight of its purpose. The risk of creating expectations in participants about what you want to hear can also be mitigated by talking about your own experiences in a very personal way, focusing on 'I felt' or 'in my experience', talking about the range of experiences that have come up elsewhere in the research, and avoiding evaluative or pejorative language.

The first problem, of influencing the data, is to my mind a non-problem that only manifests if we assume a very naive account of knowledge generation in an interview context. Given that I tend to see all interviews as encounters in which knowledge and understanding is co-constructed (see, for example, Dunn and Ives, 2010), the idea that as an interviewer I might affect the data is neither news nor at all troubling. This epistemic position needs, however, to be engaged with seriously and reflexively, especially in my own case, given that my research aims to interrogate and challenge the normative (understood in an ethical sense). I find myself, again, turning to feminist writers and research practices to help make sense of my role and my responsibilities in relation to this. Before I close with an extended quote from Leach-Scully below, which seems to tie together the various strands of this chapter neatly and far more eloquently than I could hope to, my return to feminist writers raises the question of whether, at the end of this reflection, I ought to be considering whether fatherhood researchers (or at least those with bioethical leanings) need also to be feminist researchers. Given the focus herein on the need to be conscious of how we frame our research subject and understand our research agendas, and the need to be conscious of (and draw on) our own perspectives and understandings, if the essence of feminist research can be characterised by the following quote, I think the answer is a resounding yes:

> Feminist epistemology takes social, cultural and historical position to be important to the formation of distinct epistemic perspectives that need to be taken into account when others' moral practices and choices are evaluated. But feminist epistemology also recognises that the forms of knowledge taken for granted by moral philosophy and philosophical bioethics are not immune to this epistemic distortion. Feminist bioethical approaches necessarily also involve the critical examination of the positions from which we, as bioethicists, carry out our empirical investigations and reflect normatively, of the empirical methods used, the epistemological and sociological assumptions that the use of them reveals, and so on. The inescapable human reality is that all of us are situated observers whose observations are shaped not only by explicit moral beliefs but by much of what we take for granted experientially, socially, institutionally and culturally. Feminist or any other approaches cannot offer a foolproof way around this, other than the constant and necessary reminder that all thinking is thinking from a particular vantage point. This includes the thinking of the moral philosopher: bioethics, whether empirical or theoretical, necessarily is done from a perspective that is dependent on bioethicists' own personal backgrounds and biographies, and also their disciplinary and professional training, and their institutional roles within national and cultural environments. (Leach-Scully, 2017, p 212)

Note

[1] There is, of course, more going on here, as there is an assumption that there are better spaces to engage with your children, and so it is a good thing that men are encouraged into these shared spaces – but there is not space to deal with that here.

References

Burgess, A. (2008). 'Maternal and infant health in the perinatal period: the father's role', Fatherhood Institute, available at www.fatherhoodinstitute.org/index.php?id=2&cID=736.

Burrel, A. Ives, J. and Unwin, G. (2017) 'The experiences of fathers who have offspring with autism spectrum disorder', *Journal of Autism and Developmental Disorder*, 47(4): 1135-1147.

Callahan, D. (1996) 'Bioethics and fatherhood', in L. May, R. Strikwerda and P. Hopkins (eds) *Rethinking masculinity: Philosophical explorations in light of feminism*, Lanham, MA: Rowman & Littlefield, pp 161-171.

Doucet, A. (2006) *Do men mother? Fatherhood, care, and domestic responsibility*, Toronto: Toronto University Press.

Draper, H. and Ives, J. (2009) 'Paternity testing, a poor test of fatherhood', *Journal of Social Welfare and Family Law*, 31(4): 407-418.

Draper, H. and Ives, J. (2013) 'Men's involvement in antenatal care and labour: rethinking a medical model', *Midwifery*, 29(7): 723-729.

Dunn, M. and Ives, J. (2010) 'Methodology, epistemology, and empirical bioethics research: a constructive/ist commentary', *American Journal of Bioethics*, 9(6-7): 93-95.

Fuscaldo, G. (2006) 'Genetic ties: are they morally binding?', *Bioethics*, 20(2): 64-76.

Goode, W. and Hatt, P. (1952) *Methods in social research*, London: Allen & Unwin.

Hall, B. (1999) 'The origin of parental rights', *Public Affairs Quarterly*, 13: 73-82.

Hill, J. (1991) 'What does it mean to be a "parent"? The claims of biology as the basis for parental rights', *New York University Law Review*, 66: 353-420.

Ives J, (2014) 'Men, maternity and moral residue: negotiating the moral demands of the transition to first time fatherhood', *Sociology of Health and Illness*, 36(7): 1003-10019.

Ives, J. Draper, H. Pattison, H. and Williams, C. (2008) 'Becoming a father/refusing fatherhood: an empirical bioethics approach to paternal responsibilities and rights', *Clinical Ethics*, 3(2): 75-84.

Kaebnick, G. (2004) 'The natural father: genetic paternity testing, marriage and fatherhood', *Cambridge Quarterly of Healthcare Ethics*, 13: 49-60.

Kant, I. (2012) *Groundwork of the metaphysics of morals*, translated and edited by M. Gregor and Jens Timmermann, Cambridge: Cambridge University Press.

Laqueur, T. (1996) 'The facts of fatherhood', in L. May, R. Strikwerda and P. Hopkins (eds) *Rethinking masculinity: Philosophical explorations in light of feminism*, Lanham, MA: Rowman & Littlefield, pp 173-192.

Leach-Scully, J. (2017) 'Feminist empirical bioethics', in J. Ives, M. Dunn, and A. Cribb (eds) *Empirical bioethics: Theoretical and practical perspectives*, Cambridge: Cambridge University Press.

Locke, J. (2003) 'The second treatise: an essay concerning the true original, extent, and end of civil government', in I. Shapiro (ed) *Two treatises of government and a letter concerning toleration*, New Haven, CT: Yale University Press.

Moody-Adams, M. (1991) 'On surrogacy: morality, markets and motherhood', *Public Affairs Quarterly*, 5: 175-191.

Narayan, U. (1999) 'Family ties: rethinking parental claims in the light of surrogacy and custody', in U. Narayan and j Bartkowaik (eds) *Having and raising children*, University Park, PA: Penn State University Press.

Nelson, J. (2000) 'Reproductive ethics and the family', *New Zealand Journal of Bioethics*, 1: 4-10.

Oakley, SA. (1981) 'Interviewing women: a contradiction in terms', in H. Roberts (ed) *Doing feminist research*, London: Routledge & Kegan Paul, pp 30-61.

RCM (Royal College of Midwives) (2011) *Reaching out: involving fathers in maternity care*. London: RCM.

Sarkadi, A. Kristiansson, R. Oberklaid, F. and Bremberg, S. (2008) 'Fathers' involvement and children's developmental outcome: a systematic review of longitudinal studies',
Acta Paediatrica, 97: 153–158.

Westwood, S. (1996) 'Feckless fathers: masculinities and the British state', in M. Mac An Ghaill (ed) *Understanding masculinities*, Milton Keynes: Open University Press, pp 21-34.

Wolf, S. (1982) 'Moral saints', *The Journal of Philosophy*, 79(8): 419-439.

TWO

Qualitative longitudinal research: researching fatherhood and fathers' experiences

Tina Miller

Introduction

Research on men's experiences of being fathers and fatherhood has proliferated over the past 30 years in the western world. This development reflects broader structural, cultural, economic and political shifts in family and work lives and associated theorisations around gender and caring capacities. The resulting body of research has often focused on men's experiences of becoming fathers and the early years of fatherhood. There has also been an interest in research questions that reflect an epistemological commitment to interpretivism, leading to small-scale, qualitative exploration of groups of men's experiences in particular contexts. The piecing together of these finely focused research outputs has led to collective, comparative and nuanced overviews. These have been complimented by broader, brush-stroke, quantitative research revealing statistical patterns and illuminating trends, for example, in relation to fathers' involvement in the domestic and paid work spheres. Even so, there continues to be a lack of regularly collected, national-level, large-scale data available on fathers (Nuffield Foundation[1]; Burgess, et al, 2017). In 1992, the 'first estimates of the lifetime fathering of a nationally representative sample of men living in private households' was produced from an analysis of the British Household Panel Study (Burghes et al, 1997). But in the intervening period, the lack of nationally available data – and so crucial knowledge – regarding fathers' involvement in their children's lives has continued to be noted amid calls for 'data improvement' (Burgess, et al, 2017). Of course, it is important to also acknowledge that the category 'father' operates in complex ways; for example, the biological fact of being a father may remain unknown and residency, non-residency and legal fatherhood can further complicate the category. But this should not impede research attempts to collect and improve baseline and other data; in fact, it makes the endeavour all the more necessary. Research designs that include repeat interviews or other forms of data collection *over time* are also lacking – with some notable exceptions, such as the Timescapes projects (www.timescapes.leeds.ac.uk) – in the research literature. Yet longitudinal research can be especially illuminating when complex categories and experiences are the focus of research. Only through data improvement in its various and multiple forms can our knowledge on fathers and fatherhood experiences become necessarily enhanced.

This chapter focuses on a qualitative longitudinal (QL) research project, Transition to Fatherhood (Miller, 2010, 2011), and later episodes of fathering and fatherhood experiences (Miller, 2017). It begins by examining the research design of this study and considers the inherent gendered and other assumptions made in this study, which mirrors an earlier research project on Transition to Motherhood (Miller, 2005, 2007). For example, how did I understand and employ the category 'father' and what factors influenced the research design and data collection practices? Following an examination of some of the methodological issues that arose during this qualitative longitudinal study, I turn my attention to reflect on the important question of what adding *time* into a qualitative study can do. What happens when narratives collected in later interviews are incorporated into earlier analysis and findings as lives and fatherhood experiences change? Do new versions of selves as fathers 'undo' the previous analysis and findings and/or emphasise the temporality of selves? What are the benefits of researching individuals over time and can time render the accumulated data *more* trustworthy because of its increasingly 'thick' and time-sensitive description (Geertz, 1973; Lincoln and Guba, 1985)?

Designing and developing qualitative longitudinal (QR) research

The Transition to Fatherhood QL study began in 2004, with interview data initially collected between 2005 and 2007. The study arose as a consequence of an earlier study I had conducted on Transition to Motherhood (Miller, 2005, 2007). This study had followed a group of 17 women through a year in which they became a biological mother for the first time and, as the findings were disseminated the question 'What about the fathers?' arose repeatedly. Shifting the research lens to focus on men becoming biological fathers seemed straightforward and an important undertaking for future comparative possibilities. This included using the interview schedule that had guided the motherhood interviews. The research design was based epistemologically on a view of the social world as complex and fluid, requiring an approach that facilitated collecting and exploring individual meanings and temporal practices through transition and being a father. An interpretivist approach was adopted with a particular focus on narrative practices, discursive possibilities and normative expectations and, analytically, how these remained constant and/or shifted *over time*. As Neale notes, time, and so temporality, provides the 'theoretical heart' of qualitative longitudinal enquiry (2017, chapter 2).

The focus on narrative construction and narrative possibilities was a key characteristic in the Transition to Fatherhood study and the earlier Motherhood study too. Taking a narrative approach in QL research begins from a position of assuming or accepting (although not uncritically) the storytelling and 'modernist subject' who can reflexively give an account of a life in ways that are coherent and culturally recognisable (MacIntyre, 1981; Frank, 1995; Chamberlayne et al, 2000; Miller, 2005, 2017; Riessman, 2008; Alldred and Gillies, 2012; Andrews et al, 2013). This has become a well-recognised research approach and in the fatherhood study was designed to explore selves, identities and practices of agency, through the (potentially biographically disruptive) life event of becoming a father for the first time and how this is made sense of, over time (see Miller, 2005, chapter 1, and Miller, 2017 for further details of narrative research). The particular social, cultural and, importantly, moral contexts that underpin contemporary expectations and experiences of fathering (as practice) and fatherhood (as constructed category of structural assumptions) provided an important contextual focus.

Following submission to a university research ethics review committee, permission was granted for the study to proceed, subject to the requirement that any potential participants must opt in to the study. Even though the study was then advertised widely in order to attract a diverse sample, the effect of this requirement led to the recruitment of a white, employed and older sample than had originally been intended in the research proposal. The process of recruitment was also slow and eventually getting *any* men to join a longitudinal study on fatherhood felt like a small victory. The sample of 17 men who consented to join the study had a mean age of 33.7 years at the time of the first interview (ages ranged from 24 years to 39 years) and were employed in a wide range of jobs that would mostly position them as skilled and, occupationally, middle-class. They were from dual-earner households, were partnered (some married), white (several in ethnically mixed partnerships/marriages) and heterosexual. Data was collected in the original motherhood study in three separate, individual interviews, timed to coincide with late pregnancy, at six weeks following the birth and at around nine months after birth, followed by an end-of-study questionnaire. The same design was initially adopted in the fatherhood study, but as data collection proceeded it was decided to extend this one-year time frame to include an additional (fourth) interview with the fathers, when their child reached their second birthday (Miller, 2010). In 2012, new ethics approval was gained to further extend the study and recontact the fathers as their first-born child reached primary school age (Miller, 2015, 2017). The rationale for keeping the study 'live' was both to add to a growing literature on early years fathering experiences and to return to a sample seemingly willing and comfortable ('socialised'?) with the qualitative, open-ended and iterative interview format. It has been noted elsewhere that research on parents and parenthood has tended to focus on mothers, because of their availability as main carers to provide details of family lives to researchers. It seemed important then to add fathers' voices and experiences to these descriptions.

Even though the original intention had been to follow the same format as the Transition to Motherhood study, I was aware that my assumptions about interviewing men becoming fathers differed in some ways to my expectations around interviewing women. There were aspects of shared biography and gender with the participants in the motherhood study (I was a mother too) that I could not/did not share with the men, and so I wondered how I would be positioned as I prepared to undertake the first face-to face interviews in the homes of my new participants. My (gendered) assumptions were that men would not necessarily feel comfortable or have very much to say on the novel and potentially emotive subject of experiences of transition or thoughts and hopes around their selves and the advent of first-time fatherhood. Concerned about this, I decided to take along visual materials (pictures of well-known fathers, such as footballer David Beckham, with their children) to act as easy prompts ('Tell me what this picture makes you think about') if needed. These were, I now realise, more to assuage my own fears of sitting through short, uncomfortable interviews, but I never actually needed to use these extra prompts. My assumptions about how masculinities might play out across the interviews were in many respects unfounded and on occasion, confirmed ("At the birth I was like yeah, I probably won't cry, but I cried too"). The interviews in the fatherhood study were longer than those recorded in the motherhood study. Some of the fathers spoke of the interview as a rare opportunity to "talk like this" in ways they said they said they would not talk to their male friends at the pub ("We're just blokes, we don't really speak about it, like well I do when I speak to you"). There were disclosures ("No one else knows this"), sadness, elation, anger and, over the years, reflections encompassing a gamut of experiences and emotions as the fathers in the study mostly came to feel comfortable talking about the personal and emotional aspects of their lives as new fathers (Birch and Miller, 2000; Pini, 2005; Seidler, 2006; Miller and Nash, 2016; Miller, 2017).

In order to reflect further on how gender might have played out in the early interviews (a woman and mother interviewing a 'novice' father-to-be), I added an extra question to the end-of-study questionnaire circulated to the fathers at the end of the first year of the study. This questionnaire had been designed to collect participants' experiences of being in the motherhood – and now fatherhood – studies. The question added asked 'Was there anything you felt unable to talk about in the interviews?' Under this question, one participant wrote 'I'm glad you didn't ask about sex', but this topic had been spoken about (unprompted) by some of the other fathers during the interviews. The gendered dynamics at play in the interviews shaped the data collection process as would be the case in any social interaction. Gender, of course, operates between the participant and researcher in at least two ways in the interview, both in how the researcher is placed by the participant and how the researcher places the participant and the assumptions each hold. The topic under study will also shape the interview interaction and how gender plays out (Padfield and Proctor, 1996; Pini, 2005). Specifically, this was a study conducted by a woman who was (often) positioned as having an 'innate expertise' on aspects of the research topic, for example being asked by participants for advice about the baby or their partner's 'post-natal blues', or confirmation of their own feelings, thoughts and actions. But in the interviews the male participants were both novice (in relation to fathering and fatherhood) *and* practised and expert at having available to them a range of normative, hegemonic discourses (for example, around paid work and masculinities) that provided them with more (recognisable and accepted) possibilities in their narrations and practices of agency as fathers ("I'm hoping to help out when I can") than had been the case with the women in the motherhood study (Pini, 2005). It was important then to pay attention to the doing and possible 'undoing' of gender during the interview process and data analysis, focusing on which aspects of masculine selves, practices and 'choices' were, and could be, presented and in what circumstances (Marsiglio and Pleck, 2005; Deutsch, 2007; Miller, 2011).

Researching father's experiences of fatherhood: time and QL research

The data collected in the first interviews provided a baseline of intentions, experiences and hopes, against which subsequent interviews were conducted and data analysed. The first phase of the fatherhood study followed the fathers from anticipating the birth in the first interview, to their child's second birthday in a fourth interview. The later phase of the QL study as the children reached school age served to follow up and interview 10 of the original participants[2] (see Miller, 2017 for further details). So-called 'attrition' in QL research may be reduced or avoided depending on how the study is initially designed and what participants are invited to consent to. In practical terms, social media, online or other digital media can also be used as a means to keep a sample 'involved' over time and between interview phases (Miller, 2012, 2015; Neale, in press). Time, then, is distinctive in QL research and we turn now to consider what specifically adding *time* into research on fathers can do. What might be gained from researching men's experiences of fathering as their child grows that cannot be captured in a single, one-off interview?

Neale has noted that time is 'central to the task of creating a moving picture of the lifecourse' (Neale, 2015). Those who opted into the fatherhood study anticipated and envisaged at some level a happy trajectory in which their child would be safely born and they would 'be there' as fathers in emotional and physical ways that differed from their own childhood experiences (or their memories of these). They would become 'a family', 'mature' and 'responsible'; they would 'step up to the plate', impart all sorts of knowledge, fun and sports prowess, and provide security for their child. The passage of time turns imagined trajectories into the here and now, but the past and the fathers' lives unfold in a multitude of unforeseeable ways. Across the interviews, the passage of time reveals the twists, turns and messiness of lives as individuals 'negotiate' what at the outset are envisaged as unproblematic life course (becoming a father) trajectories. Importantly, QL research illuminates subjectivity as moving and reflexive, a process in which individual stories of experience may become edited and narrated again over time, and may simultaneously illuminate broader, structural-level change (Thomson, 2009; Neale, in press).

To turn time back, the first interviews were conducted with the participants when their partner/wife was approximately seven to eight months' pregnant. In the interviews (and in spite of my own misgivings, noted earlier), the men spoke at length. But there was also some uncertainty about what was 'required' in this novel space as well as an implicit understanding that I would not/could not expect participants to be 'expert' in this arena or at this (pre-birth) time. As one participant said, "How much detail do you want me to go into?", later adding "Sorry I'm not very good with words". This uncertain landscape led some to seek from me confirmation of how their unfolding experiences overlapped with those of other men in the study, that is, how 'normal' they were ("Has anyone else said that?"). But as subsequent interviews were undertaken, the participants seemed to settle comfortably into the open-ended format ("It's a little like counselling") and gradually they became the experts on their child: being a father and parent was no longer "a new world". Going back offered opportunities for the men to edit earlier versions of themselves as a new, involved father, a good worker, a divorced father, or a caring parent as experiences accumulated and time changed plans, hopes and trajectories. The initial interest in transitional experiences around first-time fatherhood receded as being a father became incorporated into the sense of self being narrated and it was something the men just got on with (or not). It was the interview that prompted them to pause and reflect on how aspects of being a father were managed individually, in couples, across households, around work and so on, as subsequent children were born and 'time-stressed' and sometimes difficult lives were lived, made sense of, and narrated.

As the years unfolded, being a father had become everyday, mundane in some respects and incorporated into their sense of who they were ("That is now who I am, I am now a father, whereas before I was a new one. I don't feel like a new one anymore"). But at least three (of the original 17) fathers are now separated/divorced from their partner/wife and their perspectives on their selves as fathers is complex (see Miller, 2017, chapter 5 for further details). This is the case for James and the following exchange is taken from a fifth interview with him as his child reaches school age. James is now divorced from his wife and only sees his child at weekends.

Tina: "Can you remember life before being a father?"
James: "Yeah I can do sort of, but yeah, probably similar to now actually but yeah *because I mean I don't feel like a father now*, I mean that's the reality of it....

	[Later] No it isn't what I thought fatherhood was so …"[3]
Tina:	"But in one of the really early interviews … are you okay?"
James:	"Yeah I'm just texting. Cool."
Tina:	"Okay."
James:	"Perfect."
Tina:	"So in one of our earlier conversations [interviews] we did talk about what a good dad was and what a bad dad was and everyone says a good dad is someone who is there and a bad dad is a dad who's absent and you were very upset earlier [in this interview] that … and not surprisingly … that you've been called an absentee father."
James:	"Yeah that's pretty insulting isn't it?"
Tina:	"Yeah it's absolutely insulting."
James:	"And that's the category that I'm listed at, it's just unbelievable…."

This exchange illuminates several aspects of the ways in which time operates in QL research. I am able to recall what had been said in earlier interviews and relay this to James. He is categorical that he does not feel like a father now, that things have not turned out as he thought. I am also aware that he is distracted from time to time and feel comfortable enough with him (fifth interview) to check 'are you okay' and also reassure him that it's 'not surprising' that he is upset at having been called an 'absentee father' in circumstances painfully narrated as not of his choosing. So the lengthy interview produces another layer of rich data on aspects of being a father (or not feeling like one) and what post-separation parenting and here, non-residency, can look and feel like (he has just dropped his child off after a weekend together). But he also becomes exasperated (perhaps not surprisingly in the circumstances) with a question I ask about how parenting works across the households (James: "I'm struggling with this question I don't really, I mean …") and I feel that the air of comfort developed across the interviews makes this emotive outburst permissible, but I still feel anxious that I have provoked some discomfort/upset/anger in him. So, time breeds familiarity in ways not possible in a single interview and normalises the interview as an opportunity for continuing a 'conversation', for frankness and perhaps greater freedom for emotional expression. These were not things I had anticipated at the outset of the research study, nor probably what James will have envisaged when he (happily) signed up to the study anticipating first-time fatherhood, several years before.

Adding time into research and taking a long view provides descriptions and narratives of change and continuities that, through their accumulation and layering, can come to tell different stories from perhaps those originally intended or sought. Everyone grows, including the researcher, and the researcher's analytic and reflexive skills also develop. The passage of time and accumulation of research 'expertise' through designing and conducting research also inform how researchers (come to) practise. I am not the same researcher I was when I commenced the first of my qualitative longitudinal studies over 20 years ago in 1995. At that time, I was well versed in the theory of research practice and influenced in my ideas about how a sensitive and (non-exploitative) interview could be accomplished, through groundbreaking feminist literature from the period (Oakley, 1981; Roberts, 1981; Bell and Roberts, 1984; Harding, 1987; DeVault, 1990; Cotterill, 1992; Ribbens and Edwards, 1998). But since then, I have grown in my research knowledge and confidence, and in aspects of my research skills, as my longitudinal studies have unfolded. At one level, this is as uncomplicated as being able to sit through long silences in interviews and not feel compelled to fill the spaces. Similarly, I am more practised at reading body language and pursuing areas raised by a participant, rather than slavishly following the interview schedule, which in the early days provided a metaphorical 'comfort blanket' as I performed the 'competent' researcher role I thought my participants expected to see.

Analytical and theoretical competence is also accrued over the years of researching and teaching in a discipline – and in some ways there are no short cuts to becoming an experienced researcher. But this does not mean that early research endeavours are inferior to later ones, rather that the accumulation of interview materials over time can provide new opportunities for conceptualising and theorising participant practices and experiences, and the researcher's experience and engagement with the data will shift too. QL research then provides an opportunity to look back over the twists and turns of lives and to document what might have changed and what remains embedded – and why – at the individual and structural level, but alongside personal change for the researcher too. However, taking a longer view and inviting participants to (once again) reflect back on episodes in their lives, captured in earlier phases of a the study, raises new possibilities and other issues for researchers to consider.

The re-analysis/secondary analysis of QL data – either by the original researcher returning to, or adding to, previously collected accounts, or another researcher who has accessed the data from a data archive – offers opportunities for new engagement with the longitudinal data as a whole. This new engagement can offer the researcher novel opportunities to ask new questions of 'old' data and may lead to alternate and/or contradictory theorisations of aspects of the earlier research. Similarly, in QL research, the collection of data in subsequent phases of a project also offers novel opportunities through analysis of *cumulative* (over a longer time period) and so more richly layered and textured episodes of experience and narration (Henwood and Shirani, 2012a, 2012b; Miller, 2015).

This returns us to the earlier observation made by Neale, that time is 'central to the task of creating *a moving picture of the lifecourse*' (Neale, 2015, emphasis added). In collecting men's narrations of first-time fatherhood through time, a moving and dynamic picture is captured encompassing individual practices as well as the ways in which particular structural features (for example, policies) and broader cultural expectations have influenced these practices at different times. For example, the 'moving picture' of fatherhood has illuminated changing discursive and agentic practices in relation to the diminishing dominance of masculine 'breadwinner' claims (at times) and practices that increasingly emphasise caring and more emotionally attuned aspects of father identities and permissible masculine selves. But the QL approach also provides a finely focused view of the 'micro-processes' of household-level interactions and how fatherhood is choreographed and managed across home and work spheres in straightforward and complex ways as children are first anticipated, born and grow (Miller, 2017). The need for such dynamic and nuanced data, which explores complexity, contradictions and continuities, has recently been called for as a counter to the 'oversimplified, oppositional categorisations of male caring evident within policy and media portrayals' (Boyer et al, 2017, p 67).

Researcher and participant relationships overtime

Undertaking QL research presumes that a researcher–participant relationship will be fostered over a long period of time and, in interview-based research, that there will be a number of interviews with each participant. It might be expected that in such research, the opportunities to establish 'rapport' and develop friendships are amplified. The idea of rapport, as a facet of establishing a 'good' interview, has been examined and critiqued in the research literature, and interview experiences in the fatherhood study were described in friendly and positive ways by a number of the men as 'enjoyable' and 'cathartic' (Birch and Miller, 2000; Duncombe and Jessop, 2012; Oakley, 2016). As noted earlier, the participants in the study spoke of the interviews providing an opportunity to reflect on unfolding experiences in ways and spaces they said would not normally be available to them. It is interesting, of course, to reflect on how a male interviewer, perhaps also a father, may have been privy to the telling of differently presented versions of the fathers and these events, perhaps reduced in their emotional poignancy and/or potentially heightened. For example, in research on men's attendance at all-male antenatal preparation classes in Australia, led by a male facilitator, heightened performances of hegemonic masculinity were described by some of the participants (Miller and Nash, 2016).

In contrast, in the fatherhood study, as events unfolded in the men's lives, they seemed grateful for the opportunity to share their experiences and spoke openly and at length about all sorts of aspects of their lives in what had become comfortable interview exchanges, based on what could be called 'intermittent friendship'. I also came to care about the participants and had a genuine interest in their experiences. I looked forward to hearing about their lives and became familiar with the other figures who peopled their home and work spheres and featured in their narratives. I reacted in spontaneously empathetic ways to their stories, which traversed familial experiences of love, growth, sadness and loss, including separations, breakdowns and in one case the death of a young baby (Miller, 2017). There was an intensity in both the interview and experiences shared with me ("I thought I must remember to tell Tina about that"), perhaps because the experiences were distilled and crystalised into the interview space. Of course, all research is only possible with willing participants, and in a recent article Oakley (2016) reflects on what it is that participants in (QL) research give to the researcher. She uses the idea 'of the gift' to capture the time and material that participants share with us in altruistic (in some respects) ways (2016, p 208). Oakley calls for greater attention to be paid to the 'notion of friendship' and 'the gift relationship' in longitudinal studies, and goes on to note 'the dependence of researchers on what research participants are willing to contribute from the memories and stories of their lives' (2016, p 209).

It is interesting, then, to consider how those who are most vital to our research – the participants – view the enterprise they have agreed to participate in. I noted this in my earlier research for the Transition to

Motherhood project, when as a younger and less experienced researcher I was taken aback when I contacted a participant to confirm address details before sending (as agreed) a summary of the research findings, only to receive a card confirming her address details and a note saying, 'To be honest I'd forgotten about it [the study]' (Gatrell, 2009). This was an early lesson in respecting the very different perspectives researchers and their participants are likely to have about a research project. Even so, in the longer (and potentially ongoing) fatherhood study, I realise on reflection that had assumed the greater number of interviews and years of the study would make a greater impression on the participants. But as the following exchange with Nick in the fatherhood study illustrates, this is not necessarily the case. As the interview wound down with Nick[4] – a fifth interview as his eldest child reached school age – the following exchange took place.

> Nick: so how old was [son] when you first came, 2?
>
> Tina: So he was just over 2 at the last interview.
>
> Nick: 2½ last time?
>
> Tina: Yeah I mean so obviously he wasn't born when I first came, but ...
>
> Nick: I had forgotten that.
>
> Tina: That was the transition part of the project.
>
> Nick: Oh that's probably a good transcript, 'oh it will be fine, it will be great, it will be really easy'.
>
> This is interesting in part because Nick had completely forgotten about the first interview, a key interview from my perspective for the study overall, as it was where first-time fatherhood and intentions were imagined and explored as transition was anticipated. But also the fact that he has forgotten underscores the enormity of the shifts which occur in lives when individuals become parents and it's hard to recall a pre-baby life and self. And Nick's final jesting comment about the possible content of the forgotten interview *'oh it will be fine, it will be great, it will be really easy'*, confirms an earlier shared (amongst the participants), but misplaced view that caring for a baby is straightforward, but now in the knowledge of just how difficult the first year with his new baby had turned out to be. (Miller, 2017, p 160)

Going back into lives and experiences that have unfolded in unexpected ways, and reminding the participant of an earlier version of their self, can enrich theorising of temporal subjectivity, but also unintentionally reinforce feelings of sadness or expressions of failure, for example when a divorce has occurred (Shirani and Henwood, 2011; Miller, 2017). It must be hard to be reminded of earlier interview accounts – I begin interviews by reminding the participant what had been the main threads of their last interview (using the participants own words) – when expectations and hopes have been dashed. Feeling that the amount or type of fathering involvement envisaged in earlier interviews has not been managed, or that spending 'family time' together has been squeezed out through work commitments, or that relationships and marriages have failed and fathering now occurs in pockets of time decided by others, are salutary to describe and 'own'. It can also be hard for the researcher, who has been on the unfolding journey at a distance, to hear whatever version of events is shared. Failure and personal frailty can be uncomfortable to witness when things have begun years before in such hopeful ways, but this is the richness of the moving picture and thickly layered descriptions of lives that can emerge in QL research.

Conclusion

Qualitative longitudinal research is increasingly recognised as having distinctive qualities that can facilitate the collection of more nuanced and time-sensitive findings (Neale, 2013, 2017; Thomson and McLeod, 2015; Oakley, 2016). The accumulation and weaving together of episodes of experience gained through researching experiences of fatherhood described here has illuminated the tenuousness of selves and the power of discourses and associated assumptions that configure societal and cultural ideas about fatherhood, caring, family lives and (men's) paid work. The interviews conducted over time have also indicated how change at the individual, household and broader structural level occurs. The chapter has considered too what is distinctive about researching fathers and fatherhood using a QL approach and has shown the ways in which adding time into research can reveal and illuminate the micro-processes of how lives are actually lived. The more nuanced findings contribute to, and complement in important ways, broader and more quantitative descriptions of patterns and trends. Both have relevance for policy makers and others. The addition of time into research design allows the effects of structural changes such as the introduction of new policies (for example, shared parental leave) to be monitored over time and, for example, to explain the multiple factors in *why* take-up of shared parental leave by fathers has (so far) been disappointing in the UK context. In comparison with a single, one-off interview, QL research facilitates participant familiarity with the research process and the researcher, especially where the same researcher undertakes all the interviews, as in the study described here. Familiarity is not necessarily cosy as lives unfold in sometimes uncomfortably sad and distressing ways, but the development of 'intermittent friendship' does mean that these unfolding experiences are shared.

Thus our participants give us the 'gift' of their time and experiences, and QL research can document the findings in nuanced, time-sensitive and layered ways. The addition of time into this research project has enabled the ebb and flow of everyday fathering and fatherhood experiences to be traced. The findings to date have contributed to the uneven literature currently available on men's lives with their children.

Notes

[1] http://www.nuffieldfoundation.org/
[2] Contact was made with 13 of the original 17 participants. Of these, 10 fathers 'opted in' and were interviewed for a fifth time; see Miller (2017) for further details.
[3] Emphasis added.
[4] The extract from Nick and subsequent description on page 42 are taken from Miller (2017, p 160).

References

Alldred, P. and Gillies, V. (2012) 'Eliciting research accounts: reproducing modern subjects?', in T. Miller, M. Birch, M. Mauthner and J. Jessop (eds) *Ethics in qualitative research*, London: Sage Publications, pp 146-166.

Andrews, M., Squire, C. and Tamboukou, M. (eds) (2013) *Doing narrative research* (2nd edn), London: Sage Publications.

Bell, C. and Roberts, H. (eds) (1984) *Social researching: Politics, problems, practice*, London: Routledge & Kegan Paul.

Birch, M. and Miller, T. (2000) 'Inviting intimacy: the interview as a therapeutic opportunity', *International Journal of Social Research Methodology*, 3(3): 189-202.

Boyer, K., Dermott, E., James, A. and MacLeavy. J. (2017) 'Regendering care in the aftermath of recession?', *Dialogues in Human Geography,* 7(1): 56-73.

Burgess, A., Goldman, R. and Davies, J. (2017) *State of the UK's Fathers*, Full Report, London: Fatherhood Institute.

Burghes, L., Clarke, L. and Cronin, N. (1997) *Fathers and fatherhood in Britain*, JRF Social Policy Research 120, York: Joseph Rowntree Foundation.

Chamberlayne, P., Bornat, J. and Wengraf, T. (eds) (2000) *The turn to biographical methods in social science*, London: Routledge.

Cotterill, P. (1992) 'Interviewing women: issues of friendship, vulnerability, and power', *Women's Studies International Forum*, 15: 593-606.

Deutsch F.M. (2007) 'Undoing gender', *Gender & Society*, 21(1): 106-126.

DeVault, M. (1990) 'Talking and listening from women's standpoint: feminist strategies for interviewing and analysis', *Social Problems*, 37: 96-116.

Duncombe, J. and Jessop, J. (2012) '"Doing rapport"' and the ethics of "faking friendship"', in T. Miller, M. Birch, M. Mauthner and J. Jessop (eds) *Ethics in qualitative research*, London: Sage, pp 108–121.

Frank, A. (1995) *The wounded storyteller: Body, illness, and ethics*, Chicago, IL: University of Chicago Press.

Gatrell, C. (2009) 'Safeguarding subjects? A reflexive appraisal of researcher accountability in qualitative interviews', *Qualitative Research in Organizations and Management*, 4(2): 110-122.

Geertz, C. (1973) *The interpretation of cultures: Selected essays*, New York, NY: Basic Books.

Harding, S. (1987) 'Is there a feminist method?', in S. Harding (ed) *Feminism and methodology: Social science issues*, Bloomington, IN: Indiana University Press, pp 1-14.

Henwood, K. and Shirani, F. (2012a) 'Researching the temporal', in H. Cooper (ed) *Handbook of research methods in psychology: Volume 2*, Washington, DC: APA Publications, pp 209-224.

Henwood, K. and Shirani, F. (2012b) *Extending temporal horizons*, Timescapes Methods Guides Series No. 4. (online).

Lincoln, Y.S. and Guba, E.G. (1985) *Naturalistic inquiry*, Newbury Park, CA: Sage Publications.

MacIntyre, A. (1981) *After virtue: A study in moral theory*, Notre Dame, IN: University of Notre Dame Press.

Marsiglio, W. and Pleck, J. (2005) 'Fatherhood and masculinities', in M.S. Kimmel, J. Hearn and R.W. Connell (eds) *Handbook of studies on men and masculinities,* Thousand Oaks, CA: Sage Publications.

Miller, T. (2005) *Making sense of motherhood: A narrative approach*, Cambridge: Cambridge University Press.

Miller, T. (2010) *Making sense of fatherhood: Gender, caring and work*, Cambridge: Cambridge University Press.

Miller, T. (2017) *Making sense of parenthood: Caring, gender and family lives*, Cambridge: Cambridge University Press.

Neale, B. (2013) 'Adding time into the mix: stakeholder ethics in qualitative longitudinal research', *Methodological innovations Online*, 8: 6-20.

Neale, B. (2015) 'Time and the lifecourse: Perspectives from qualitative longitudinal research', in N. Worth & I. Hardill (eds) *Researching the lifecourse: Critical reflections from the social sciences*, Bristol: Policy Press.

Neale, B. (In press) *What is qualitative longitudinal research?*, London: Bloomsbury.

Oakley, A. (1981) 'Interviewing women: a contradiction in terms', in H. Roberts (ed) *Doing feminist research*, London: Routledge & Kegan Paul, pp 30-61.

Oakley, A. (2016) 'Interviewing women again: power, time and the gift', *Sociology*, 50 (1): 195-213.

Padfield, M. and Proctor, I. (1996) 'The effect of interviewer's gender on the interviewing process: a comparative enquiry', *Sociology*, 30(2): 355-366.

Pini, B. (2005) 'Interviewing men: gender and the collection and interpretation of qualitative data', *Journal of Sociology*, 41(2): 201-216.

Roberts, H. (ed) (1981) *Doing feminist research*, London: Routledge & Kegan Paul.

Ribbens, J. and Edwards, R. (1998) *Feminist dilemmas in qualitative research*, London: Sage Publications.

Riessman, C.K. (2008) *Narrative methods for the human sciences*, Thousand Oaks, CA: Sage Publications.

Seidler, V. (2006) *Transforming masculinities*, London: Routledge.

Shirani, F. and Henwood, K. (2011) 'Taking one day at a time: temporal experiences in the context of unexpected life course transitions', *Time & Society*, 20: 49-68.

Thomson, R. (2009) *Unfolding lives: Youth, gender, change*, Bristol: Policy Press.

Thomson, R. and McLeod, J. (2015) 'New frontiers in qualitative longitudinal research: an agenda for research', *International Journal of Social Research Methodology*, 18(3): 243-250.

THREE

Researching fathers through surveys: methodological challenges

Maria Letizia Bosoni and Sara Mazzucchelli[1]

Introduction

Research on fatherhood has increased in recent years, especially in the form of qualitative studies that allow a deeper understanding of specific aspects of fatherhood, such as fathers' representations and expectations, paternal care practices and relationship with the mother. In this chapter, while confirming the benefits of qualitative research, we discuss how a quantitative approach to researching fatherhood can highlight interesting aspects, giving a brief overview of the topic in large and important surveys.

Researchers agree that the transition to parenthood, long treated mainly as a female issue, is relevant today for both mothers and fathers; in fact, broad trends point to men's increasing desire to participate in their children's lives and their involvement in childcare practices (Day and Lamb, 2004; Gregory and Milner, 2011; Miller, 2011; O'Brien and Wall, 2015).

As a consequence, in recent years, fathers have become more visible in the parenting landscape, and scientific literature on their involvement in childcare has grown (Burgess and Russell, 2004; Doucet, 2006; Mahwah et al, 2009; Bosoni, 2014a, 2014b; Miller and Dermott, 2015; Crespi and Ruspini, 2016). The father's role is now widely acknowledged in policy discourse, and a recognition of fathers' rights and responsibilities is increasingly – although heterogeneously – reflected in social policy systems. Alongside changes taking place in many areas of social life (economic crisis, gender equality issues, transformation in work time and space, the rise of the dual-earner family model and so on), fathers want to share children's education and growth within the family, and the role of work–life balance policies is also crucial in creating new patterns of family relations and gender roles (Lamb and Sagi, 2001; Meth and McClymont, 2009).

Although, in terms of childcare practices, research indicates that fathers engage in a wider range of activities (and to a greater extent) than in the past, they still play a secondary role in childcare, where they are mainly involved in domestic and playing activities but less in physical care, with the mother acting as primary caregiver (Bosoni, 2014b; O'Brien, 2009; Tanturri and Mencarini, 2009). Moreover, studies highlight fathers' increased emotional connection with children; nurturing and emotionally involved fathers thus seem to suggest a new model of masculinity, although the traditional breadwinner role is still strong in many countries (Gillies, 2009; Perra and Ruspini, 2013). In such a context, where tradition and modernity coexist, changing gender roles require more articulated strategies in the division of responsibilities.

Moreover, changes in fathers' practices are strictly linked to the cultural dimension of fatherhood, that is, the 'norms, values, beliefs, and expressive symbols pertaining to fatherhood' (LaRossa et al, 2000, p 375). **Fatherhood norms** include the norms that men are expected to follow when they become fathers and that distinguish them from non-fathers. For example, in western industrialised societies, three sets of fatherhood norms historically have come to define fatherhood: the 'father as the economic provider for the family', the 'father as male role model for both daughters and sons', and the 'father as children's playmate and companion' (LaRossa, 2007, p 89). **Fatherhood values** concern the salience and relevance levels of being fathers. To assess fatherhood values, we would ask: How important are fathers in a particular situation? Are fathers held in high or low esteem? Are fathers viewed as competent or incompetent caregivers? **Fatherhood beliefs** concern what fathers think about their role, and come from stories about what fathers did in the past and what they are capable of doing in the future. These stories may or may not be accurate. However, valid or not, their impact is significant for valuing themselves as good fathers or otherwise. Young fathers can erroneously believe, for example, that men in the past did not change nappies, thus proudly considering themselves as the first generation to engage in infant care. **Fatherhood symbols** are potent elements in the culture of fatherhood. Ceremonies intended to honour fathers (such as Father's Day) are expressive symbols, as are the words used to talk about fatherhood (LaRossa, 2007). So as LaRossa and colleagues (2000) show, the images of fathers in culture may affect the social reality of fatherhood, thus influencing men's expectations about the father role.

Crucial in this regard are questions about whether the culture of fatherhood has changed. LaRossa and colleagues (LaRossa and Reitzes,

1993; LaRossa et al, 2000), by content analysis of 490 Father's Day and Mother's Day comic strips published from 1940 to 1999, reported a loss of the patriarchal fatherhood, with less 'incompetent fathers' starting to appear from the 1950s, and nurturing and supportive fathers most evident in the late 1940s and early 1950s as well as in 1990s. They agreed that there has been a change in the culture of fatherhood, but did not agree on how much of a change had occurred, when the change occurred, or how the change could be characterised in terms of linear shifts or oscillating fluctuations. What is beyond doubt is that the culture of fatherhood changes over decades, but not in a linear or simple way.

As a consequence, fathering practices vary a lot across cultures and history; different social, economic and political contexts have produced different types of father involvement (Coleman and Ganong, 2003). It is interesting to note that some scholars have used the study of cultural artifacts to provide information about what a culture holds as valued as well as insight into how the participants of a culture make meaning: artefacts such as media, books and comic strips are possible sources of role identity information for male parents and may provide a model of fathering behaviours (LaRossa and Reitzes, 1993; Quinn, 2006).

However, such a cultural dimension is not easy to detect, mainly as the operationalisation of values and orientations behind the paternal role is ambiguous; the definition of the concept of value is so complex that some authors speak of a 'terminological jungle' (Halman, 1995) and a 'black box' (Hechter, 1993), highlighting that in social research we can only grasp beliefs, attitudes and opinions, which are assumed to refer to the values as a profound guide to human action[2] (Cipriani, 2012). Few studies have examined how men come to define their fatherhood[3] – the act of being a father – as opposed to merely 'fathering' a child, finding a variety of factors influencing it: men's relationship with their own fathers, their perception of what a father *ought* to be, their spouse's perception of fathering responsibilities, the portrayal of fathers in the media and social expectations. So fatherhood also reflects ideas about the rights, duties and activities of men in families and society, and in other social and symbolic relationships. Thus fatherhood reflects a normative set of social practices and expectations that are institutionalised within religion, politics, law and culture. Social theories, moreover, refer to social fatherhood to explain how the institution of fatherhood links a particular child to a particular man in order to secure a place for that child in the social structure; fathering – in contrast to fatherhood – refers more directly to what men do with and for children, and fathers must learn how to be a parent (Hobson, 2002; Coleman and Ganong, 2003; Dermott, 2008; Featherstone, 2009).

Moreover, the link between cultural aspects or values and practices requires further discussion; the causal–linear relationship between some values/opinions and actions is not given, as human behaviours are always derived from a complex mix of both cultural and structural factors. Qualitative and quantitative research methods are often presented as different paradigms in research, based on different epistemological assumptions and research cultures; however, these techniques are often used in a combined way to better grasp complex and multidimensional phenomena (Gabb, 2009). The methodological issue in sociological research is extremely relevant as it refers to techniques to be used in relation to the specific object analysed. The results in fact are closely related to the methodological choices made to investigate the field of study.

Qualitative research allows us to grasp daily personal life, experiences and motivations, and is aimed at understanding action courses rather than searching for causal relationships to make sense of personal biographies. Quantitative research instead intends to explain and generalise phenomena by an extensive method based on a significant number of cases analysed with statistical procedures; its results are numerically expressed and they can be extended to similar phenomena. Choices related to the methodological issue, however, require an accurate reflection in order to capture the complexity of today's social world, which can be grasped by combining different methods and techniques.

From a quantitative perspective, large international surveys have been used to investigate relevant topics, including family life, gender roles and care. Such topics are addressed with ad hoc scales and variables, covering many European countries, thus allowing a useful comparison between them. Additionally, statistically representative samples are very relevant methodological elements. However, qualitative methods (narrative and biographic) have largely been used, at least recently – for studying fatherhood and how/if it has changed (Thompson, 2004; Brannen and Nilsen, 2006; Latshaw, 2011). This is partly because of a lack of detailed questions on fatherhood or small numbers of items (questions) in large-scale, nationally representative surveys.

Moreover, some caveats need to be taken into consideration when researching complex issues through large surveys: What are the theoretical and methodological orientations inside a survey? What are the aims? Which variables are used to investigate a specific issue (that is, family, fathers, gender role, or care?). The concept of fatherhood is multifaceted and complex and in the same society various concepts of the father's role can coexist, with different defining ideas over time, from breadwinning to involvement and nursing, as well as 'absent' and 'new' fathers. Thus, the ways in which fatherhood have been defined and consequently operationalised have changed in important ways. Lamb (2000) describes a shift from a focus on qualitative dimensions, in studying masculinity and male identity, to a more quantifiable dimension for exploring the concept of involvement – for example, the amount of time spent by fathers with their children – producing a restricted focus on paternal nurturance with little attention to the cultural variation in the definition and understanding of fatherhood.

If it is certainly true that different methods are better suited to grasping complex concepts, it is also true that the method we use to investigate social reality influences the results themselves in terms of our knowledge of the object. So, methodological attention is required in researching fatherhood. This chapter asks why and how to investigate fathers from a quantitative perspective, using large and sophisticated surveys providing large amounts of interesting data – without incurring costs, as these datasets have been collected as part of nationally funded initiatives and available to scholars for further analysis – that have not, however, been designed merely to investigate fatherhood.

In this chapter, we focus on researching fatherhood within a quantitative approach, first, giving a brief overview of the topic, scales and aspects of fatherhood and gender roles in some important surveys (the European Values Study [EVS], the Generations and Gender Programme [GGP] and the International Social Survey Programme [ISSP][4]) and second, providing critical methodological considerations about researching fathers. Even if these large datasets do not specifically focus on fathers, they can be used by scholars to learn more about fathers and fathering.

We chose to focus on these three particular surveys as they have high-quality features: they are longitudinal and transnational, they use well-structured methodology and instruments, and they provide a specific pool of questions on family life.

Overview of surveys

European Values Study

The EVS is a large-scale, transnational, longitudinal research programme on human values in Europe (www.europeanvaluesstudy.eu).

The study began in 1981 and is updated every nine years, involving an ever-growing number of countries; the fourth wave (2008) covers 47 European countries/regions. It is based on representative multi-stage or stratified random samples of the 18-year-old+ population of each country, totalling 67,492 interviewees. It investigates the moral, religious, societal, political, work and family values of Europeans. This is obviously not the only existing survey on values, nor is it the only possible way to explore this issue (other interesting examples are Schwartz's Theory of Basic Human Values, the Rokeach Value Survey, the Allport-Vernon-Lindzey Study of Values, the Hartman Value Inventory and the World Values Survey). This programme, however, has some peculiarities and definitely noteworthy aspects that can be identified and summarised by means of a simple analytical grid.

The first survey was intended to respond to the above questions by focusing on a small number of countries.

The EVS programme, however, has some peculiarities and noteworthy aspects, summarised in Box 3.1.

Box 3.1: Identifying features of the European Values Study
Structural features

An extended temporal dimension (1981–) and ever-expanding reference pool:

- **1981**: first EVS wave (16 countries);
- **1990**: second EVS wave (29 countries);
- **1999**: third EVS wave (33 countries);
- **2008**: fourth EVS wave (47 countries/regions).

A wide, well-structured survey instrument, with the following principal investigative domains:

- **life**: wellbeing, happiness, life satisfaction, locus of control;
- **family**: marriage, children, unconditional love, role of women, transmission of values;
- **work**: importance, work qualities, job satisfaction, work ethos, obedience to one's superior;
- **religion**: church attendance, confidence in the church, importance of God, traditional beliefs;
- **politics**: political interest, willingness to join in political actions, left-right placement, post-materialism, support for democracy;

• **society**: social networks, confidence in others, solidarity, tolerance, permissiveness.

Strong methodological structure: the EVP is governed by the Council of Program Directors, discussing the project's guidelines and approving the questionnaire and the surveying method. Day-to-day management is entrusted to an Executive Committee. The questionnaire is developed by a Theory Group, while the project's quality is the responsibility of a Methodology Group.

Cultural features

Clarity and relevance of the original objectives: the EVS started off as the European Value Systems Study Group (EVSSG) at the end of the 1970s, from an informal group of scholars[5] interested in studying and understanding the process of secularisation as Europe was being formed. **This early research unit adopted the following questions emerging from a conference organised by bishops, who formed one of the interest groups:**

• Do Europeans share common values?
• Are values changing in Europe and, if so, in what directions?
• Do Christian values still permeate European life and culture?
• Is a consistent alternative meaning system replacing Christianity?
• What are the implications of secularisation for European unity?

The first survey was intended to respond to these questions by focusing on a small number of countries.

From its very beginning as the EVSSG to the present day, the EVS has aimed to study the values of Europeans and the possible convergences and divergences between ever-changing cultural contexts. How? In the EVS, values are investigated mainly in terms of detected attitudes, beliefs and opinions. Behind this choice, doubtless dictated by the complexity of definitions and operationalisation, there is a functional idea of value. Values are not defined by what they are, but by what they do (Halman, 1995), namely as deeply rooted motivations or orientations that direct actions and can explain people's beliefs, norms and opinions (Lidz, 1981).

EVS is a complex survey influenced by **internal** and **external** drivers. As **internal** drivers, we could identify a specific and explicit theoretical perspective, a methodological attention on variable construction and a different articulation of domain in the questionnaire.[6] It is important to deepen the theoretical perspective; the questionnaire design in fact took into account the transformative processes of western societies – modernisation, individualisation, globalisation, secularisation, the EU enlargement process – according to the theoretical approach developed by different authors and in particular by Inglehart (1977, 1997, 2003, 2008) and Giddens (1991). As **external** drivers, the scientific community (EVS data users) influences the EVS's methodological and theory group choices.

Generations and Gender Programme

The GGP is a longitudinal survey of 18- to 79-year-olds in 19 countries (www.ggp-i.org). More precisely, wave 1 (2003-04) data is available for 19 countries: Australia, Austria, Belgium, Bulgaria, Czech Republic, Estonia, France, Georgia, Germany, Hungary, Italy, Japan, Lithuania, Netherlands, Norway, Poland, Romania, Russian Federation and Sweden. Wave 2 (2007-12) data is available for 10 countries: Australia, Austria, Bulgaria, Czech Republic, France, Georgia, Germany, Hungary, Lithuania and the Netherlands.

The GGP survey has an average of 9,000 respondents per country, making cross-national comparability possible.

This research programme aims to improve the **understanding of the various factors** – including public policy and programme interventions – that **affect the relationships between parents and children (generations) and between partners (gender)**.

A broad array of topics, including fertility, partnership, the transition to adulthood, economic activity, care duties and attitudes, are covered by the survey, which is available online; this also allows some simple online analysis.

International Social Survey Programme

The ISSP is a continuing annual programme of cross-national collaboration on surveys covering topics important for social science research (www.issp.org). It brings together pre-existing social science projects[7] and coordinates research goals, thereby adding a cross-national, cross-cultural perspective to individual national studies. Currently, 45 countries[8] are members of the ISSP, alongside the ISSP secretariat and the ISSP archive. As is the case for the EVS, the GESIS-Leibniz Institute for the Social Sciences, Germany, is responsible for archiving, integrating and documenting data, and for the distribution of the merged international datasets for the programme. Since 1997, the

GESIS Data Archive has been supported in the processing of data by the Spanish ISSP partner *Análisis Sociológicos, Económicos y Políticos.*

The ISSP sub-groups drawn up within the ISSP comprise drafting groups for modules and a methodology research group – a special group that is responsible for defining the methodological criteria and comparability between countries.

The annual topics for ISSP are developed over several years by a sub-committee and pre-tested in various countries. The topics include the following:

- role of government (1985, 1990, 1996, 2006, 2016);
- social networks (1986, 2001, planned 2017);
- social inequality (1987, 1992, 1999, 2009);
- family and changing gender roles (1988, 1994, 2002, 2012);
- work orientations (1989, 1997, 2005, 2015);
- religion (1991, 1998, 2008, planned 2018);
- environment (1993, 2000, 2010);
- national identity (1995, 2003, 2013);
- citizenship (2004, 2014);
- leisure time and sports (2007);
- health (2011).

ISSP marks several new departures in the area of cross-national research. First, the collaboration between organisations is not special or intermittent, but routine and continual. Second, ISSP makes cross-national research a basic part of the national research agenda of each participating country. Third, by combining a cross-time with a cross-national perspective, two powerful research designs are being used to study societal processes.

Structural critical analysis of surveys: how fathers are investigated

In this section, we consider which and how different aspects of fatherhood are addressed in each of the three surveys.

European Values Study

As previously mentioned, the amount of space devoted in the questionnaire to different domains (national identity; religion and morality; policy and society; family; work; environment; life perception) is not constant. Over time, some domains of life have been given more weighting than others (for example, environment; national identity; policy and society), while others have seen their weighting reduced (family; religion and morality).

Figure 3.1 compares the different weightings allocated to the different domains in each wave.

The content of the domains has also changed, with some questions being replaced by others.

Figure 3.1: Changes over time in research domains

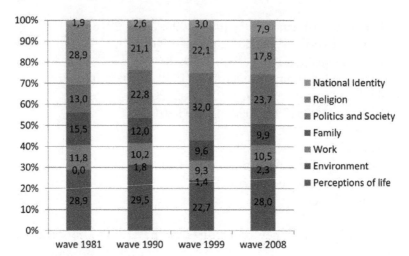

With regard to the family domain, some changes are of particular interest. The first wave (1981) included a substantial battery (10 items) on the situations in which divorce was considered acceptable. These questions were successively discarded (1990), to make room for the increasingly topical theme of equality between men and women; its six-item-strong battery in 1990 was increased to seven items in 1999 and eight in 2008. The eight areas where questionnaire respondents can express degrees of agreement are shown in Table 3.1.

The first six items are common to other surveys born in the late 1970s (such as the ISSP), while items relating to the fathers (seven and eight) were included only in the later waves, as a result of greater social and scientific debate on the role of the father and parental roles. In Table 3.2, we can identify several questions in the integrated dataset (1981–2008) for domain and wave. As can be seen from a quick count, there is an item imbalance favouring the mother figure (14 items, compared with eight for fathers) and a predominance of items in the **family** domain, where orientations towards work and care are investigated

Table 3.1: Equality between men and women in EVS

Q48 People talk about the changing roles of men and women today. For each of the following statements I read out, can you tell me how much you agree with each? Please use the responses on this card.

	Agree strongly	Agree	Disagree	Disagree strongly
A working mother can establish just as warm and secure a relationship with her children as a mother who does not work	1	2	3	4
A pre-school child is likely to suffer if his or her mother works	1	2	3	4
A job is alright but what most women really want is a home and children	1	2	3	4
Being a housewife is just as fulfilling as working for pay	1	2	3	4
Having a job is the best way for a woman to be an independent person	1	2	3	4
Both the husband and wife should contribute to household income	1	2	3	4
In general, fathers are as well suited to look after their children as mothers	1	2	3	4
Men should take as much responsibility as women for the home and children	1	2	3	4

for men and women. The other domains involved are **perceptions of life**, which gathers some judgments related to motherhood and abortion; **religion and moral**, which analyses the relevance, for the respondents, of their relationship with their father and mother; and **life experience**, where respondents are asked whether they had to face a parent's death at an early or later age.

Generations and Gender Programme

In its section on parents and the parental home, the GGP gathers structural data on parents (level of education, type of employment), and examines aspects such of the type of relationship and the existing level of formalisation between parents (marriage, cohabitation, separation), the time spent by interviewees with their parents, judgements about parental effectiveness or the ability of each parent to take care of survey respondents, and respondents' levels of satisfaction with their relationship with each parent.

In the section on partner's activity and income, the most relevant areas for our purposes concern maternity leave, parental leave or childcare leave, and the degree of satisfaction and the impact of such leave on the return to work or the intention to resume work. The richest section,

Table 3.2: EVS integrated dataset (1981-2008), overview of domains over time

EVS (integrated dataset 1981-2008)	Both EVS and WVS (World Values Survey)	EVS1 (1981)	EVS2 (1990)	EVS3 (1999)	EVS4 (2008)
Perceptions of life					
Abortion if the mother's health is at risk	x	x	x		
Abortion if a woman is not married	x	x	x	x	x
Don't like as neighbours: unmarried mothers	x	x			
Family					
Women need children in order to be fulfilled	x	x	x	x	x
Men need children in order to be fulfilled	x			x	x
Female single parent, no stable relationship with man	x	x	x	x	x
Working mother warm relationship with children	x		x	x	x
Being a housewife as fulfilling as paid job	x		x	x	x
Husband and wife contribute to household income	x		x	x	x
Men make better political leaders than women do	x			x	
Pre-school child suffers with working mother	x		x	x	x
Women really want home and children	x		x	x	x
Job best way for women to be independent	x		x	x	x
Fathers **are** as well suited to look after children as mothers	x			x	x
Men should take the same responsibility **as women** for home and children					x

EVS (integrated dataset 1981-2008)	Both EVS and WVS (World Values Survey)	EVS1 (1981)	EVS2 (1990)	EVS3 (1999)	EVS4 (2008)
Men are less able to handle emotions in relationships than women	x			x	
Religion and morality					
Relationship between you and your mother	x	x			
Relationship between you and your father	x	x			
Life experience					
Experienced death of father					x
Age experienced death of father					x
Experienced death of mother					x
Age experienced death of mother					x

however, is that concerning value orientations and attitudes; here, many points are investigated, some of which mirror items covered in EVS. In addition to marriage, cohabitation and divorce, this sections investigates opinions about gender roles and care (Box 3.2).

Box 3.2: Value orientations and attitudes of gender roles in GGP

1107. To what extent do you agree or disagree with each of the following statements?

a. Marriage is an outdated institution.
b. It is alright for an unmarried couple to live together even if they have no interest in marriage.
c. Marriage is a lifetime relationship and should never be ended.
d. It is alright for a couple with an unhappy marriage to get a divorce even if they have children.
e. A woman has to have children in order to be fulfilled.
f. A man has to have children in order to be fulfilled.
g. A child needs a home with both a father and a mother to grow up happily.

h. A woman can have a child as a single parent even if she doesn't want to have a stable relationship with a man.

i. When children turn about 18-20 years old they should start to live independently.

j. Homosexual couples should have the same rights as heterosexual couples do.

1113. To what extent do you agree with the following statements?

a. In a couple it is better for the man to be older than the woman.

b. If a woman earns more than her partner, it is not good for the relationship.

c. On the whole, men make better political leaders than women do.

d. Women should be able to decide how to spend the money they earn without having to ask their partner's permission.

e. Looking after the home or family is just as fulfilling as working for pay.

f. A pre-school child is likely to suffer if his/her mother works.

g. Children often suffer because their fathers concentrate too much on their work.

h. If parents divorce it is better for the child to stay with the mother than with the father.

1114. To what extent do you agree or disagree with the following statements?

a. When jobs are scarce, men should have more right to a job than women.

b. When jobs are scarce, younger people should have more right to a job than older people.

c. When jobs are scarce, people with children should have more right to a job than childless people.

In a section on children, GGP also analyses care practices and distribution of tasks between mothers and fathers (Box 3.3).

A longitudinal analysis, however, is almost impossible because the GGP has only two waves.

Box 3.3: Childcare practices and distribution of tasks in GGP

Could you just tell me which of the other household members?

(R = respondent P = partner) Always R/usually R/R and P about equally/usually P/always P/always or usually other persons in the household/always or usually someone not living in the household/children do it themselves/not applicable

a. Dressing the children or seeing that the children are properly dressed.

b. Putting the children to bed and/or seeing that they go to bed.

c. Staying at home with the children when they are ill.

d. Playing with the children and/or taking part in leisure activities with them.

e. Helping the children with homework.

f. Taking the children to/from school, day care centre, babysitter or leisure activities.

International Social Survey Programme

As already mentioned, the ISSP is a continuing annual programme of cross-national collaboration on surveys covering topics important for social science research. These topics, in chronological order of the first survey in each area, cover family and changing gender roles (1988, 1994, 2002, 2012); work orientations (1989, 1997, 2005, 2015); religion[9] (1991, 1998, 2008, planned 2018) and leisure time and sports[10] (2007).

Table 3.3: Family and changing gender roles in ISSP

1988 – the significance of family and changing sex roles	1994 – the significance of family and changing sex roles	2002 – family and gender roles	2012 – family and changing gender roles
Attitude to employment of women (scale)	x		
Preferred extent of employment of women during various stages of child raising	x	x	x
Attitude to single fathers and mothers			
Employment of mother during childhood of respondent	x	x	x
Extent of employment during various stages of child raising	x	x	x
Income of both spouses			
Attitude to children (scale)	x		
	Attitude to role distribution of man and woman		
	Attitude to paid maternity leave		
	Preferred measures to care for babies of working couples		
	Ideal number of children		
	Attitude to single fathers and mothers		
	Partner or respondent as manager of household income		

We focus on the surveys on family and changing gender roles (in 1988, 1994, 2002, 2012) (Table 3.3) and work orientations (in 1989, 1997, 2005) (Table 3.4) as the two topics most relevant to our investigation, in order to identify not only the specific areas surveyed but also the changes undergone in the survey over time.

As can be seen from the analysis of family and changing gender roles (Table 3.3) there are no specific sets of variables for fathers; the central focus is the mother or at most the parental couple.

Table 3.4: Work orientations in ISSP

1989	1997	2005
Attitude to work. Work orientation and description of work responsibilities.	Attitude to work. Work orientation and description of work responsibilities.	Attitude to work. Work orientation and description of work contents.
desired division of time for selected activities such as work, leisure time etc.;	x	x
work orientation accomplishment of work in household;	x	
part-time employment;	x	
interest in full-time employment;	x	
expected difficulties in looking for work;		
description of personal commitment at work;		
preference for more work and more pay or more leisure time;		
significance of career possibilities and flexible organization of working hours;	x	
personal opportunities to influence the form of the work day or the course of work;		
job satisfaction;		
		preference for full-time employment or part-time employment;
		difficulties in handling personal matters during working hours;
		frequency of the impairment of the family life by the work requirements and vice versa;

The broadening of questions over time is also evident: the first wave (1988) focused on employment along the life course; the second wave (1994) analyses the role distribution of men and women and preferred measures to care for babies of working couples; the third one (2002) deepens shared housekeeping, attitudes towards children and introduces the theme of stress (caused by family, work and household duties) and satisfaction with employment situation and family life; and the last wave (2012) looks in particular at 'attitude' towards paid leave for full-time working parents, preferred duration and best way of organising paid leave.

Even for work orientations (Table 3.4), existing sets of variables concern both men and women. It is interesting to highlight the focus of the first sets of variables (1989, 1997) on attitude to work (paid, housework), work orientation (part-time, full-time, career possibilities and flexible organisation of working hours) and description of work responsibilities, and the predominance of the third (2005) on work contents, preference for full-time employment or part-time employment and frequency of the impairment of family life by work requirements and vice versa.

Critical analysis of items: what can we learn about fathers from surveys

In this section, we critically reflect on items previously identified in order to see which aspect of fatherhood they refer to and how they contribute to an understanding of fatherhood. The **EVS** is based on a bidimensional articulation of human value and cultural orientation, so questions are conceived to investigate opinion over a continuum, where, for example, acceptance of authority is opposed to freedom and individual choice, and compliance with rules and moral standards is opposed to personal interest. With reference to gender roles, questions refer mainly to equality between men and women, fathers and mothers, with six items investigating opinions about the mother as a main caregiver and her job (see Table 3.1). The basic idea emerging here is that the mother is the primary – or sole – caregiver and that work has a negative impact on care and family responsibilities. The father is thus entitled as a caregiver, by assimilating fatherhood to the maternal care model (item 'Fathers are as well suited to look after children as mothers') and engaging in domestic activities ('Men should take the same responsibility as women for home and children'). However, some authors have argued that this scale shows a traditional orientation towards gender role and suggest caution in comparing these items in different countries with diverse cultural orientations towards 'traditional gender role' (Braun, 2008; Philipov, 2008; Braun and Scott, 2009).

Also the idea that having children is a natural fulfilment for both male and female identity arises from the item 'A woman/man has to have children in order to be fulfilled', but also the irrelevance (or lesser importance) of the father in parenting with the question about whether a woman can have a child as a single parent even if she does not want to have a stable relationship with a man. Note that only in wave 3 (1999) of this survey did a couple of questions address the political dimension of men ('On the whole, men make better political leaders than women do') and that they are unaccustomed to emotional expression ('Men are less able to handle emotions in relationships than women'), a current issue in contemporary thinking about fathers.

In the **GGP**, in the session on value orientations and attitudes, items do not expressly concern fathers, but by pointing out some of the differences between men and women (with regard to age, status, power and couple decision-making processes) they highlight some gender stereotypes articulated – here, too, according to a bidimensional and oppositive logic, with men as the breadwinners with power in decision making both inside the home and in the public domain, and women as less powerful in general. Family care is also addressed in comparison with work engagement ('Looking after the home or family is just as fulfilling as working for pay'), thus referring to the extent to which family duties and work are really of equal importance.

Here an interesting item is present, different from those in the other surveys considered and questioning the conflictual link between parenting and work for fathers ('Children often suffer because their fathers concentrate too much on their work'), while typically the consequences for children are considered in relation with the maternal presence (see EVS items), where the breadwinner model is problematised as potentially negative for children. The issue of absent fathers and the impact of divorce is highlighted through the question of whether it is better for the child to stay with the mother than with the father if parents divorce; this is a relevant and increasingly discussed topic as transformation processes and increased variability in family forms creates a variety of contexts in which fathers perform their role (biological/non-biological, resident/non-resident, in couple/single fathers) (Kalmijn, 2015).

In the session on children, care practices and task distribution between mothers and fathers are explored in detail. The GGP is the only survey among those here considered that specifically investigates this topic. Care is distinguished in **physical tasks** (dressing the children or seeing that the children are properly dressed, putting the children to bed and/or seeing that they go to bed, staying at home with the children when they are ill), **recreational activities** (playing with the children and/or taking part in leisure activities with them) and **organisational aspects** (taking the children to/from school, day care centre, babysitter or leisure activities, and helping the children with homework). Thus, it covers not only ideas and orientation about fatherhood, but also practical and concrete aspects on what fathers do with their children.

The **ISSP** session on family and changing gender roles (2012) addresses the following topics: attitude towards employment of mothers; role distribution of men and women in occupation and household; preferred extent of employment for women during different stages of child raising; attitude towards paid leave for full-time working parents; preferred division of paid leave period between mother and father; allocation of duties in the household and in family matters; and estimation of fair share of the household work. A specific interest in fathers does not clearly emerge here, with items oriented more towards the couple's allocation of tasks and care. However, some dimensions of fathering (in comparison with mothering) are addressed, especially attitudes towards paid leave for working parents, preferred duration of leave and the best way to organise such leave.

Conclusion

The three surveys considered here have in common the fact that they are not designed specifically to investigate fathers; however, they contribute to such investigations by addressing different aspects of the paternal role. While the EVS focuses on orientations and conceptions about fatherhood in general, the GGP appears more complete, mixing both orientations (fatherhood) and care practices (fathering), and the ISSP is focused less on fathers but more on care practice (family practices in terms of what parents do) and household organisation. In this closing section, we reflect critically on researching fathers using large comparative surveys, highlighting strengths and weaknesses and what we can or cannot learn from them.

One of the main advantages in using such data is the possibility of comparing large populations in different cultural and geographical contexts and over time (through a longitudinal perspective). However, while such surveys allow investigation of some specific content (such as family practices), they struggle to grasp aspects related to the identity of persons and the fundamental reasons for actions. The analysis of specific items has highlighted the fact that, in all three surveys considered, some aspects are overestimated, while others are missing, risking parenthood being defined on the basis of stereotypes or partial visions (that is, traditionalism versus equity) and set according to an appositive and dichotomous logic, failing to capture nuances and transformative processes. For example, the image of fathers as main breadwinners is still very present; at most, its persistence is questioned but there is no investigation into how fathers are involved in caring. The paternal identity is conceived as constituted mainly by work, with care as secondary and assessed according to maternal codes (the EVS even asks if fathers are able to look after their children *as mothers*). If a specific male role in care remains underestimated, the risk is that these surveys are overcoming a traditional view – based on distinction – in favour of one based on gender neutrality and non-discrimination. So, when to use this data and when other methods? One initial consideration is that large surveys allow comparison of practices and services, from a transnational and longitudinal perspective, thus revealing uses for policy and intervention implementation; with deeper investigation, it is also possible to grasp the representation and the imagery on which practices are built. In addition, a focus on fathering practices, often prevalent in these surveys, does not fully consider the identity dimension and meaning of such practices, aspects that could most profitably be investigated through qualitative methodologies (life stories, narrative interviews and discussion groups). In conclusion, although these surveys are very interesting and allow an exploration of various aspects of families and fathers, quantitative ad hoc surveys on fathers are still missing and therefore necessary.

Notes

[1] Paragraph attribution: Bosoni: 'Introduction' and 'Critical analysis of items'; Sara Mazzucchelli: 'Overview of surveys' and 'Structural critical analysis of surveys'. Conclusion written jointly by both authors.

[2] For this reason, in surveys on values, including the European Values Study, values themselves are investigated by measuring opinions, beliefs, attitudes and behaviours.

[3] An exception is given by scholars from the Oxford Network of European Fatherhood Researchers (www.brookes.ac.uk/onefar). For further information, see Miller and Dermott (2015).

[4] We will focus on family and changing gender roles (1988, 1994, 2002, 2012) and work orientations (1989, 1997, 2005).

[5] Particularly, Jan Kerkhofs (Catholic University of Leuven, Belgium) and Ruud de Moor (Tilburg University, the Netherlands).

[6] Although the interests of the survey were always the same, the space devoted to different domains (national identity; religion and morality; policy and society; family; work; environment; life perception) investigated by the questionnaire is not constant.

[7] The German General Social Survey (ALLBUS/GGSS), Zentrum für Umfragen, Methoden, und Analysen (ZUMA) of Mannheim, Germany; National Opinion Research Center (NORC) of Chicago; Social and Community Planning Research (SCPR) of London; Research School of Social Sciences (RSSS), Australian National University.

[8] Argentina; Australia; Austria; Belgium; Bolivia; Bulgaria; Canada; Chile; China; Croatia; Czech Republic; Denmark; Estonia; Finland; France; Georgia; Germany; Great Britain; Hungary; Iceland; India; Ireland; Israel; Japan; Latvia; Lithuania; Mexico; Netherlands; Norway; Philippines; Poland; Portugal; Russia; Slovakia; Slovenia; South Africa; South Korea; Spain; Suriname; Sweden; Switzerland; Taiwan; Turkey; US; Venezuela.

[9] The waves relating to religion (1998, 2008), focusing on attitude to religious practices, using substantially the same aspects, or more precisely judgements, on distribution of roles in marriage and attitude to working women.

[10] It explores the meaning of time and leisure, and its relation to work and other spheres of life; it also investigates the concept of the ideal man and woman.

References

Bosoni, M.L. (2014a) 'Breadwinners or involved fathers? Men, fathers and work in Italy', *Journal of Comparative Family Studies*, XLV(2): 293-315.

Bosoni, M.L. (2014b) 'Men, fathers and work: the challenge of reconciliation. Case studies in some Italian companies', in E. Carrà (ed) *Families, care and work-life balance services: Case studies of best practices*, Milan: Vita e Pensiero, pp 11-30.

Brannen, J. and Nilsen, A. (2006) 'From fatherhood to fathering: transmission and change among British. Fathers in four-generation families', *Sociology*, 40(2): 335-352.

Braun, M. (2008) 'Using egalitarian items to measure men's and women's family roles', *Sex Roles*, 59: 644-656.

Braun, M. and Scott, J. (2009) 'Gender-role egalitarianism – is the trend reversal real?', *International Journal of Public Opinion Research*, 21(3): 362-367.

Burgess, A. and Russell, G. (2004) 'Fatherhood and public policy', in *Supporting Fathers: Contributions from the International Fatherhood Summit 2003*, The Hague: Bernard van Leer Foundation.

Cipriani, R. (2012) 'La religione dei valori' ('The religion of values'), in S. Belardinelli and L. Gattamorta (eds) *I valori hanno ancora bisogno della religione? (Do values still need religion?)*, Soveria Mannelli: Rubbettino, pp 87-106.

Crespi, I. and Ruspini, E. (2016) *Balancing work and family in a changing society. The fathers' perspective*, Basingstoke: Palgrave Macmillan.

Coleman, M. and Ganong, L.H. (eds) (2003) *Handbook of contemporary families: Considering the past, contemplating the future*, London: Sage Publications.

Day, A. and Lamb, M. (eds) (2004) *Conceptualising and measuring father involvement*, Mahwah, NJ: Lawrence Erlbaum Associates.

Dermott, E. (2008) *Intimate fatherhood*, London: Routledge.

Doucet, A. (2006) *Do men mother? Fathering: Care and domestic responsibility*, Toronto: University of Toronto Press.

Featherstone, B. (2009) *Contemporary fathering: Theory, policy and practice*, Bristol: Policy Press.

Gabb, J. (2009) 'Researching family relationships: a qualitative mixed methods approach', *Methodological Innovations Online*, 4(2): 37-52.

Giddens, A. (1991) *Modernity and self-identity: Self and society in the late modern age*, Cambridge: Polity Press.

Gillies, V. (2009) 'Understandings and experience of involved fathering in the United Kingdom: exploring classed dimensions', *The Annals of the American Academy of Political and Social Science*, 624(1): 49-60.

Gregory, A. and Milner, S. (2011) 'What is "new" about fatherhood? The social construction of fatherhood in France and the UK', *Men and Masculinities*, 6: 1-19.

Halman, L. (1995) 'The need for theory in comparative research on values', Tilburg: Tilburg University, Work and Organization Research Centre.

Hechter, M. (1993) 'Values research in the social and behavioral sciences', in M. Hechter, L. Nadel and R.E. Michod (eds) *The origin of values*, New York, NY: De Gruyter, pp 1-28.

Hobson, B. (2002) *Making men into fathers: Men, masculinities and the social politics of fatherhood*, Cambridge: Cambridge University Press.

Inglehart, R. (1977) *The silent revolution: Changing values and political styles among western publics*, Princeton, NJ: Princeton University Press.

Inglehart, R. (1997) *Modernization and post modernization: Cultural, economic, and political change in 43 societies*, Cambridge: Cambridge University Press.

Inglehart, R. (2003) *Human values and social change: Findings from the values surveys*, Leiden: Brill Academic Publishers.

Inglehart, R. (2008) 'Changing values among western publics from 1970 to 2006', *West European Politics*, 31(1-2): 130-146.

Kalmijn, M. (2015) 'Father-child relations after divorce in four European countries: patterns and determinants', *Comparative Population Studies*, 40(3): 251-276.

Lamb, M.E. (2000) 'The history of research on father involvement', *Marriage and Family Review*, 29(2-3): 23-42.

Lamb, M. E., and Sagi, A. (2001) *Fatherhood and family policy*, London: Routledge.

LaRossa, R. (2007) 'The culture and conduct of fatherhood in America, 1800 to 1960', *Japanese Journal of Family Sociology*, 19(2): 87-98.

LaRossa, R. and Reitzes, D. (1993) 'Symbolic interactionism and family studies', in P. Boss, W. Doherty, R. LaRossa, W. Schumm, and S. Steinmetz (eds) *Sourcebook of family theories and methods*, New York, NY: Plenum, pp 135-163.

LaRossa, R., Jaret, C., Gadgil, M. and Wynn, G.R. (2000) 'The changing culture of fatherhood in comic-strip families: a six-decade analysis', *Journal of Marriage and the Family*, 62: 375-387.

Latshaw, B. A. (2011) 'Is fatherhood a full-time job? Mixed methods insights into measuring stay-at-home fatherhood', *Fathering*, 9(2): 125-149.

Lidz, V. (1981) 'Conceptions of value-relevance and the theory of action', *Sociological Inquiry*, 51(3-4): 371-408.

Mahwah, N.J., Daly, K.J., Ashbourne, L. and Brown, J. L. (2009) 'Fathers' perceptions of children's influence: implications for involvement', *The Annals of the American Academy of Political and Social Science*, 624(1): 61-77.

Meth, P. and McClymont, K. (2009) 'Researching men: the politics and possibilities of a qualitative mixed-methods approach', *Social & Cultural Geography*, 10(8): 909-925.

Miller, T. (2011) *Making sense of fatherhood: Gender, caring and work*, Cambridge: Cambridge University Press.

Miller, T. and Dermott, E. (2015) 'Contemporary fatherhood: continuity, change and future', *Families, Relationships and Societies*, 4(2): 179-181.

O'Brien, M. (2009) 'Fathers, parental leave policies, and infant quality of life', *The Annals of the American Academy of Political and Social Science*, 624(1): 190-213.

O'Brien, M. and Wall, K. (eds) (2015) *Comparative perspectives on work-life balance and gender equality: Fathers on leave alone*, Dordrecht: Springer.

Perra, M. S. and Ruspini, E. (eds) (2013) 'Men who work in 'non-traditional' occupations', *International Review of Sociology*, 23(2): 265-270.

Philipov, D. (2008) 'Family-related gender attitudes', in C. Höhn, D. Avramov and I.E. Kotowska (eds) *People, population change and policies*, Netherlands: Springer, pp 153-174.

Quinn, S.M.F. (2006) 'Examining the culture of fatherhood in American children's literature: presence, interactions, and nurturing behaviors of fathers in Caldecott Award Winning Picture Books (1938-2002)', *Fathering*, 4(1): 71-96.

Tanturri, M.L. and Mencarini, L. (2009) *Fathers' involvement in daily childcare activities in Italy: Does a work-family reconciliation issue exist?*, CHILD Working Paper No. 22/2009, Torino: University of Torino.

Thompson, P. (2004) 'Researching family and social mobility with two eyes: some experiences of the interaction between qualitative and quantitative data', *International Journal of Social Research Methodology*, 7(3): 237-257.

FOUR

Fatherhood research on the internet: methodological reflections from a literature review

Lars Plantin and Kristian Daneback

Introduction

An increasing number of parents are today turning to the internet for information on children and parenting (Daneback and Plantin, 2008). Many are also living part of their family lives, and forming their identities as parents, in various chat forums and online communities and on social media (Plantin and Daneback, 2009). Against this background, the number of sites specifically directed at parents has grown substantially over the past decade. These sites provide opportunities to access large quantities of information on parenting from public sector agencies and experts, but first and foremost, they provide the opportunity for parents to share and obtain experience-based information among themselves. It has been found, however, that many of these sites attract mothers to a greater extent than fathers (Sarkadi and Bremberg, 2005; Pedersen and Smithson, 2013), while more fathers instead appear to be active on social media such as Facebook and various blog sites. Statistics on parents' use of social media show, for example, that a majority of American fathers with internet access use Facebook on a daily basis, and almost half of these state that this provides useful parenting information (Pew Research Center, 2015). New fathers in particular appear to be active on Facebook, where they establish contacts with other parents, post pictures of their children and develop an important source of social support in their parenting (Bartholomew et al, 2012).

The internet has thus become a very interesting arena for studying how fatherhood is expressed and modelled online, as well as a source for other forms of data collection. It provides opportunities to quickly and simply collect large-scale questionnaire data, to conduct interviews or focus groups, to conduct ethnographic studies of discussions in various chat forums, or to follow the reflections of individual fathers on parenthood via blogs or personal web pages. The internet also provides the opportunity to collect large amounts of data on specific groups of fathers that are too small to study in the context of more broadly focused surveys. The internet opens up a world populated by fathers who are visible, and who can be reached and observed. But what characterises the fatherhood research that makes use of the internet to develop an improved knowledge of fathers? What arguments have been presented on the advantages and disadvantages of conducting studies online, and to what extent does this research contribute to the development of new knowledge about fathers? This chapter discusses these questions in more detail on the basis of a literature review of this research field.

Background

When the general public started using the internet, and particularly the World Wide Web at the beginning of the 1990s, it also became an object of interest for researchers within the social sciences: in part as a technology for data collection, in part as a research field in its own right. Some researchers conducted ethnographic field studies directing a focus at the social interactions and communication found in different web arenas (Markham and Baym, 2009). These studies employed the methodological approaches and data collection techniques of conventional ethnographic studies, namely observation, interviews and document studies, which were documented over a long period of time in the form of field notes and memos. The difference was that the researchers no longer had to travel to distant locations in order to study unfamiliar cultures – all that was required was to make one's way to the nearest computer with internet access. Other researchers instead used the internet as a data collection technology for the distribution of questionnaires and to conduct qualitative interviews. The internet made it possible to collect large quantitative data sets with fast response times and at very low cost (Ilieva et al, 2002). The electronic questionnaires employed also made it technically possible to check the data collection process more easily. For example, it became possible to obtain an overview of time the respondents spent on particular questions and to see at which point they stopped completing the survey (Ross et al, 2003; Malhotra, 2008). It also became possible to reduce the internal dropout rate by constructing the survey in such a way that one question has to be answered before you can continue to the next question (Frippiat and Marquis, 2010). Being able to guide the respondents through the questionnaire also minimises the risk of incorrect responses, and the fact that surveys are completed directly online reduces the risk of coding errors. Web surveys also provide the possibility of giving more information and instructions via pop-up windows or links (Shropshire et al, 2009). The primary disadvantage is often the low response rate. A number of studies show that while there are large variations in response rates depending on which approach is employed, web surveys generally have lower response rate than other survey methods (Manfreda et al, 2008; Frippiat and Marquis, 2010). An explanation for this is the increase in the number of online surveys and the difficulty of distinguishing scientific studies from other types of internet survey (Munoz-Leiva et al, 2010). Internet surveys have also been criticised for only reaching out to individuals with access to a computer, and this leads to bias in the data.

Thus there are both advantages and disadvantages associated with using the internet for research purposes, a picture that has emerged successively over the period of just over 20 years in which it has been used in this way. To begin with, however, the research community in general viewed such studies with a great deal of scepticism. One key point of contention related to the study population – how could the researcher know who was being studied, since the involved parties could not see one another? Who could the researcher make statements about? This is a relevant and interesting question, since it also illustrates the way in which the same problem also exists in the context of other more traditional research methods, where there has generally been a relatively uncritical assumption that the person who has filled in the questionnaire or who has answered the telephone is actually the intended study object – something that is difficult to prove if the researcher has not been present with the person at the time. And even when we meet interview subjects face-to-face, it may be impossible to determine the veracity of their statements, even though we tend to believe that this type of situation contributes to higher data quality. This leads into a more theoretical discussion about whether people ever answer completely honestly in research contexts, and whether there is a true personality or identity, or whether these shift over time and depending on the context. Researchers' views on this issue will in turn depend on their ontological and epistemological points of departure, but this discussion lies beyond the framework of this chapter.

Another methodological problem that was quickly identified related to issue of samples, namely the question of who is reached when the internet is used as a means of recruiting research participants. Here too a parallel may be drawn with more conventional sampling methods. In order to be included in a postal questionnaire study, you must have an address, while for a telephone interview, you must have a registered phone number – and it is clear even here that there are individuals who will not be included in the sample. While it is true that in certain countries and age groups, the level of internet penetration lies at almost 100%, the trends described above mean that web environments have become increasingly fragmented over time and appeal to certain groups with regard to age, gender, ethnicity and interests. Further, there are always people who for various reasons lack access to the internet, or do not even desire such access. Those who lack internet access primarily comprise individuals from groups who are marginalised in other respects (van Dijk, 2008). This means that researchers must have some knowledge of the group that is to be studied, and must pose a large number of background questions in order to develop an understanding of the nature of the sample and of possible biases.

In other words, internet research appears to be subject to problems similar to those associated with other research methods. One factor that distinguishes online research from more traditional methods, however, is the degree to which it has changed over time. This is in part a question of the way in which the composition of internet users has changed substantially over the past 20 years, and in part the way in which internet environments have also changed and become more fragmented, specialised and focused on specific target groups. The time chosen to conduct online research is also crucial, and must always be discussed in relation to research findings and the possible conclusions that may be drawn by a given study, which is also true with regard to study samples and populations – in the final analysis, these factors are central to issues of validity, reliability and generalisability.

Questions relating to research ethics are often raised in the context of discussions of internet research (see, for example, McKee and Porter, 2009). This is also related to the fact that we have only been conducting research online for a relatively short period of time, and also that the internet has been constantly changing throughout this period. Ethical discussions often result in the emergence of two camps: those who feel that existing ethical guidelines are sufficient, and those who feel that specific guidelines are required for internet research. The issue that has probably been discussed most often is that of the relationship the public and private spheres, namely which environments it is possible to study. Thereafter come discussions of the provision of research information and informed consent – and how these questions might be dealt with when researchers do not know who is present in the arena they wish to study. These questions are primarily of relevance in relation to ethnographic studies that involve some element of observation. In studies based on questionnaires and interviews, the ethical issues are relatively similar to those associated with offline research. One ethical issue that is discussed less often relates to how easy it has become to conduct research on or with the help of the internet, something that may have led to the conduct of less well-planned studies and the use of ethically questionable research methods. The same is the case with regard to the publication of identifiable excerpts from web forums and chat sites. As with other methodological issues, continuous reflection is required with regard to potential ethical problems linked to all phases of the research process, and also regarding how these problems might relate to the nature of the internet at a specific point in its development.

How then is the internet used in fatherhood research? Is it used as an arena for studying fathers and if so, what are the advantages or disadvantages of collecting data on fathers online? Does the internet research give us something new that we were previously unable to see?

The methodology employed in the literature review

As a means of providing a basis for a more detailed discussion of these issues, we have conducted a literature review of fatherhood research conducted on the internet. Since our questions relate to methodology, the literature review has focused on the methodological descriptions contained in each article. In this sense, our review should be regarded as scope oriented rather than as a meta-analysis with a focus on the quality of the existing research (Arksey and O'Malley, 2005). The literature review is restricted to scientific articles and is based on a search strategy known as the 'building block' approach, which builds on similar and related terms combined into blocks. Seven databases have been used in the search process: ERIC, ProQuest Sociology, PsycARTICLES, PsycINFO, Social services abstract, Sociological abstract and Pubmed. The database searches were conducted during the period 11-15 April 2016, and the search was limited to title and abstract, to English and to peer-reviewed articles in all seven databases. The search strategy involved building two blocks that included terms related to fatherhood and the internet respectively and then combining the two blocks to capture the most relevant articles. The first block, whose use was restricted to a search of article titles, comprised the terms father★ and dad★. The second block, whose use was restricted to a search of abstracts, comprised the terms online, internet, cyber, cyberspace★, 'web community', 'online forum' and Facebook. This resulted in a third block that was simply a combination of all the father-related terms and all the internet-related terms. Consequently, at least one term in the first block had to be combined with at least one term in the second block for an article to be considered relevant in this search. In the first and the second blocks, terms were separated by OR and in the third block by AND.

The articles identified by the literature search were analysed by the researchers in order to assess their relevance. In addition to the requirements that the articles had been peer reviewed, were in English and had an abstract, one important inclusion criterion was that the articles were based on a study that had collected data on fathers via the internet. This means that we have excluded research reviews about what fathers do online, evaluations of specific websites containing information for fathers, studies that have only made use of the internet in order to recruit fathers and studies that focus on children's views about their fathers. The search of Pubmed also excluded articles that had nothing to do with fathers, but which were identified by the search process since they included the abbreviation DAD in descriptions of various molecular structures. We also excluded articles that were not available in full-text versions. The database searches identified a total of 114 articles, of which 36 were assessed as relevant and were included in the study. Nine of the articles had been identified repeatedly across several databases, which means that the searches produced a total of 27 unique articles. In order to further strengthen the basis of the study material, a special search was also conducted to identify internet research in all issues of the scientific journal *Fathering*. For the past decade, this has been the only journal that has specifically focused on compiling and publishing research on fathers. This search was conducted among the journal's abstracts using the same search terms employed in the research databases, and identified an additional six articles.

Thus the study finally included a total of 33 articles, primarily from the social science disciplines and for the most part published during the past 10 years. The subject focus of the articles is very varied, but four central themes emerged. The first subject area relates to **becoming a parent** and first-time fathers' experiences of fatherhood. Here we find studies on fathers' experiences of pregnancy and the birth process, as well as on the practices of fathers during their first year as parents. The second subject area relates to **how fathers experience the support provided by various types of professionals** and professional interventions, as well as how fathers provide support to one another in their parenting role with the help of these interventions. The third subject area identified **focuses on various aspects of gender equality and examines questions relating to the work–family conflict, the division of labour or parental leave**. Finally, the material includes a cluster of articles whose interest is directed at more or less **specific groups of fathers**, such as the fathers of children with serious or unusual illnesses. This group of articles also includes studies of gay fathers, young fathers, adoptive fathers and non-residential fathers.

A large majority of the studies are quantitative and have employed web questionnaires as the data collection method. These questionnaire studies have primarily been conducted in the US and have been published over the course of the entire period from which the articles are drawn, that is, 2003-2016. The qualitative studies identified in the study, which are usually based on analyses of blogs and threads/messages published in various online forums, have often been conducted in Scandinavia, and have been published more recently, from 2008 onwards. This is also the point at which a marked increase can be observed in the number of published studies in this area. But what does this mean, and what was it that produced this change?

Netnography and studying fathers online

A cursory overview of the articles included in the review thus indicates the presence of a trend, from the internet primarily having been used as a data collection technology towards it emerging as a research field in its own right, with a clearer focus coming to be directed at how fathers and fatherhood are modelled and described online. One of the powerful motors behind this shift has been a growing interest among parents in blogging, reading others' blogs, posting on Facebook or engaging in discussions in various online forums (Daneback and Plantin, 2008; Plantin and Daneback, 2009). The most recent survey of Swedes' internet use, for example, found that 50% of all internet users visited Facebook every day, and that 40% sometimes read blogs (Findahl, 2013). In this regard, the internet appears to be satisfying an increasingly powerful need among people to continually evaluate and reflexively negotiate their personal identity projects (Bauman, 2000; Beck, 2009). Expanding choices and increased risk awareness, combined with reduced opportunities to rest on previously accepted norms and traditions, are contributing to an insecurity that is leading parents to constantly search for information, advice and opportunities to communicate about their situation (Madge and O'Connor, 2006). Thus the internet provides substantial opportunities not only to collect information, but also to present and express parenting in relation to other parents. At the same time, this need to display one's parenting is nothing new, but may rather be viewed as an important element in the process of creating one's identity as a parent and constructing one's family life. Janet Finch (2007) argues that the need to display parenting is a manifestation of the 'fundamentally social nature of family practices where the meaning of one's actions has to be conveyed to and understood by relevant others if those actions are to be effective as constituting "family" practices' (p 66). What is new is the way in which the internet today provides much greater opportunities to expose one's parenting to the gaze of large numbers of people, from friends and family to complete strangers. This in turn creates enormous quantities of online data that is often easy to access at minimal cost. Diaries, blogs and discussion forums are accessible for observation and analysis without the need for a great deal of preparation or effort. They often provide an uncontrived, naturalistic (Lincoln and Guba, 1985), insight into men's reflections and discussions about their parenting. Blogs provide access to a unique combination of long, diary-like reflections that are published over time and comments from and conversations with other people. It is much more difficult, and more expensive, to capture such a rich variety of information from a single data source offline. Thus the accessibility and diversity of the online material attracts large numbers of researchers to ethnographic online research, so-called netnography (Kozinets, 2009), in which they either openly or from a position of concealment examine and analyse the lived online experiences of fathers. At the same time, as was noted earlier, these opportunities also give rise to a large number of ethical questions about what may be viewed as a public arena or as part of the private sphere, what may be regarded as texts or conversations (which in turn also has implications for copyright issues), how to ensure confidentiality and whether, and when, informed consent should be required (Kozinets, 2002; Sveningsson-Elm, 2009; AoIR, 2012).

The question, however, is how diverse the data available online actually is, not least with regard to socioeconomic status, education marital status and age. The research on fathers has previously been criticised for having too much of a middle-class focus, and for being dominated by older men with high levels of education and good incomes (Plantin, 2007; Miller, 2011). For obvious reasons, this type of information is not always available in the context of netnographic research. Blogs and discussion forums rarely include a presentation of the participants' demographic backgrounds, and this information instead appears more sporadically or is found embedded in the texts themselves. Thus few of the netnographic studies included in our literature review present any socio-demographic information on the fathers' backgrounds. Boman and colleagues (2013) merely note briefly that the fathers in their online groups had mid-range or higher levels of education, whereas Johansson and Hammarén (2014) describe the presence of variation in their study with regard to marital status. Otherwise we are given no idea about who the studied fathers are. Previous research shows, however, that there is a general predominance among bloggers of individuals with high levels of resources who have integrated digital technologies into their everyday lives (Schradie, 2012). This not only involves differences in levels of resources and skills, but also in 'the ability to control the digital means of content production, and multiple gadgets and resources that those from higher classes are more likely to have' (Schradie 2012, p 557). Thus there is much to indicate that the research describing fatherhood online, in the same way as offline fatherhood research, is characterised by a strong middle-class focus. It is also unclear whether the research that observes fathers online provides new knowledge that could not have been developed using data collected in other, more traditional, ways. None of the studies in the literature review included a discussion of this question.

But if we instead look at the research that does not primarily make use of the internet in order to observe fathers but instead uses it to reach out to fathers with various questions, how does this research discuss the internet as an arena for the collection of data?

Using the internet to reach fathers

The quantitative studies included in our review that have employed the internet as a data collection technology are most often non-representative, non-random and in most cases based on very small samples of between 100 and 250 respondents. Only one of these studies (Cohen-Israeli, 2016) discusses why the internet was chosen for conducting the research rather than other data collection methods. This study argues that the internet makes it easier to contact hard-to-reach parents and that it is easier to communicate information about the study electronically than by manual means. As disadvantages, the study notes the risk for bias in the data, since fathers from an academic background, and who work in professional occupations, have a greater online presence, especially on social forums, and also display greater willingness to participate in social studies (Cohen-Israeli, 2016). The risk for bias is also confirmed at a general level in our own data, since all of the studies are based on skewed samples with regard to the participants' socioeconomic status. They are almost exclusively focused on white/Caucasian middle-class men with relatively high levels of education and income. In 19 of the 22 studies that report the participants' ethnicity, educational background and socioeconomic status, 70-90% of the fathers are white/Caucasian with a background in higher education. The average age of the respondents is around 40 in the majority of studies, and the vast majority are also married or cohabiting with a partner. This means that the quantitative studies that contact fathers online follow in the footsteps of earlier fatherhood research and have a clear bias towards a focus on white, well-established fathers from the middle class. Thus in this respect there is no clear direct support for the view that online studies contribute to broadening our knowledge on different groups of fathers or on hard-to-reach fathers.

At the same time, the literature review shows a clear and growing genre of research with a focus on specific groups of parents. These include, for example, studies on fathers of children with genetic disorders (Rivard and Mastel-Smith, 2014), brain tumours (Nicholas et al, 2012) or spina bifida (Nicholas et al, 2003), as well as gay fathers (Tornello and Patterson, 2012; Tornello et al, 2011), young fathers (Eerola and Huttunen, 2011), adoptive fathers (Foli et al, 2013) and non-residential fathers (Erera and Baum, 2009). Common denominators in this research are that it has almost exclusively been produced in the past five years, is often based on small datasets and is dominated by a social and behavioural science perspective. The fact that an increasing number of studies are focusing an interest on a range of specific groups of fathers in this way suggests a growing breadth in the fatherhood research, even though the data is based on fathers with similar levels of education, ethnic background and socioeconomic status.

The results manifest patterns that have also been found in research on parenthood and the internet, namely research that also includes mothers. Daneback and Plantin (2008) and Plantin and Daneback (2009), for example, found that an increasing number of studies focused on specific groups of parents had been conducted during the period 2002-08 and that these studies were often based on small, non-representative datasets. They also noted that the majority of these studies were characterised by a strong focus on mothers and not fathers. It is thus possible that we are now seeing further development of this research, but with a shift towards a greater focus on fathers.

This trend can also be understood in relation to the theoretical frameworks of modernism, with a diversity of performances and possibilities also leading to an increasing number of descriptions of different experiences among fathers. The increased diversity may also be viewed in relation to an increasingly powerful focus on the family as practice, 'rather than [as] a thing like object of detached social investigation' (Morgan, 1996, p 16). This point of departure leads to the inclusion of an increasing number of family forms, family members and family practices. The construction of parenthood is also extended and need not necessarily be based on blood ties, continuous physical presence or traditional behaviours. Fathers in prison, fathers who do not have custody of their children, fathers who work at long distances from their families and so on have all attracted more interest, since in spite of their situation they are nonetheless included in the family and in parenthood. This has opened the way for a greater degree of diversity in fatherhood research over the past 15 years, with articles and books describing the parenting experiences of different types of fathers (Seward and Richter, 2008). Over recent years, fatherhood research has also developed a broader global base and has come to include the experiences of fathers from a large number of different countries and cultures (Roopnarine, 2015). At the same time, this is not reflected in the research that makes use of the internet to examine various specific groups of fathers. In our literature review, these studies have exclusively been conducted the US, Canada and Scandinavia. A similar pattern emerges in the studies based on netnographic research. Given the increased levels of internet access and the advantages of conducting studies online, with the distribution of questionnaires being both easier and cheaper, for example, we would in time expect to see internet-based fatherhood research being produced in an increasing number of different countries.

Conclusion

The aim of this chapter has been to present a relatively detailed examination of how fatherhood research has used the internet both as a research field and a data collection technology. One overarching question has been that of the types of methodological questions that have been considered when deciding to make use of the internet, while another has been how this online research has influenced our knowledge about fathers. Our literature review shows that, viewed over time, relatively few studies of fathers have been conducted with the help of the internet. The majority of studies have made use of the internet as a means of contacting fathers in connection with various questionnaire studies. At the same time, the past five years have seen a marked increase in the research that has used the internet in order to study fathering online.

Hardly any of the studies that utilised the internet as means of distributing questionnaires directed at fathers have discussed the decision to use the internet as a data collection arena, which may be viewed as somewhat remarkable given that there are both advantages and disadvantages associated with the use of postal or online questionnaires respectively. The advantages of online questionnaire studies include, among others, improved opportunities to come into contact with hard-to-reach-fathers, the ease with which questionnaires can be posted online, low costs and improved opportunities for monitoring and checking the data collected (Frippiat and Marquis, 2010). At the same time, postal surveys also have certain advantages by comparison with web surveys. For example, postal surveys often provide a better overview of the study, because the respondent can easily browse through the survey and quickly get an understanding of its scope and content. In addition, postal surveys may also be perceived as more personal and exclusive, because they arrive with the regular mail, which has a positive effect on the response rate (Frippiat and Marquis, 2010). Discussing these methodological considerations is thus an important factor in understanding why a particular arena and method have been chosen for the data collection process.

The risk for bias and skewed samples that has been found in other internet research was also clearly visible in our literature study of the internet-based fatherhood research. The study samples are often small and unrepresentative, and for the most part comprise white fathers with relatively high levels of education and income, who are cohabiting with a partner. This constitutes the same group that has dominated much of the existing offline fatherhood research (Plantin, 2007). Thus in this respect, there is a risk that internet-based fatherhood research will be unable to contribute new knowledge about the large number of fathers who are not part of this particular social and socioeconomic stratum. This means, so to speak, that even a new method may still encounter 'old' problems of finding some groups of men harder to reach. At the same time, the past five years have witnessed an increasing number of studies of specific groups of fathers with somewhat different characteristics and experiences. These include, for example, young fathers, single fathers, fathers in prison or fathers of children with various disabilities or illnesses. This trend suggests a development towards a broader picture of men's perceptions and experiences of parenthood than we have seen to date. The increasing proportion of studies that are employing a netnographic approach to studying fatherhood on the internet, via various forms of social media, are also providing a basis for a more detailed understanding of fathering. However, the fact that the internet-based fatherhood research, in the same way as offline fatherhood research, is almost exclusively focused on fathers in the western world constitutes a significant constraint on our knowledge of how parenthood is lived and experienced by today's fathers.

References

AoIR (Association of Internet Researchers) (2012) 'Ethical decision-making and internet research: recommendations from the AoIR Ethics Working Committee (version 2.0)', available at www.aoir.org.

Arksey H., O'Malley, L. (2005) 'Coping studies: towards a methodological framework', *International Journal of Social Research Methodology: Theory and Practice*, 8(1): 19-32.

Bartholomew, M.K, Schoppe-Sullivan, S.J., Glassman, M. and Kamp Dush, C.M. (2012) 'New parents' Facebook use at the transition to parenthood', *Family Relations*, 61(3): 455-69.

Bauman, Z. (2000) *Liquid modernity*, Cambridge: Polity Press.

Beck, Ulrich (2009) *World at risk*, Cambridge: Polity Press.

Boman, Å., Povlsen, L., Dahlborg-Lyckhage, E., Hanas, R. and Borup, I. (2013) 'Fathers' encounters of support from paediatric diabetes teams; the tension between general recommendations and personal experience', *Health and Social Care in the Community*, 21(3): 263-270.

Cohen-Israeli, L. (2016) 'Care and career: work and parenting among Israeli men', *Fathering*, 13(3): 203-218.

Daneback, K. and Plantin, L. (2008) 'Research on parenthood and the internet: themes and trends', *Cyberpsychology: Journal of Psychosocial Research on Cyberspace*, 2(2), article 1.

Eerola, J.P. and Huttunen, J. (2011) 'Metanarrative of the new father and narratives of young Finnish first-time fathers', *Fathering*, 9(3): 211-231.

Erera, P.I. and Baum, N. (2009) 'Chat-room voices of divorced non-residential fathers', *Journal of Sociology and Social Welfare*, 36(2): 63-83.

Finch, J. (2007) 'Displaying families', *Sociology*, 41(1): 65-81.

Findahl, Olle (2013) *The Swedes and the internet 2013: A yearly study of the internet use among the Swedish population*, http://www.soi2013.se/en/

Foli, K.J., South, S.C., Lim, E. and Hebdon, M. (2013) 'Depression in adoptive fathers: an exploratory mixed methods study', *Psychology of Men & Masculinity*, 14(4): 411-422.

Frippiat, D. and Marquis, N. (2010) 'Web surveys in the social sciences: an overview', *Population*, 65(2): 285-312.

Ilieva, J., Baron, S. and Healey, N.M. (2002) 'Online surveys in marketing research. Pros and cons', *International Journal of Market Research*, 44: 361-376.

Johansson, T. and Hammarén, N. (2014) '"Imagine, just 16 years old and already a dad!" The construction of young fatherhood on the internet', *International Journal of Adolescence and Youth*, 19(3): 366-381.

Kozinets, R.V. (2002) 'The field behind the screen: using netnography for marketing research in online communities', *Journal of Marketing Research*, 39 (February): 61-72.

Kozinets, R.V. (2009) *Netnography: Doing ethnographic research online*, Thousand Oaks, CA: Sage Publications.

Lincoln, Y.S. and Guba, E.G. (1985) *Naturalistic inquiry*, Newbury Park, CA: Sage Publications.

Madge, C. and O'Connor, H. (2006) 'Parenting gone wired: empowerment of new mothers on the internet?', *Social & Cultural Geography*, 7(2): 199-220.

Malhotra, N. (2008) 'Completion time and response order effects in web surveys', *Public Opinion Quarterly*, 72(5): 79-104.

Manfreda, K.L., Bosnjak, M., Berzelak, J., Haas, I. and Vehovar, V. (2008) 'Web surveys versus other survey modes. A meta-analysis comparing response rates', *International Journal of Market Research*, 50: 79-104.

Markham, A.N. and Baym, N.K. (2009) *Internet inquiry: Conversations about methods*, Thousand Oaks, CA: Sage Publications.

McKee, H.A. and Porter, J.E. (2009) *The ethics of internet research: A rhetorical, case-based process*, New York, NY: Peter Lang Publishing.

Miller, T. (2011) *Making sense of fatherhood*, Cambridge: Cambridge University Press.

Morgan, D. (1996) *Family connections: An introduction to family studies*, Cambridge: Polity Press.

Munoz-Leiva, F., Sanchez-Fernandez, J., Montoro-Rios, F. and Ibanez-Zapata, J.A. (2010) 'Improving the response rate and quality in web-based surveys through the personalization and frequency of reminder mailings', *Quality & Quantity*, 44: 1037-1052.

Nicholas, D.B., Chahauver, A., Brownstone, D., Hetherington, R., McNeill, T. and Bouffet, E. (2012) 'Evaluation of an online peer support network for fathers of a child with a brain tumor', *Social Work in Health Care*, 51(3): 232-245.

Nicholas, D.B., McNeill, T., Montgomery, G., Stapleford, C. and McClure, M. (2003) 'Communication features in an online group for fathers of children with spina bifida: considerations for group development among men', *Social Work with Groups*, 26(2): 65-80.

Pedersen, S. and Smithson, J. (2013) 'Mothers with attitude – how the Mumsnet parenting forum offers space for new forms of femininity to emerge online', *Women's Studies International Forum*, 38: 97-106.

Pew Research Center (2015) 'Parents and social media', available at www.pewinternet.org/2015/07/16/parents-and-social-media.

Plantin, L. (2007) 'Different classes, different fathers? On fatherhood, economic conditions and class in Sweden', *Community, Work & Family*, 10(1): 93-110.

Plantin, L. and Daneback, K. (2009) 'Parenthood, information and support on the internet. A literature review of research on parents and professionals online', *BMC Family Practice*, 10(1): 34.

Rivard, M.T. and Mastel-Smith, B. (2014) 'The lived experience of fathers whose children are diagnosed with a genetic disorder', *Journal of Obstetric, Gynecologic & Neonatal Nursing: Clinical Scholarship for the Care of Women, Childbearing Families & Newborns*, 43(1): 38-49.

Roopnarine, J.L. (2015) *Fathers across cultures: The importance, roles and diverse practices of dads*, Santa Barbara, CA: Praeger.

Ross, M.W., Daneback, K., Månsson, S., Tikkanen, R. and Cooper, A. (2003) 'Characteristics of men and women who complete or exit from an online internet sexuality questionnaire: a study of instrument dropout biases', *Journal of Sex Research*, 40(4): 396-402.

Sarkadi A. and Bremberg, S. (2005) 'Socially unbiased parenting support on the internet: a cross-sectional study of users of a large Swedish parenting website', *Child: Care, Health and Development*, 31(1): 43-52.

Schradie, J. (2012) 'The trend of class race and ethnicity in social media inequality', *Information, Communication & Society*, 15(4): 555-571.

Seward, R.R. and Richter, R. (2008) 'International research on fathering: an expanding horizon', *Fathering*, 6(2): 87-91.

Shropshire, K., Hawdon, J. and Witte, J. (2009) 'Web survey design: balancing measurement, response and topical interest', *Sociological Methods & Research*, 37(3): 344-370.

Sveningsson-Elm, M. (2009) 'How do various notions of privacy influence decision making in qualitative internet research?', in A.N. Markham and N.K. Baym (eds) *Internet inquiry: Conversation about method*, Thousand Oaks, CA: Sage Publications, pp 69-87.

Tornello, S.L. and Patterson, C.J. (2012) 'Gay fathers in mixed-orientation relationships: experiences of those who stay in their marriages and of those who leave', *Journal of GLBT Family Studies*, 8(1): 85-98.

Tornello, S.L., Farr, R.H. and Patterson, C.J. (2011) 'Predictors of parenting stress among gay adoptive fathers in the United States', *Journal of Family Psychology*, 25(4): 591-600.

van Dijk, J. (2008) 'The digital divide in Europe', in *The handbook of internet politics*, London: Routledge, pp 288-304.

FIVE

Researching fatherhood and place: adopting an ethnographic approach

Therése Wissö

Introduction

This book is a unique collection in that it brings different methodological perspectives to the study of contemporary fatherhood and fathering. Although there is a growing body of fatherhood research, it is argued that fathers, especially those who are viewed as vulnerable, such as poor fathers and fathers with a migrant background, are hard to reach in qualitative studies (Hemmerman, 2010; Shiriani and Henwood, 2010). As a family researcher, I have experienced gender as well as class bias in previous studies as more mothers than fathers have volunteered, and to a large extent, the research participants have been middle-class parents. This encourages reflection on how to design studies for exploring the everyday lives of fathers. In this chapter, I present an ethnographic approach as a potential way of gaining knowledge about disadvantaged fathers, including poor fathers, fathers with insecure employment and fathers from minority ethnic groups. My starting point was to find places where fathers are located, yet also available for a female researcher. The research project was situated in a district of Gothenburg, the second biggest city in Sweden. The fathers in the study are thus embedded in a Swedish welfare state context. However, being a dad can have different meanings even within the same country. In research about poverty and inequality, there is increasing interest in the neighbourhood as an influential factor for individual life circumstances (Wacquant, 2008; Österberg, 2013; Rostila et al, 2013). Neighbourhood effects can be studied using quantitative data, for example, to investigate and compare unemployment rates, income, health, educational level and so on. The aim of the study described in this chapter is to gain knowledge of what it is like to be a father in a neighbourhood that is known for its high concentration of social problems. The research design is characterised by an inductive approach and research questions formulated along the way.

By using an ethnographic design including observations, field notes and various forms of interviews with fathers and professional actors, this chapter discusses ethnographic methods in the study of fatherhood. The main focus of the chapter is on methodological aspects of the study, but I also present some results. The ethnographic method is familiar from family research in the UK and the US, especially in studies relating to marginalised and vulnerable groups. In Sweden, the ethnographic method has been used to a limited extent in fatherhood studies. Usually, researchers use qualitative interview studies and quantitative methods such as register studies of parental leave or the employer's attitude to cash and care dimensions of fathers' involvement in caring work (for example, Plantin, 2007; Klinth and Johansson, 2008; Haas and Hwang, 2009). My study is, therefore, unique in Swedish fatherhood research.

As a fatherhood researcher, I use various theoretical concepts in order to understand and interpret empirical data. Bourdieu's concept of habitus has guided my understanding of how masculinity and fatherhood are practised. By spending time and participating in social environments, people acquire different forms of habitus, ways of acting and naturally relating to one or more social situations (Bourdieu, 1977, 1990). Thus, individuals' thoughts and actions are of a social and collective nature, and in this respect, place is a major factor. Habitus as concept incorporates multiple levels of analysis; it involves bodily elements such as the actor's posture, demeanours and doings, as well as cognitive elements. Habitus may be viewed as a useful concept for analysing how masculinity and fatherhood are reproduced and transformed within different social fields (Coles, 2009; Doucet, 2009).

What is ethnography and how can it be used in fatherhood studies?

A presumption for the study is the ability to explore fatherhood by coming close to environments in which it is set. The idea of researchers getting close to people and situations was a core matter in early ethnographic studies. Today, there is variation in the ethnographic research tradition. For example, a large part of everyday life is played out 'online' in various digital environments. The term 'netography' (Kozinets, 1997, 2010) has been coined to describe how ethnographic methods can examine social life online, in different communities and social media. However, ethnography is still about researchers taking on an educational role so as to try to understand what is going on in a particular context, by visiting the environments and meeting the people who live there (Agar, 1986).

Ethnography combines different data collection methods, such as observations, interviews in various forms, documents, diaries, photographs and recordings (Tedlock, 2003). A challenge in this consists of achieving 'thick descriptions', to get beyond photographic reproductions of what people said or did (Hammersly and Atkinsson, 1995). Following Geertz (1973), thick descriptions should provide detailed knowledge of how people feel, think, imagine and perceive their world. Within what is called action research, or critical participatory action research (Grubenmann, 2015), knowledge is considered as something that is done in collaboration between the researcher and participants in a particular field. According to Whyte (1994), participatory action research means that people within an organisation or a group of individuals actively collaborate with the researcher throughout the research process, from the initial design to the final presentation of results. Method literature for participant observation and ethnography is relatively extensive, both as part of the qualitative research tradition, but also because of its uniqueness (Burgess, 1984; Denzin and Lincoln, 2005; Hammersly and Atkinson, 1995; Atkinson, 2001).

Background to the research project

My study is an ethnographically inspired study, where place and fatherhood are the key themes. The overall aim was to study how fatherhood is practised and which forms of fathering habitus are visible in the district of Biskopsgården. Hence, the aim was twofold: to explore the neighbourhood, including observations of geographical sites, and what it is like to be a father in the district, including fathers' accounts of their everyday lives.

The study was conducted for a year, in which an average of one day a week was devoted to fieldwork. The observed district, called Biskopsgården, has 10,000 inhabitants. The residential buildings of the area were constructed in the 1950s and '60s, but there are also several wooded areas. About half of the population is foreign-born, and the majority live in rented apartments. The district has few high-income individuals, but high numbers for income support, unemployment, poor health and lower educational level than the average in Gothenburg. During the 2000s, the Biskopsgården was described as a neighbourhood with a high concentration of social problems, including crime. In 2012, the National Crime Prevention Council in Sweden concluded that suburban-based criminal networks were active in the area (BRÅ, 2012). These networks consist of loose constellations of individuals, and their activities involve control of criminal markets, violent crimes and drug offences. Their presence in the district constitutes a risk to children and young people, who risk being drawn into criminality (BRÅ, 2012).

In a previous study (Wissö, 2012), Biskopsgården was one of three districts where parents of young children were interviewed about their everyday life. However, it was difficult to recruit fathers from the area, and the professional actors interviewed, such as social workers and child health nurses, expressed concern that the fathers were too absent in their children's lives, both physically and mentally. In 2015, a non-governmental organisation (NGO) in Gothenburg opened a meeting place for fathers and their children, an open space where resident and non-resident fathers can talk about things related to life and parenthood.

Research methods

The study described in this chapter has some parallels with action research, since it was initiated by professionals within the NGO that created the meeting place for fathers, with a desire for greater knowledge of fathers' perception of their situation, thoughts on fatherhood, work and the living environment. The design of the research project – themes, data collection, selection and ethical considerations – were settled in collaboration with volunteers and professionals in the area. The professional actors (social worker, youth worker and psychologist) were also involved in the formulation of the aim and research questions of the study, which were of quite an open nature: what is it like to be a father in Biskopsgården? A variety of methods – observations, city walks and interviews – were used to answer the research questions. **Observations** were chosen as they can give us information about fathering practices and interactions, while **city walks** with participants provided an opportunity to talk about the physical and social environment. In individual **interviews**, the participants had the opportunity to develop their thoughts and ideas.

Gatekeepers

In ethnographic studies, especially within closed environments, you need permission and access as a researcher. Gatekeepers are people who allow or prevent physical and social access. They are sometimes termed door openers, people who help once you are out in the field, introduce you to people to interview and help with valuable information (Whyte, 1994, 1993, 1992; Wolcott, 2009; Agar,1980; Hammersley and Atkinson, 1995). According to Raymond M. Lee (1993), the question about access should not be viewed as a detached initiation or rite of passage into fieldwork, rather as an ongoing negotiation about the researchers right of 'being there'. As the gatekeepers in ethnographic fieldwork may affect the research sample, it is important to reflect on their function, and how their involvement might affect the research process and the empirical material.

In my study, several gatekeepers and door openers appeared, including two fathers living in the neighbourhood whom I met as volunteers in the NGO mentioned earlier. Their social network and status in the area became necessary for the legitimacy of the study and for access. Gatekeepers can, however, hinder the research process by denying researchers access to some locations and situations. For example, I was not permitted to attend a management meeting where I wanted to listen to what sort of questions concerning the district were being discussed in the municipality.

Observations

An important issue in ethnographic studies is the degree of interactivity between researcher and informant. Hammersley and Atkinson (1995) point out that social interaction is an essential element of ethnography; it is a strategy to build trust and venues for small talk with research participants. Although the degree of participation and activity often varies over time and the research process, it can also be influenced by the personal characteristics, skills and sympathies of the researcher. At times, researchers can position themselves at a distance from what is going on. At other times, the researcher is 'one of the gang', who jokes and participates on similar terms to the other participants. Many field researchers are seldom fully participant; it is rather a form of partial participation.

Another issue in ethnographic studies is whether the observation is open or hidden (Gold, 1958 [2006]). Completely hidden observation, where the researcher in particular cases acts under a false identity, stands in stark contrast to current ethical guidelines for modern research, where openness, information and consent are keywords. Most observational studies are characterised, however, by more transparency, where the researcher informs the informants about the study, its purpose and problems, and asks for the consent of potential participants. In practice, however, a series of situations arise in which the researcher role is not clear and the observations are partially hidden from the participants.

Site selection

Data collection in ethnography is less standardised, which may mean that validity and reliability are not as easy to control as in quantitative studies (see, for example, Golafshani, 2003). Many questions arise during a study, such as how to identify the right things to be observed and how to know that the interpretations of the observations are adequate. The choice of location for the observation is a critical issue and should be guided by the aims and objectives of the study. The overall aim of my study – what it is like to be a father in Biskopsgården – guided my site selection. Other aspects were the inclusion of formal and informal places, as well as sites that are open to anyone and places that restrict access. Site selection is, however, partly a matter of access, which can be affected by the researcher's gender, age and ethnicity. Some sites were not accessible during the project period, for example, Friday prayer at the mosque, an important meeting place for many fathers in the neighbourhood.

In some ethnographic studies, the physical location is well defined – for example, a waiting room –while other studies move over a larger geographic area. In my study, I wanted to observe and interview fathers at different locations in the neighbourhood. I wanted to avoid sites for mothers, such as maternity clinics, sites that researchers often utilise to reach fathers and fathers-to-be. My aim was to find fathers in other surroundings, where they gather with or without their children. Research on family life and the shifting focus on family practices pinpoint the fact that parenthood takes place in several arenas, and that the home is not automatically the most important one (Morgan, 2011).

Using a system described by Gerell (2015), I distinguished three geographical units: district, neighbourhood and microsites. These units are partially intertwined and affect each other. The district is the overall unit (the district of Biskopsgården), while the neighbourhood is defined as a distinct part of the district that is used in everyday life. The microsites are places close to people's homes, such as courtyards and staircases.

The café

The café is an open space anyone can visit. I went there for a cup of coffee, and could not help notice that most of the visitors were men of different ages. Initially, the observations at the café had the lure of hidden observation. These repeated observations aimed to get an idea of what happened at the café, who the visitors were and what types of social interaction took place there. Unlike infiltration research where researchers are trying to emulate and blend into the group without being noticed, I, as a white woman, deviated from the crowd. It did not take long for the café's owner to recognise me and it seemed natural to inform visitors about the study. I was welcomed to spend time at the café, but it was not possible to inform all the visitors of my purpose. I still considered it ethically justifiable, because the environment was relatively public and I had not appeared under a false identity.

The café was also a perfect place to observe, together with the fathers, what was happening in the plaza outside. Several interviews with fathers were conducted here, and we could talk about things that happened outside the window, as the following extract from an interview at the café demonstrates.

Father:	"The police should do more here. Usually, they only show up after something has happened, after a shooting or a fight. You know, or they come here to pick someone up and take them in for interrogation at the police station. But now you see them more often. Like those you see over there [points at two police officers standing outside the café]."
Researcher:	"What do you think and feel when you see the police officers? Do you get worried or do they make you feel safe?"
Father:	"Well, I don't know what I feel. But you see what I mean; they are not doing anything. They are just standing there with their arms crossed. Observing. They should be walking around talking to people, to get to know them. If we are to rely on them, they need to build relationships with the people living here."

The playground

A playground close to the district shopping area was another site selected for observation. This is also an open space, although it is mostly mothers and fathers with their children who go there. As an observer, it is hard to blend in at the playground; it was important to present myself to visiting parents as a researcher. There was no obvious place for me to sit, and, as a single adult, it was easy to be viewed with some suspicion, like a crazy person who planned to kidnap a child. On some occasions, my observations had the lure of hidden observation, for example, when on sunny days I had a picnic lunch on the lawn close to the playground.

The observations I made focused on the interactions that took place between fathers and their children. I observed direct interactions between father and child, such as talking, pushing the swing and playing in the sand, but also actions where fathers directed their attention to other things, for example, looking at their smartphones, reading a magazine, talking to other adults and so on.

I found that the playground was not a natural meeting place for parents and their children, since the number of visitors was quite small. The finding generated questions for my interviews, and I could ask fathers about their reasons for not going there with their children. The playground had recently been upgraded, yet many of the fathers considered it to be too small and have too few visitors. The surrounding area and neighbouring plaza were another reason why it was deemed an unsuitable meeting place. The playground is just 50 metres from a restaurant where two men were shot to death at the beginning of my fieldwork, and so for many people, the name of the restaurant had negative associations. Some of the shootings in the district had taken place in the daytime, which is why the area was viewed as potentially unsafe at all times of the day.

Open preschool/meeting place for fathers

I made observations at one open preschool operated by the local municipality, and one meeting place for fathers and their children, run by an NGO. The open preschool is an arena for all parents in the neighbourhood and their children. Open preschools are part of the general support for parents and children in Sweden, offered to children who have no place in the regular preschool system (SFS ['The Education Act'] 2010: 800). The site provides a meeting place for parents who stay at home with their children. No registration is required to attend, but children must be accompanied by an adult. The meeting place for fathers was not an official open preschool, but the fathers interviewed argued that it was more or less the same thing, just that the meeting place was for fathers only. Another difference is that preschool was open four days a week, while the meeting place for fathers was open once a week.

The professional actors at the preschool and the meeting place for fathers (preschool teachers, youth workers, social worker, psychologist and volunteers) were informed about the study and relaxed about my presence. The open preschool consists of several rooms. I often kept to the kitchen area where there are often personnel nearby and where visitors sit down for coffee. The meeting place for fathers only had two rooms. To clarify my position as a researcher, I wore a nameplate with my name and the information that I was a researcher from the University of Gothenburg. When I started talking to fathers, I always presented myself in this way. It was important not to be perceived as a person from the municipality or social services. I was not an inspector who would examine how well they interacted with their children.

The open preschool is well attended, with an average of 30 children and parents per day. The meeting place for fathers was not as well known in the neighbourhood, since it was newly opened. Sometimes there was only one father present, at other times four fathers.

Field notes

Taking field notes is a vital part of the ethnographic method, not least because there may be practical difficulties regarding voice recordings. It makes writing a distinct part of the research; writing is not primarily about a completing or reporting the study. Richardson (2005) describes field notes as an aid for the researcher to be 'here and now'. Taking notes help to clarify and put words to observations, reflections and interpretations. The boundary between data collection and interpretation becomes more blurred; it becomes a circular process where analysis occurs everywhere you go. In this respect, it is important to clarify the theoretical framework that influences interpretations and forms the basis for the analysis. As a paternity and family researcher, you put on particular academic glasses that limit what you see (and do not see) and how to interpret it. Field notes can be discussed from a validity perspective (Chan, 2003). It is impossible to record everything that is said and happens in a room. Field notes are a selection of what is said and done. Field notes can be coded in a similar way to interview printouts, according to topic or theme (see, for example, Bernard, 1994). There are currently several different computer programmes that are helpful in providing an overview of the process of taking and analysing field notes.

City walks

During the study, I developed a strategy called city walks, where I walked around the neighbourhood accompanied by one or several fathers. The fathers decided the route around the blocks and the walks lasted for about an hour, adapted to the number of participants and whether children were accompanying us. The walks and talks had 'place' as a guiding theme, and covered the following aspects:

- Site value: What makes the place interesting for you?
- Usage: How do you use this site? What do you usually do when you come here?
- What defines the beginning and ending of this place for you?
- Attendance: Who else is more frequently present here? Who will never come here?
- Freedom: What is it possible to do at this site?
- Conflict zones: Are there any conflicts of interest around this location you know of?
- Requests: Is there something that should be different with this location? Where and why?

The city walk was an excellent method to observe different geographical units, the meanings these sites have for fathers and how fathers act at various places in the district. Undertaking interviews while walking turned out to be beneficial, and I experienced that some of the conversations ran more smoothly than face-to-face interviews. Some potentials and practical aspects of 'walking interviews' are described by Riley and Holton (2016). One disadvantage compared with indoor interviewing is that the conversations are harder to record if you only use a simple recording device. I used photographs and field notes to document the city walks. Some of the themes were later followed up by interviews with the fathers.

Interviews

The observations and city walks were complemented with individual interviews with professional actors in the neighbourhood, and personal interviews with 15 different fathers. Ten of these fathers also took part in city walks. Interviewing is a way of validating observations and field notes, a way to let the informants have insight and contribute to the interpretations of the material.

The fathers were known to me from their visits to one or several of the observed sites and I invited them to participate in the interviews. The sample was partly strategically chosen, since I aimed for diversity in the data material considering the father's age and ethnicity. All fathers interviewed were residents of the district, and they had lived there for one to 10 years. The respondents were relatively heterogeneous and consisted of fathers born in Sweden (about half of the interviewees), fathers born outside Europe (about half of the interviewees), cohabiting fathers (11), single fathers (four), fathers who lack higher education (10) and college-educated fathers (five). The common denominator was that everyone lived in a rented apartment and had at least one child. The children were aged one to 11 years. In addition, I also completed a number of interviews with professional actors and volunteers in the district.

The ethnographic interview is characterised by open-ended questions. Research participants are encouraged to talk about the topics of interest in depth, to gain insight not only into what the participants say, but also into the meaning made of those phenomena (Spradley, 1979). The interviews with fathers were relatively open and revolved around the following themes:

- Activities: What do you usually do in the neighbourhood, individually and together with the children? Where do you do it?
- Objectives and outcomes: What do you do when you are here (open preschool/ café/meeting place for fathers)? Why are you doing this? Why do you come here?
- Understanding of dads in the neighbourhood: What is your view on the conditions for fathers and fathering in the area?
- Problems: What issues affect you as a father in this area?

The individual interviews also included questions about housing, work and the family (forms, functions and relationships). The fathers spoke about fatherhood in retrospect; they talked about the present, and they also shared their thoughts about the future.

Ethical aspects

The local Ethical Review Board approved my study and hence it could be argued that the participants were protected against mental injury or violation of their integrity. However, ethical issues are delicate and are not settled once and for all. In this respect, Pittaway and colleagues (2010) discuss aspects of participatory research and how stories told are conveyed. Their discussion is based on research that took place in a refugee camp, and how visiting professionals, many of them working for NGOs, conducted interviews and observations at the site. The respondents later reported that they had felt that they were being researched 'like monkeys in a cage', and hence questioned the objectives of the interviews and observations. They suspected that their stories were being exploited or 'stolen', so as to generate money for the organisation, for example, from funders such as the European Union or other donors, and that any such funds would not automatically benefit those living in the refugee camps. These suspicions touch on ethical issues that can be discussed in relation to my study: Who gains from trying to get close to dads in a suburb? Who benefits from their stories about everyday life, and how are the stories they tell broadcast? It is not easy to give a short answer to these questions. Researchers can sometimes be considered as people with the power to effect change, both at an individual and societal level, and it is thought that research results actually can enhance change. It is possible that the various actors and participants in my study had somewhat different ideas and expectations on this matter. I discussed these issues with the participants, and some dads said that they appreciated the fact that someone was interested in listening to their thoughts and opinions about living in the district. A few dads wanted me to send messages to politicians and decision makers. Others hoped that the written report could help people form another (better) image of the district. The objectives for the NGO to participate and help the study could have financial motives. Its business is based on donations, and my report could serve as a proof of the fact that its actions in the district are crucial for fathers and their children. Although I was clear that the study had no evaluative function, it is hard to remove such expectations completely.

Informed consent

Even if ethical guidelines about informed consent are followed, it is difficult to be certain that research participants have fully understood the scope of the study. As the researcher, you often handle situations where you need to assess quickly whether it is ethically right or not to conduct an interview, as the following excerpt from field notes on the open preschool shows.

> I have on several visits observed a father who is there for his daughter. She looks as if she is a year and a half. The staff say that the man speaks very little Swedish, and they

do not think it will work to interview him. The man himself has not taken any initiative to contact me, and I rarely see him interact with other parents at the open pre-school. About six months into the data collection, one of the preschool teachers says that the man is looking for work and is disappointed at how hard it is to get a job in Sweden if you were not born here and have Swedish as their mother tongue. They say his Swedish has got much better. I decide to try to make contact with the man at the open pre-school. I introduce myself as a researcher and talk about my research; I study dads in the district and their thoughts about everyday life. I see him first as cautious, but when I mention the issue of the work and family life, he turns his gaze towards me and looks interested. The man is called Omid, says he has no job and asks if I still want to talk to him. I say that I do. Then I talk to Omid for about 15 minutes. During this time, it is mainly Omid talking. He says he is very upset that he did not get any help to find a job. He is disappointed in his officer at the employment officer; that he does not want to help him. Omid mentions he plans to contact a lawyer to sue the employment office. During our conversation, Omid asks me several times "can you help me?" And "how can you help me?" I feel that Omid is frustrated, angry and sad. It feels as if he wants concrete help from me, help that I cannot offer.

Omid is a father whose experience it is important to capitalise on, as he is expressing a feeling of being excluded from Swedish society. However, I decided not to ask for an interview, because it was difficult to judge the degree of informed consent given his current desperate situation.

Analysis

Individual interviews, city walks and observations generate different data. The multiple datasets that were collected in this study were analysed separately. Within the scope of this chapter, I cannot present details of the analysis, but merely a brief view on my thoughts on analysing ethnographic data. Alvesson and Deetz (2000, p 204) have inspired me, as they argue that analytical work is about modifying dominating beliefs and 'theoretical creativity'. Among other things, they talk about the 'interpretation repertoire', that is, the researcher's understandings of theories, assumptions and vocabularies, and the empirical material (Alvesson and Deetz, 2000, p 204). Bourdieu is another source of inspiration, as he advocates that researchers should refrain from prearranged means of categorisation and interpretative patterns that are common in the area studied (Bourdieu and Wacquant, 1992; Emirbayer and Williams, 2005). However, there is always a risk that subjective social categories are perceived as unbiased categories (Bourdieu, 1999). The analysis in the project has been inspired by the 'listening guide', which includes four thorough readings (or listenings) of the material (see Mauthner and Doucet, 2003; Doucet and Mauthner, 2008). To increase the validity of observational studies, it would have been delightful if there had been a collaborating team of researchers to read and check interview printouts, field notes and analysis (Chan, 2003). In this case, however, I could only discuss the material with my informants. In research that strives to give a voice to marginalised groups, it is important to involve participants in the analysis (Guba and Lincoln, 2005). I met the informants on several occasions, discussing observations and field notes with them. Sometimes the fathers would confirm an idea or thought, and at other times they would contribute to an alternative interpretation.

Guba and Lincoln (2005) speak of fairness as an aspect of a study's validity, that is, the researcher's quest for all participants to have the same opportunity to be heard in the text, and for stories to be given equal weight. As a researcher, you have a power advantage in this respect, with the result that some informants' contributions may receive more attention than others' in the results section. It is difficult to do the complete material justice, especially in situations where copious amounts of detail must be summarised.

Does the method contribute to an in-depth knowledge of fatherhood?

The ethnographic method is a way to study at first hand what fathers do and say in a particular context, and can be productive in fatherhood research as a means of understanding fatherhood in a social and cultural context. The results of the study show that it is not possible to locate one fathering habitus, even within a limited geographical area. There is still variety in the ways of being a father. For some fathers, their presence at the open preschool with their children is a result of an active choice; they are on parental leave or work part-time because they want to. These fathers describe positive aspects of being at home with their children, even though they can also pinpoint the stresses and ambiguities of being a 'stay-at-home dad'. For others, the situation is not self-chosen, as in the case of fathers who are unemployed and longing for a 'real job'. Although they can describe positive aspects of being with the children, and the children enjoy being with them, they would rather have a job and be the breadwinning adult in the family. One unemployed father said in an interview, "It is okay to stay home, I have my wife's job right now, but I want to do what I am trained for." Bourdieu argues that habitus is formed in interactions, and in this sense, my study has several limitations as I could only observe interactions between fathers at a few selected sites. As previously highlighted, ethnographic studies often focus on a small number of units, and hence it is not possible to apply the results from the study to all fathers in Biskopsgården.

The results, however, give us some insight into what it can be like to be a father in a deprived area. Many of fathers in Biskopsgården are satisfied with their neighbourhood and the services available there, such as the open preschool, as well as with their everyday lives as fathers. The fathers also declared a concern for the district as a whole and for developments in the area that might affect their children in a negative way, such as criminality, segregation and other social problems. All fathers were aware that schools in the district had a bad reputation, and this is something that concerned them all, even those whose children were not yet in school.

The results of interviews and city walks indicate that several factors influence whether a place and a situation is perceived as safe or unsafe. Such factors include both physical elements (roads, traffic and so on) and social elements (people and events). Feelings of security and insecurity also vary depending on whether the fathers are accompanied by their children in various situations, or are on their own, as highlighted in the following excerpt from field notes from a city walk.

> A few weeks ago I was here with the kids (a playground near a wooded area in the district) and a police helicopter came and began to hover over the area. Considering everything that happened, I looked at my smartphone to see if anything had happened. I immediately saw a notice that there was a shooting in the neighbourhood, very close to the tram stop where the children and I got off half an hour earlier. Then it felt a little uncomfortable, that like 'shit, we could have been there.' So then I said indeed to the kids that we have to go home. I tried not to transfer my anxiety to them, more like; 'now it's time to go home' but it felt weird. I did

not tell the kids about it, but talked to my girlfriend in the evening. It is in situations like this you know, you think, 'damn, we cannot live here'.

Later on in the interview, this father says that he feels that the area close to their apartment building and the yard around it is safe for him and his family. He thinks, for example, that it is okay that his six-year-old son goes to the supermarket to shop for milk or other minor items. The microsites thus feel safe. The father mentions that they lived in another city a year ago, and that he probably would not have been comfortable with his son walking to the shop alone in that area, because of a heavily trafficked road. He would not have been comfortable to let the boy cross the road on his own there.

The study indicates that factors such as ethnicity, class and educational background are crucial for the everyday life of a father in Biskopsgården. An issue such as whether the decision to live in Biskopsgården is an active choice or not differs between the respondents. Some of the fathers have a financial and operational capacity to move to a different (better) area. In the interviews, they lean on ideological arguments as reasons to stay. Several of the Swedish-born fathers mentioned such aspects; as one father put it: "I believe that segregation is not good for the city, so I feel that I have to stay here; it would not be good if all Swedes moved to other areas. But, you know, sometimes it seems like I am experimenting with my kids and that's not satisfying." Nevertheless, they conceded that as fathers they had to deal with paradoxes and ambiguities to deal; they had to negotiate between ideological ideas and everyday realities. All fathers agreed that they wanted to act in the child's 'best interest', but that it was difficult to define what that was. Some of the foreign-born fathers who lack economic resources and cannot move to better areas discussed the possibility of letting their children go to school elsewhere, in an area where the schools have a better reputation. They are prepared to spend a considerable time on buses and trams just to make sure that their children are equipped with a high-quality education. These fathers also mentioned that their foreign origin had an adverse impact on the possibilities of obtaining a flat to rent elsewhere.

Mats Alvesson and Stanley Deetz (2000, p 20) argue that critical research aims to present alternative views to dominant ideals and understandings rather than conclusively establish 'how it is'. In this respect, this study contributes to a more nuanced picture of a district that the public perceives as deprived, but also what it is like to be a father there.

References

Agar, M. (1980) *Professional stranger*, New York, NY: Academic Press.

Agar, M. (1986) *Speaking of ethnography. Qualitative Methods Series 2*, Beverly Hills, CA: Sage Publications.

Alvesson, M. and Deetz, S. (2000) *Kritisk samhällsvetenskaplig metod* (*Critical Methods in Social Sciences*), Lund: Studentlitteratur.

Atkinson, P. (ed) (2001) *Handbook of ethnography*, London: Sage Publications.

Bernard, H.R. (1994) *Research methods in anthropology: Qualitative and quantitative approaches* (2nd edn), Thousand Oaks. CA: Sage Publications.

Bourdieu, P. (1977) *Outline of a theory of practice*, Cambridge: Cambridge University Press.

Bourdieu, P. (1990) *The logic of practice*, Cambridge: Polity Press.

Bourdieu, P. (1999) 'Site effects', in P. Bourdieu (ed), *The weight of the world: Social suffering in contemporary society*, Cambridge: Polity Press, pp 123-9.

Bourdieu, P. and Waquant, L. (1992) *An invitation to reflexive sociology*, Chicago, IL: University of Chicago Press.

BRÅ (Brottsförebyggande rådet) (2012) *Brottslighet och trygghet i Malmö, Stockholm och Göteborg* (*Crime and security in Malmö, Stockholm and Gothenburg*), Stockholm: BRÅ.

Burgess, R.G. (1984) *In the field: An introduction to field research*, London: Allen & Unwin.

Chan, J. (2003) 'Ethnography as practice: is validity an issue?', *Current Issues in Criminal Justice*, 25(1): 503-516.

Coles, T. (2009) 'Negotiating the field of masculinity: the production and reproduction of multiple dominant masculinities', *Men and Masculinities*, 12(1): 30-44.

Denzin, N.K. and Lincoln, Y.S. (2005) *The Sage handbook of qualitative research* (3rd edn), Thousand Oaks, CA: Sage Publications.

Doucet, A. (2009) 'Gender equality and gender differences: parenting, habitus and embodiment', *Canadian Review of Sociology*, 46(2): 103-121.

Doucet, A. and Mauthner, N.S. (2008) 'What can be known and how? Narrated subjects and the listening guide', *Qualitative Research*, 8(3): 399-409.

Emirbayer, M. and Williams, E.M. (2005) 'Bourdieu and social work', *Social Service Review*, 79(4): 689-724.

Geertz C. (1973) 'Thick description: toward an interpretive theory of culture', *Interpretations of cultures*, New York, NY: Basic Books, pp 3–30.

Gerell, M. (2015) 'Collective efficacy, neighborhood and geographical units of analysis: findings from a case study of Swedish residential neighborhoods', *European Journal of Criminal Policy and Research*, 21(3): 385–406.

Golafshani, N. (2003) 'Understanding reliability and validity in qualitative research', *The Qualitative Report*, 8: 597–607.

Gold, R.L. (1958 [2006]) 'Roles in sociological fieldwork', *Social Forces*, 36: 217–223.

Grubenmann, S. (2015) 'Collaborative research for the improvement of digital journalism practice', *Digital Journalism*, 4(1): 160–176.

Guba, E.G. and Lincoln, Y.S. (2005) 'Paradigmatic controversies, contradictions, and emerging confluences', in N.K. Denzin and Y.S. Lincoln (eds) *The Sage Handbook of qualitative research*, Thousand Oaks, CA: Sage Publications, pp 163–187.

Haas, L. and Hwang, P. (2009) 'Is fatherhood becoming more visible at work? Trends in corporate support for fathers taking parental leave in Sweden', *Fathering*, 7(3):303–321.

Hammersly, M. and Atkinson, P. (1995) *Ethnography: Principles in practice* (2nd edn), London: Routledge.

Hemmerman, L. (2010) 'Researching the hard to reach and the hard to keep: notes from the field on longitudinal sample maintenance', in F. Shirani and S. Weller (eds) *Conducting qualitative longitudinal research: Fieldwork experiences*, Timescapes Working Paper Series No. 2, Leeds: University of Leeds, -.Klinth, R. and Johansson, T. (2008) 'Caring fathers: the ideology of gender equality and masculine positions', *Men and Masculinities*, 11(1): 42–62.

Kozinets, R.V. (1997) '"I want to believe": a netography of the X-Philes' subculture of consumption'. *Advances in Consumer Research*, 24: 470–475.

Kozinets, R.V. (2010) *Netography: Doing ethnographic research online*, London: Sage Publications.

Lee, R.M. (1993) *Doing research on sensitive topics*, London: Sage Publications.

Mauthner, N.S. and Doucet, A. (2003) 'Reflexive accounts and accounts of reflexivity in qualitative data analysis', *Sociology*, 37(3): 413–431.

Morgan, D. (2011) *Rethinking family practices*, Basingstoke: Palgrave Macmillan.

Österberg, T. (2013) 'The increasing importance of place: neighbourhood differences in metropolitan Sweden, 1990-2006', *China Journal of Social Work*, 6(3): 244-261.

Pittaway, E., Bartolomei, L. and Hugman, R. (2010) '"Stop stealing our stories": the ethics of research with vulnerable groups', *Journal of Human Rights Practice*, 2(2): 229-251.

Plantin, L. (2007) 'Different classes, different fathers? On fatherhood, economic conditions and class in Sweden'. *Community, Work and Family*, 10(1): 93-110.

Richardson, L. (2005) 'Writing: a method of inquiry. Part I: qualitative writing', in *The Sage handbook of qualitative research* (3rd edn), in N.K. Denzin and Y.S. Lincoln (eds) Thousand Oaks, CA: AltaMira Press

Riley, M. and Holton, M. (2016) 'Place-based interviewing: creating and conducting walking interviews', *Sage Research Methods Cases*, DOI: 10.4135/9781446273050155595386.

Rostila, M., Almquist, Y.B., Östberg, V., Edling, C.R. and Rydgren, J. (2013) 'Network characteristics and daily smoking among young adults in Sweden', *International Journal of Environmental Research and Public Health,* 10(12): 6517-6533.

Shiriani, F. and Henwood, K. (2010) 'Continuity and change in a qualitative longitudinal study of fatherhood: relevance without responsibility', *International Journal of Social Research Methodology*, 14(1): pp 17-29.

Spradley, J.P. (1979) *The ethnographic interview*, Fort Worth, TX: Holt, Rinehart & Winston.

Tedlock, B. (2003) 'Ethnography and ethnographic representation', in N.K. Denzin and Y.S. Lincoln (eds) *Strategies of qualitative inquiry* (2nd edn), Thousand Oaks, CA: Sage, pp 165-213.

Wacquant, L. (2008) *Urban outcasts*, Cambridge: Polity Press.

Whyte, W.F. (1943 [1993]) *Street corner society: Social structures of an Italian slum*, Chicago, IL: Chicago University Press.

Whyte, W.F. (1992) 'In defense of street corner society', *Journal of Contemprorary Ethnography*, 21(1): 52-68.

Whyte, W. F. (1994) *Participant observer: An autobiography*, Ithaca, NY: Cornell University Press.

Wissö, T. (2012) *The everyday lives of parents of small children: Care, moral and social capital*, Gothenburg: University of Gothenburg.

Wolcott, H.E. (2009) *Writing up qualitative research* (3rd edn), Thousand Oaks, CA: Sage Publications.

SIX

Teleconference focus groups with fathers: 'You're on the line with ...'

Simon Burnett and Caroline Gatrell

Introduction

> Recently teleconferencing has been used to conduct focus groups in research ... where distance makes face-to-face [interactions] difficult and where anonymity of participants is important. (Tolhurst and Dean, 2004, p 1)

> I admire machinery as much as any man [sic], and am as thankful to it as any man can be for what it does for us. But, it will never be a substitute for the face of a man, with his soul in it, encouraging another man to be brave and true. Never try it for that. It will break down like a straw. (Dickens, 1857 [2008], p 24)

This chapter explores methodological issues experienced in the employment of audio **teleconference focus groups** in fatherhood research. Between 2009 and 2012, seeking to understand how easily (or otherwise) employed fathers were able to access flexible working, we undertook a research project entitled 'Work–Life Balance: Working for Fathers?', exploring how men with dependent children combine work and family commitments (Burnett et al, 2010a, 2010b). As part of this research, when recruiting fathers for face-to-face interviews and focus groups proved difficult, we utilised the medium of recordable teleconferencing technology. This enabled us to convene cross-UK qualitative focus groups. In what follows, we explain how fathers were recruited and assured anonymity, and how the teleconference focus groups were chaired and convened. In the context of research on fatherhood, we evaluate the emergent complexities integral to the entire process of running 'teleconference' (telecon) focus groups.

In undertaking this evaluation, we offer a reflexive appraisal of our experiences of using the telecon facility. The first section of our chapter describes the technological and procedural challenges in the commissioning of telecon focus groups. The second reflects on fathers' confession-like admissions, and the challenges for the research team of managing sensitive and emotional conversations among and between fathers 'on the line'.

Research design

Our research project comprised an empirical study on the impact of flexibility on the stress, health and wellbeing of working fathers. It was conducted between April 2009 through to March 2012 by a research team from Lancaster University (Simon Burnett, Caroline Gatrell, Cary Cooper and Paul Sparrow) and their partners from the renowned charity and lobbyists Working Families (led by Sarah Jackson OBE, and Policy and Research Officer Jonathan Swan). The research was financed by the Lottery Research Fund (Hill, 2010).

The initial phase of our empirical research was quantitative and comprised a stress analysis survey known as 'ASSET', the intellectual property of Robertson Cooper (Faragher et al, 2004; Donald et al, 2005; Johnson et al, 2005). We conducted this phase of the research drawing our sample from two large UK organisations, one public and one private sector, jointly employing over 40,000 workers and spread across a wide geographical area. Both organisations offered relatively generous flexible working options including part-time, full-time flexible hours and (more particularly in the case of the private sector) home and remote working. Both organisations hosted effective employee communications systems and each invested in promoting the survey, as they were interested to learn how their flexible working policies were experienced, in practice, by fathers in their employ.

The call for fathers to participate in the quantitative survey was met with an enthusiastic response. Within four weeks, more than 1,100 working fathers, split evenly between the two organisations, were enrolled onto the survey, spanning a range of high to low income levels. These fathers filled in and submitted a 15- to 20-minute anonymous online survey in which demographics (such as paternal income level and numbers of dependent children) were collected, along with data about attitudes and behaviours regarding flexible working, and health and stress-related behaviours (for example, smoking and alcohol consumption). Statistical analysis of this quantitative data offered broad measurements, for example regarding how far flexible working might mediate stress levels, and whether it enhanced workplace engagement among employees. In many respects, the findings from the quantitative research highlighted potential areas for further examination – for example, we sought to explore qualitatively our finding that fathers who shared housework with partners were happier, and experienced better work–life balance, than fathers who did not contribute to domestic chores. We also sought to understand more about the (in our view surprising) finding that employed fathers with two children were less stressed than those with only one child (Hill, 2010).

We thus planned to investigate, in greater depth and through qualitative research, how fathers felt about access to flexible working, and how they conducted their personal and everyday lives. As part of our qualitative research design, it was agreed that we would first share with participant fathers our general findings regarding paternal stress, numbers of children, housework and so on, and then seek their views about the relevance of, and explanations for, such findings. Initially, we planned to conduct our qualitative research through face-to-face focus groups (or, if preferred, one-to-one interviews) with fathers, held on workplace premises (or in suitable halls and meeting rooms nearby), with the research team travelling to meet respondents. Again, the participating organisations engaged in extensive and concentrated advertising (which had proved so successful in relation to the quantitative survey).

After four weeks, however, and in contrast to the successful recruitment onto our quantitative survey, less than a handful of fathers had come forward. This was despite several re-runs of the promotional campaigns via emails, newsletters, plasma screen advertisements and posters in dining and social areas. To try to understand the reasons for this, we approached those few fathers who had volunteered to take part in interviews/focus groups, and sought their views on why so few of their colleagues had signed up for the qualitative element of the research. Those fathers who had agreed to take part in the qualitative research apprised us of some key deterrents that might have discouraged their colleagues from signing up. These barriers included three observations: that fathers were likely to be concerned about the logistics of taking part in interviews and focus groups, that they might worry about retaining anonymity, and that they might feel reluctant to share personal matters with others (including the research team). It was further suggested that men might find it especially difficult to discuss issues that made them feel and appear emotional in the presence of other fathers (men perhaps preferring the solitary activity of filling in a survey). With regard to logistics, it was pointed out to the research team that – especially for remote and home workers – the obligation to visit the office specifically to attend the focus group might be simply inexpedient – just another appointment to be fitted in with busy lives.

In relation to sharing personal experience, fathers felt that colleagues might be reluctant to be seen, at work, entering rooms where focus groups or interviews were being held (because of drawing attention to their participation in the research project and thus compromising anonymity). Arguably, this apparent disinclination, on the part of fathers, to share feelings about family and work was unsurprising, given research evidence that some men find it difficult to express emotion in qualitative research contexts (McKee and O'Brien, 1983, p 153). In their work on the gender and emotion in households, Duncombe and Marsden (1993) describe men as unable or unwilling to reveal feelings, not only in research situations, but in relationships in general. It has been argued (by Connell, 2005), that men's reluctance to disclose emotions might be due to social expectations relating to 'hegemonic masculinity', in which displays of 'emotional self-control' are regarded as desirable among men.

Having acknowledged this possible male reluctance to share feelings, however, members of the 'Work–Life Balance: Working for Fathers?' research team had previous, personal experience of interviewing paternal participants where (once recruited onto research projects) fathers were equally as open and forthcoming as mothers. As Gatrell (2006) observed, fathers who took part in her Hard Labour project seemed keen to share their experiences and appeared neither embarrassed nor constrained about being emotional in qualitative interview situations. As one father noted: 'I am just so grateful for the opportunity to get things off my chest' (2006, p 245).

Following our reflections on the poor recruitment of fathers to the qualitative element of our study (and especially the comments offered by those fathers who had volunteered to take part, but could see why colleagues might feel reluctant to do so), the research team agreed to revisit the qualitative research design. At this point, we sought guidance from the senior managers at both participating organisations and we agreed on a different approach, inspired by one manager who is a communications specialist: we would continue our idea to run both single interviews and focus groups, but we would offer this in a different format – via telephone conferencing. This telecon facility would be audio only, and available across the UK (thus protecting anonymity and greatly reducing the likelihood of fathers meeting up with colleagues in the focus group setting).

The qualitative telecon focus groups and interviews were advertised afresh, and the opportunity for working fathers to sign up to these was embedded in each of the research organisation's intranet news feeds. In this 'call for fathers', a hotlink was provided, leading to a secure section of the Working Families website on which self-selecting participants could discreetly provide their first names and email addresses against a preferred, available time slot. Fathers were then contacted with confirmation and necessary sign-in details: a telephone number and pass code to access the teleconferencing facility. The response to this redesigned initiative was in marked contrast to the previous invitation. Within less than a fortnight, 100 fathers (the maximum requirement) opted to contribute, all of whom were guaranteed anonymity as names would not be shared with employers, nor any comments attributed to individuals.

The qualitative research interviews and focus groups ran for a period of approximately 15 available sessions over four weeks. The telecon focus groups for each organisation were kept separate from one another, and then all of the sign-up details were deleted. The majority of fathers signed up for the focus group option only; a small number (five) requested an individual conversation either in addition to or instead of the focus groups. Each focus group session catered for between two and eight fathers, and was chaired by at least one member of the research team, who took responsibility for outlining and orchestrating the proceedings for all participants. Given that we were running the focus groups as teleconferences, rather than as face-to-face events, the research team needed to think carefully about how these would be managed. Even so, the experience of convening these, and the challenges we faced, proved different from what we might have anticipated. Our preparations, and our reflections on what happened in practice when the teleconferences took place, are described after the following brief outline of the literature on focus groups.

The literature on focus groups

As discussed in depth by Morgan, customary face-to-face focus groups 'are not really new' and have a long, well-established history, having been introduced as a tool in social science as early as 1926, and being embraced by subsequent 'applied social research programs' during the Second World War (1988, p 4). More recently, however, they have become an increasingly 'common method' (Tolhurst and Dean, 2004, p 1), particularly in the realms of marketing where a range of ideas and opinions may be collected in a single meeting (Morgan, 1988, p 4).

Notably, early forms of teleconferencing technologies have been embraced in focus group interaction since the 1990s, as evidenced particularly by the employment of telecon facilities in the provision of medical care (MacIntosh, 1993; Schattner et al, 1993; Cho et al, 1995) and distance learning (Anderson and Garrison, 1995; Wildsoet et al, 1996). More modern developments have even seen the incorporation of video (Greenhalgh and Benford, 1995, p 240) and 'augmented reality' holographic projections, creating 'fundamentally new forms of remote collaboration' (Billinghurst et al, 2002, p 11).

In the case of our fatherhood research, our team followed similar procedural guidelines to those associated with traditional focus groups. We agreed a prearranged set of questions and ran the focus groups with fewer than 10 participants for less than 90 minutes, seeking a homogenised group of contributors 'in terms of at least one research factor', with permission to record sought from all involved (Tolhurst and Dean, 2004, p 2; Schattner et al, 1993; Cho et al, 1995; Appleby et al, 1999).

Despite their relative under-usage compared with face-to-face groups, the obvious, functional benefit of focus groups in a telecon environment is that they alleviate possible constraints arising from time, geography and finance issues (Tolhurst and Dean, 2004, p 2; Egido, 1988; Kuramoto and Dean, 1993; Tudiver et al, 2001). This assisted with the 'convenience' problem outlined by the fathers who advised us about why recruitment to the originally proposed face-to-face focus groups had been so slow. Fathers participating in 'Work–Life Balance: Working for Fathers?' could thus contribute from their homes, offices or even cars, from anywhere in the country, without having to travel or book prohibitively long periods of time out from work (Tolhurst et al, 1997).

Furthermore, the cloak of privacy and anonymity was tightly veiled, as only first names (or pseudonyms) were to be used, and any concerns among fathers over lack of anonymity due to their faces being recognised from previous or at future encounters were effectively addressed (White and Thompson, 1995; Schopler et al, 1998) as the teleconferences were audio only. Finally, the technology typically allowed for recordings to be downloaded almost immediately on completion of the session. Background noise could be cancelled out and voice volumes could be equalised, moving researchers on from the need to huddle their subjects around a dictaphone mounted on a table. Telecon focus groups thus afforded an array of 'opportunities', but with these, a contingent cluster of 'challenges' emerged (Billinghurst et al, 2002, p 11). We detail these in the following sections, beginning with the complexities of chairing the focus groups.

Complexities of the chair

> Email, instant messaging, and cell phones give us fabulous communication ability, but because we live and work in our own little worlds, that communication is totally disorganized. (vos Savant, 2010)

Despite experiencing the typical benefits inherent in telecon focus groups, a number of procedural, technological and unpredicted complexities arose during their commissioning. These 'technical hitches' began with problems not directly caused by, but perhaps pertaining to, technology. First, although participants were able to book timed places via the secure website, the focus groups suffered an approximate 30% attrition rate between those fathers who scheduled themselves onto a slot and who (virtually) attended in practice. While no-shows are of course not uncommon in face-to-face proceedings, we wondered whether the comparative lack of commitment and effort required of the participants actually to join one of their chosen telecon focus group – not necessarily needing to organise sanctioned time physically away from the workplace or travel out to a collective point – lessened pressure on them to attend, or even provide forewarning. (A minority of those who absented themselves did subsequently rearrange to phone in to another group on a following day.) The matter of attendance (or otherwise) proved an interesting issue during the running of the focus groups. In the experience of the research team, respondents participating in face-to-face focus groups were unlikely to get up and leave without warning. This was different in the telecon context. Once online with the telecon focus group, all fathers could voluntarily remove themselves from proceedings at any point by simply hanging up; this would be heralded by an automatic voice interjecting and announcing to all that, for example, 'John has left the conversation'. We saw this as a potential benefit of the technology – participants could exit the conversation if they wished without explanation (although we also felt it could be difficult to manage the subsequent discussions if participants left without notice).

However, on two separate occasions the technology conspired to erroneously eject chairing members of the research team who had not wished to leave. During the first, there were two researchers online so the other was able to continue the focus group without significant disruption until the outcast member dialled back in. On the second occurrence, though, there was only one chair present, leaving the participating fathers alone for the circa 60-second period it took to reconnect, rejoin and apologise. Interestingly, all fathers had remained present (albeit a little confused) rather than disbanding, enabling the focus group to be recovered. Indeed, the recording facility, which was not interrupted despite the loss of the chairing member, showed that the conversation between these otherwise unconnected individual fathers had continued organically.

Related to these accidental dismissals, another session experienced an unscheduled addition. During one of the focus groups for the private sector company, a father from the public sector organisation mistakenly joined. As detailed below in the discussions between the researchers, the private sector employees (Stephen and James), and the unexpected public sector worker (Ben), it took the research team a moment to identify what was occurring:

Researcher 1:	"Do you think working flexibly allows ..."
[Voiceover:	Now joining the conversation: Ben]
Ben:	"Hello, yeah it's Ben here from [organisation]."
Researcher 2:	"Oh, I think we must have got a crossed line."
James:	"Yeah have you got the right call you're on?"
Ben:	"I've typed in the number which was on the email."
Researcher 1:	"Oh right, there might have been a bit of a mix up in terms of the times."
Ben:	"Oh, I'm sorry, I've got totally the wrong date, it's not until this time next week."
Researcher 2:	"We would very much like to speak to you then, though! Please do phone back."
Ben:	"Ok, sorry again!"
[Voiceover: Ben has left the conversation]	
Steven [laughing]:	"The power of technology, eh? Was he one of our chaps?"
Researcher 1:	"No I don't think he is actually."

This transpired as a consequence of (for the particular brand of telecon technology being used) there being no lock-down facility once a meeting was in progress. While a specific telephone number and pass code are required to join, anyone with these has the ability to enter an ongoing discussion, whether inadvertently or otherwise. This had the potential to undermine the guarantee of anonymity. Fortunately, though, the private sector employees seemed unaware of the origins of the accidental caller, and Ben was sufficiently motivated to dial back the following week at the allotted time, alongside employed fathers from his own organisation.

A further technological issue encountered arose in attempts to close down some of the sessions. Once all the contributing members other than the chair had hung up, the recording facility had to be disengaged and the meeting formally declared over through the interactive menu system. Unfortunately, on two occasions (possibly through human error) this did not occur, resulting in the subsequent recording of the focus groups in question detailing everyone, including the chair, leaving, but continuing to run without any participants for up to three more hours. This resulted in a large mp3 data file to be downloaded and stored, not to mention the impact on the chairperson's telephone bill.

Procedural issues

Turning to procedural issues, the researchers had to be very organised (not to say regimented) in outlining the necessary introductory information, and ensuring that all fathers on the line had the opportunity to answer all the questions. The focus groups had a designated and well-publicised start time but, understandably, not all participating fathers arrived at exactly this point. The chairperson would always log in well in advance in order to greet all those who had consented to join, and the contributing fathers would log in over the next five or even 10 minutes. This sometimes resulted in the salutary greetings, requests of permission to record, assurances of anonymity and procedural details being repeated several times to ensure all had heard them. Those fathers who arrived early were thereby unavoidably subjected to a number of repetitions that could have possibly been avoided in a face-to-face format, assuming participants might be more likely to arrive at the allotted time.

Further, with each new joiner there was a necessary recap of the first names of all the other speakers, to ensure their awareness that they were not in a private interview and that others would be able to hear their responses. Instilling this fine balance between disclosure and privacy was complicated in one instance when it quickly became apparent that two individuals had the same forename. This was abated though by their agreeing to be known as 'Jack' and 'John'. However, a further complication, detailed below, emerged when two participants fathers discovered they were colleagues, calling from the same office:

Jack:	"There was a general agreement in my unit that we could work on that basis if needs be."
Researcher:	"Right, fantastic, thank you. And the same question to John, please?"

John: "Err, yeah I'm full-time, too.... I've just looked up
                     and looked to my left and Jack, erm, just sits next
                     to me ..."
[Both Jack and John laugh]
John: "... so I've got a very similar answer to him: full-
                     time, flexible ..."

While in this instance neither Jack nor John was overly concerned
at being 'identified', it could have been problematic to compromise
anonymity in this way. The situation had not been predicted (because
between them the employing organisations employed over 40,000
staff across a variety of locations), but could potentially have caused
discomfort to one or both fathers under different circumstances.

There were ten standard questions (sometimes more if required)
asked of all participant fathers, but participants were invited to answer
in a different order after each question, to vary the amount of time
individuals had to wait before giving their responses. Such variation
led to a richer, more dynamic and involved process, but required the
chair to direct every question at the required respondent by name each
time for the benefit of the recording. However, on one occasion, due
to the unavoidable reliance on non-physical, 'paralinguistic cues', such
as voice pitch, loudness, rhythm, inflection and hesitations (Graetz et
al, 1997, p 2; Tolhurst and Dean, 2004, p 3), confusion led to one
father who had just finished speaking then being asked to offer his
insights. With the researchers almost utterly reliant on these difficult,
ethereal cues, and patently aware that they provide a majority of not
only 'important information regarding the meaning of a message [but
also] the emotional state of the speaker' (Graetz et al, 1997, p 2), certain
issues raised had to be treated with a due sense of caution.

As noted earlier, the preliminary interviews with fathers who had
volunteered to participate in face-to-face focus groups suggested that
men would be more comfortable discussing personal and emotional
issues in a situation where their own and others' identities would not
be revealed (hence the idea of the telecon groups). While we did not
set out to 'prove' this to be the case, the research team did notice a
propensity for fathers to discuss personal matters in a manner that
appeared to us to be notable for its openness. If it is the case that telecon
focus groups are beneficial in encouraging confidences among male
participants, we would argue that the limitations of this method, for
the chair, were a lack of ability to read expressions or for one of the
research team physically to offer coffee and other breaks to individual
fathers when this seemed appropriate. We reflect next on the challenges

of managing telecon groups when the experiences of participant fathers become confessional in nature, and when the confessions of one party appear to discomfit another.

Chairing the confessional

In addition to the various disgruntled railings against employers discussed later in this section (whether related to flexibility, fatherhood or anything else), fathers responded to our questions with examples of personal experience, sometimes becoming emotional in their responses. One father, for example, explained he was "registered disabled" due to being "bipolar", and related the difficulties of parenting his four children under such circumstances. Another father, not having been asked directly, divulged that: "My ex walked out on me, had an affair with someone else within the office so that wasn't very pleasant." Such overt openness, in a forum populated by unknown colleagues and researchers, and being recorded for the purposes of transcription, came as something of a surprise to us. In our view, such open approaches among participating fathers were facilitated by the teleconference technology.

Like the internet, teleconferences offer space in which identity of the confiding individual remains undisclosed (Whitty and Carr, 2003; Whitty and McLaughlin, 2007). As noted earlier, within the 'Work–Life Balance: Working for Fathers?' project, participants could exercise the in-built capacity to withdraw, vanishing at any point into the electronic ether, thus providing a degree of removal and locating them within a relatively safe and 'friendly' environment (Gatrell, 2009a, p 163; Langan et al, 2006). Belli and colleagues argue that, due to the advance of information and communication technologies, there now exist forms of correspondence or 'performances' that have expedited a 'new' fusion between the expression of human emotion and the delivery medium of advanced technology (2009, p 6; Whitty and Carr, 2003). These socio-technical developments are referred to as the rise of the 'affective machine' (Brown, 2005; Michael, 2006), the 'cyborg' and 'technological disembodiment' (Harraway, 1989; Hollinger, 2000) or, as most relevant here, 'disclosure' and 'expression of emotions' via a technological interface (Belli et al, 2009, p 6).

This notion of participants using technologies as a private and anonymous medium for disclosure conjures the image and iconography of a confessional. Whether confessions take place in person (perhaps in a religious setting), online or within a telephonic multi-user interview, the confessor and the confessee cannot look one another in the eye. Technologically mediated social interactions have, hence, been described as constituting:

> a series of mechanisms from which emerge our most intimate thoughts and feelings ... [and 'disclosure'] helps us to explain how we love to talk with strangers, or someone that we already know but only through a screen we dare telling them things we would never say vis à vis, specially things we only express in private. (Belli et al, 2009, p 8)

Our experiences of chairing the telecon focus groups involved, from at least one father in every group, an exchange that could have been described as emotional in that it involved the sharing of feelings that were deeply felt, sometimes to the point of tears. For example, in one teleconference interview, as early opening gambit from one participant, Anthony, was the forewarning that:

> "Just before we go on, I do have a daughter that's not well so if I become emotional in this conversation please understand. As for 'flexible working', wow! What on earth is flexible working?! Never heard of it."

Anthony went on to explain that he had received very little help with his situation from his human resources department or line manager, which was having a detrimental effect on his stress levels and relationships with his partner and children to the point where social services had intervened. Anthony sought help from his employer and expressed resentment that this was not forthcoming:

> "Err, because my child is ill I found it very, very stressful and there was never any break [for me]. It would be work and home, work and home. Social services were so concerned they said I shouldn't go home at the weekend. And when I asked [for a shift pattern change] so that I could have one day every two weeks when I wasn't at work and when my family weren't home, just so I could have a break, I got told 'No.'"

Anthony's desire to share his experiences with the research team and other participants in his teleconference accords with the accounts of other scholars who discuss the potential effects qualitative interviews can yield on respondents (Finch, 1993; Hollway and Jefferson, 2000;

Haynes, 2006). As Gatrell (2009b), observes, some participants regard qualitative research as a form of catharsis, taking the opportunity to share emotions in an apparently safe environment with listeners offering space to talk. Perhaps the desire to engage in such sharing, in the case of fathers, was heightened by the anonymous setting of the teleconference setting. Anthony was one of several fathers who talked openly about personal issues that were intensely felt.

In our telecon group, Anthony was, audibly, very upset about his situation, yet desired to volunteer all the information. Very little prompting was needed and Anthony continued with his story, clearly seeking to share his emotions with the online team and perhaps facilitated in so doing by the anonymous setting of the teleconference. However, as a result of the inherent difficulty in providing (or even judging the need for) appropriate levels of support, and due to the presence of the others on the line, pressing the matter further was considered inappropriate by the chairperson. In a deliberate act of caution and concern, Anthony was sincerely thanked for his contributions and the questioning moved on to the next father. Due to the inherent 'challenges' (recall Billinghurst et al, 2002, p 11) of running audio-only telecon focus groups, it was difficult to judge whether or not Anthony would have wanted to continue talking and this remains a matter of speculation. So, too, does wondering if moving on to the next participant father could have left Anthony feeling silenced and rejected. This situation was something that the research team reflected on with concern at the end of the focus group, and we still are uncertain whether our chosen course of action was the best one. This was a clear example of an instance where the distance and lack of face-to-face contact felt to the team to be problematic. We could not see Anthony's face and there was no option for one of us to ask if he wanted to take a break from the focus group and get a coffee or similar course of action, which we might have done in a face-to-face focus group where two researchers were present. In retrospect, we viewed this as an instance where the technology (and audio-only nature of the teleconference) might have facilitated (or even invited) a participant father to disclose his feelings in a manner that might not have occurred in a face-to-face situation. However, the lack of personal contact with Anthony posed a challenge for the focus group chair, who would have preferred to offer a more personal form of support from the team.

The research team also found difficult a situation where fathers entered into a disagreement 'on the line'. In one session comprising six fathers, there emerged a situation where participants clashed regarding the appropriateness (or otherwise) of criticising their employer during the telecon group. Regarding time spent with his son, Peter was describing the wrangle he was experiencing with his line manager over flexibility:

> "My manager offered me overtime which I declined, this was after I'd done the work, I said, 'No thanks, but there could be a time when I would like to go early.' A week later my son was playing football. I wanted to go and watch him play football. An hour and a half is all I wanted from them. It was so difficult, so many questions were being asked. I said, 'Forget it, don't even bother.'"

Another participant, Jason, then interjected with a rather pointed response. He stated that:

> "I'm flexible within the confines of business needs, my end. It's not as though I can ring up my boss and say, 'I don't want to go to work today because I want to go and watch my son play rugby.'"

Peter was unperturbed and continued to explicate his grievance at length. Meanwhile, and without prior warning, Jason was reported by the automated voiceover as having left the conversation. Not wishing to disrupt the proceedings, and uncertain of whether Jason had left the conversation voluntarily or been unexpectedly ejected, the chair encouraged Peter to continue.

While the focus group was still in progress, however, Jason emailed the chairperson to apologise for purposefully leaving, explaining that he had not wished to 'play a part in a bitching session' about his employer, especially when he felt they were generally 'very amenable' to family life and requests for flexibility. Not wishing to lose his input, the researchers offered Jason the opportunity of a one-to-one telephone interview using the same telecon technology, to which he consented. It was during this interview that Jason's ambivalence about flexible working and his employer became clearer. As a senior manager with control over his diary but little access to flexible working, Jason did not battle with his employers for family time, but just discretely took it, 'slipping out' unnoticed from his workplace:

> "... you know with one child and especially him coming from a broken home ... I spoil him. Nothing is too much trouble for me. I make sure he doesn't miss out on any

opportunity with sport or to do with school just to ensure that he has as full a life as possible to make up for the upset. And I probably overdo it. And I'm very conscious of that. Yeah it is stressful. Like yesterday, you know, I slipped out of work, I worked from home, I slipped away from work early to go and watch him play the end of a school cricket match, and then took him from that to cricket practice."

So, while Jason had criticised Peter for having formally requested to use his available flexible hours to watch his son play football, he later admitted in private to having informally left work for a similar reason. This may have occurred because Jason appeared to be employed several hierarchical rungs above Peter. He thereby had greater capacity and freedom on occasion to work from home and manage his own hours. Furthermore, despite Jason's claim over email that he did not wish to 'bitch' about his employer, and his declaration in the teleconference that the organisation was a caring one, he went on to present in the one-on-one interview a different, personal set of circumstances. Perhaps reassured by the fact that we could only hear, but not see Jason, and we had no means of knowing his identity other than his first name, he 'confessed' his private feelings of anger and resentment towards his employer for what he considered to be a personal betrayal, the employer having reneged on a promise to facilitate Jason's divorce through relocation. Jason recounted how his employer had guaranteed, in writing, that both he and his ex-wife (who also worked for the organisation) could relocate to a different office in another part of the country where they could more easily afford to run two households. Having managed to sell both of their houses and each separately purchasing another in the new desired location, Jason continued, the newly separated couple were told that their employer had "changed their mind", and despite having nowhere to live in their original location they were all forced to stay in that area. This cost them "tens of thousands of pounds", and resulted in the divorced couple and their child having to live "in the same house back down here for nearly three years". This put strain on family relations, when the intention had been to manage the divorce amicably and smoothly. Regardless of receiving an "*ex gratia* payment" as consolation, Jason confessed that his loyalties to his organisation had been compromised and he (still) bore "huge resentment" against his employer as a consequence.

This reflection on Jason's differing portrayal of his situation compared with his comments while on the line with Peter recalls our reflections, earlier in the chapter, concerning participants' propensity towards open discussion in the anonymised telecon environment. Jason's interview alerted the research team to the fact that, on occasion, and despite being unaware of the identities of other participants, individual fathers might still have felt constrained in terms of what they felt able to talk during the teleconference. Although the situation was 'worked through' in the end, the chair found the audio conflict between Jason and Peter difficult to manage, partly because (as in Anthony's situation discussed earlier) there was no opportunity for another member of the team to offer to take Jason for a coffee at the point of exit.

It is worth noting, however, that Jason was remained keen to continue his narrative, and talk about his feelings towards his employers as part of an individual phone call with the research team. We cannot be sure whether he would have pursued this opportunity had he been identifiable as part of a person-to-person focus group, or in a situation where he was interviewed face-to-face. As a team, we were glad that Jason called back and we were able to listen to his story. However, had he not decided to email us following his exit from the teleconference, there would have been nothing we could do.

Conclusion

The preceding sections have, in turn, summarised the specific utilisation of telecon focus groups within the project 'Work–Life Balance: Working for Fathers?'; the likely benefits of teleconferencing in terms of recruiting fathers; a description of the technical and procedural complexities inherent in telecon focus groups; and our reflections on the enhanced tendency for fathers to share personal and emotional issues within teleconference focus groups. We have observed how, in some cases, the anonymous setting of the teleconference may have facilitated paternal 'confessions' regarding feelings of anger, frustration and unhappiness, either with other fathers as part of the telecon focus group event or sometimes on a one-to-one basis, as in Jason's interview. In our reflections on the emotional discussions that took place during the telecon focus groups, we have considered the challenges facing the research team when the need to provide due and appropriate care to participants was recognised, but difficult to implement using telephone technologies.

One question raised by our research is whether things would have been different had we investigated maternal experiences. Given that our research participants were fathers, we cannot know whether mothers would have been keen to join the originally planned face-to-face focus groups, as first advertised. Nor can we be sure whether mothers would have been more or less open than fathers to sharing emotions and thoughts about work and family within the teleconferences. What we do know, however, was that while fathers were reluctant to sign up to any research events requiring presence in person (whether focus groups or one-to-one interviews), we had no trouble in recruiting participants to the teleconferences and easily exceeded our target number of 100 participants. While we might have anticipated that men would be cautious about sharing personal issues (Duncombe and Marsden, 1993), in practice we found that fathers introduced to the conversations their experiences of divorce, bereavement and family illness without prompting from the research team. Perhaps the sharing of intensely felt emotions, within the telecon context, was facilitated by the anonymous environment of an audio-only focus group, where fathers could not see one another (or the research team) and could not be positively identified by internet searches, or recognised by other participants or members of the research team.

In conclusion, reflecting on the utility of teleconferencing as a method for reaching fathers when conducting qualitative studies, we suggest that this has significant benefits. Nevertheless, in crossing the divide between face-to-face and telephone research, teleconferences do raise methodological concerns. We suggest that as part of future research designs, research teams (including ourselves, should we use such technologies again) need to consider how best to manage not only the technical and procedural hitches that arise, but also the complex emotional interactions between participants and researchers. While it is possible that fathers who might avoid face-to-face research situations may feel more comfortable about sharing feelings in the anonymous setting of a teleconference, new ways need to be developed to support participants who become distressed or overwhelmed (for example, a facility that allows fathers and interviewers to switch to a separate one-to-one telephone line). More research, too, needs to be conducted on how contemporary fathers feel about sharing emotion in qualitative research, thus enabling research teams to be flexible and supportive in research environments that are changing rapidly in keeping with new technologies.

Acknowledgements

The authors would like to acknowledge their research partners, Working Families (especially Chief Executive Sarah Jackson OBE and Policy and Research Officer Jonathan Swan), and to express their gratitude to the Lottery Research Fund for financing this project.

References

Anderson, T.D. and Garrison, D.R. (1995) 'Critical thinking in distance education: developing critical communities in an audio teleconference context', *Higher Education*, 29: 183-199.

Appleby, N.J., Dunt, D., Southern, D.M. and Young, D. (1999) 'General practice integration in Australia. Primary health services provider and consumer perceptions of barriers and solutions', *Australian Family Physician*, 28(8): 858-863.

Belli, S., Harre, R. and Íñiguez, L. (2009) 'Emotions in technoscience: the performance of velocity', in C. Peter, L. Axelrod, S. Afzal, H. Agius, E. Crane and M. Balaam (eds) *Emotion in HCI – Real world challenges*, Proceedings from 5th International Workshop on Emotion in Human-Computer Interaction, available at http://uam.academia. edu/SimoneBelli/Talks/19266/Emotions_in_Technoscience_the_ performance_of_velocity.

Billinghurst, M., Cheok, A., Prince, S. and Kato, H. (2002) 'Real world teleconferencing', *IEEE Computer Graphics and Applications*, 6: 11-13.

Brown, S.D. (2005) 'Collective emotions: Artaud's nerves', *Culture and Organization*, 11(4): 235-247.

Burnett, S.B., Gatrell, C.J., Cooper, C.L. and Sparrow, P.R. (2010a) 'Fatherhood and flexible working: a contradiction in terms?', in S. Kaiser, M.J. Ringlstetter, M. Pina e Cunha and D.R. Eikhof (eds) *Creating balance? International perspectives on the work-life integration of professionals*, Berlin/Heidelberg: Springer.

Burnett, S.B., Gatrell, C.J., Cooper, C.L. and Sparrow, P.R. (2010b) 'Well balanced families? A gendered analysis of work-life balance policies and work family practices', *International Journal of Gender in Management*, 25(7): 534-549.

Cho, T.K., Davis, A., Sullivan, S. and Fisher, J. (1995) 'A review of five existing guidelines for planning focus groups in GP research', *Australian Family Physician*, 24(2): 184–86.

Connell, R.W. (2005) *Masculinities*, Oakland, CA: University of California Press.

Dickens, C. (1857 [2008]) *The wreck of the Golden Mary*, San Diego, CA: Icon Group International Inc.

Donald, I., Taylor, P., Johnson, S., Cooper, C.L., Cartwright, S. and Robertson, S. (2005) 'Work environments, stress, and productivity: an examination using ASSET', *International Journal of Stress Management*, 12(4): 409-423.

Duncombe, J. and Marsden, D. (1993) 'Love and Intimacy: The gender division of emotion and "emotion work": A neglected aspect of sociological discussion of heterosexual relationships', *Sociology*, 27(2): 221-241.

Egido, C. (1988) 'Videoconferencing as a technology to support group work: a review of its failure', in *Proceedings of the 2nd ACM Conference on Computer-Supported Cooperative Work*, New York, NY: Association for Computing Machinery, pp 13-24.

Faragher, E.B., Cooper, C.L. and Cartwright, S. (2004) 'A shortened stress evaluation tool (ASSET)', *Stress and Health*, 20(4): 189-201.

Finch, J. (1993) '"It's great to have someone to talk to": ethics and politics of interviewing women', in M. Hammersley (ed) *Social research: Philosophy, politics and practice*, London: Sage Publications, pp 166-180.

Gatrell, C. (2006) 'Interviewing fathers: feminist dilemmas in fieldwork', *Journal of Gender Studies*, 15(3): 237-251.

Gatrell, C.J. (2009a) 'Policy and the pregnant body at work: strategies of secrecy, silence and supra-performance', *Gender Work and Organization*, 18(2): 158-181.

Gatrell, C.J. (2009b) 'Safeguarding subjects? A reflexive appraisal of researcher accountability in qualitative interviews', *Qualitative Research in Organizations and Management: An International Journal*, 4(2): 110-122.

Graetz, K.A., Kimble, C., Thompson, P. and Garloch, J. (1997) 'Information sharing in face-to-face, teleconferencing, and electronic chat groups', Report for the United States Air Force Armstrong Laboratory, available at www.dtic.mil/cgi-bin/GetTRDoc?AD=A DA333568&Location=U2&doc=GetTRDoc. pdf.

Greenhalgh, C. and Benford, S. (1995) 'MASSIVE: a collaborative virtual environment for teleconferencing', *ACM Transactions on Computer-Human Interaction*, 2(3): 239-261.

Harraway, D.J. (1989) *Primate visions: Gender, race, and nature in the world of modern science*, New York, NY: Routledge.

Harre, R. (1998) *The singular self: An introduction to the psychology of personhood*, London: Sage Publications.

Haynes, K. (2006) 'A therapeutic journey? Reflections on the impact of research on researcher and participant', *Qualitative Research in Organisations and Management: An International Journal*, 1(3): 204-221.

Hill, A. (2010), 'Fathers are happier when doing more housework, says study', *The Guardian*, available at www.guardian.co.uk/lifeandstyle/2010/nov/04/fathers-happier-more-housework-study.

Hollinger, V. (2000) 'Cyborgs and citadels/between monsters, goddess and cyborgs', *Journal of Women in Culture and Society*, 25: 577-601.

Hollway, W. and Jefferson, T. (2000) *Doing qualitative research differently: Free association, narrative and the interview method*, London: Sage Publications.

Hughes, J. (1990) *The philosophy of social research* (2nd edn), London: Longman.

Johnson, S., Cooper, C.L., Cartwright, S., Donald, I., Taylor, P. and Millet, C. (2005) 'The experience of work-related stress across occupations', *Journal of Managerial Psychology*, 20(2): 178-187.

Lagan, B., Sinclair, M. and Kernohan, W.G. (2006) 'Pregnant women's use of the internet: a review of published and unpublished evidence', *Evidence Based Midwifery*, 4(1): 17-23.

Kuramoto, A.M. and Dean, J.L. (1993) 'Audiographics teleconferencing: a method of distance learning', *Journal of Nursing Staff Development*, 13(1): 13-17.

MacIntosh, J.A. (1993) 'Focus groups in distance nursing education', *Journal of Advanced Nursing*, 18: 1981-1985.

McKee, L. and O'Brien, M. (1983) 'Interviewing men: taking gender seriously', in E. Gamarnikov, D.

Michael, M. (2006) *Technoscience and everyday life: The complex simplicities of the mundane*, Maidenhead: Open University Press.

Morgan, J. Purvis and D. Taylorsone (eds) *The public and the private*, London: Heinemann, pp 147-161.

Morgan, D. (1988) *Focus groups as qualitative research*, Newbury Park, CA: Sage Publications.

Schattner, P., Schmerling, A. and Murphy, B. (1993) 'Focus groups: a useful research method in general practice', *Medical Journal of Australia*, 158: 623-625.

Schopler, J.H., Abell, M.D. and Galinsky, M.J. (1998) 'Technology-based groups: a review and conceptual framework for practice', *Social Work*, 43(3): 254-268.

Tolhurst, H. and Dean, S. (2004) 'Networking: using teleconferencing to enable general practitioner participation in focus groups', *Primary Health Care Research and Development*, 5: 1-4.

Tolhurst, H., Bell, P., Baker, L., Talbot, J. and Cleasby, L. (1997) *Educational and support needs of female rural general practitioners. Discipline of general practice*, Bathurst: School of Nursing and Health Administration, Charles Sturt University.

Tudiver, F., Brown, J., Medved, W., Herbert, C., Guibert, P., Haggerty, J., Goel, V., Smith, J., Obeirne, M., Katz, A., Molin, P., Ciampi, A. and Williams, J.I. (2001) 'Making decisions about cancer screening when the guidelines are unclear or conflicting', *Journal of Family Practice*, 50(8): 674-682.

vos Savant, M. (2010) 'Multitasking!', available at www.marilynvossavant.com/articles/multitasking.html.

White, G.E. and Thomson, A.N. (1995) 'Anonymized focus groups as a research tool for health professionals', *Qualitative Health Research* 5(2): 256-262.

Whitty, M.T. and Carr, A.N. (2003) 'Cyberspace as potential space: considering the web as a playground to cyberflirt', *Human Relations*, 56(7): 869-891.

Whitty, M.T. and McLaughlin, D. (2007) 'Online recreation: the relationship between loneliness, internet self-efficacy and the use of the Internet for entertainment purposes', *Computers in Human Behavior*, 23: 1435-1446.

Wildsoet, C., Wood, J. and Parke, J. (1996) 'Audio-teleconferencing as a medium for distance learning: an application for continuing education in optometry', *Australian Journal of Rural Health* 4(1): 18-27.

SEVEN

Using visual technologies: young children's perspectives on fathers

Susan Milner and Rita Chawla-Duggan

Introduction

The idea that children are expert informants on family life is now widely accepted within the policy and academic communities, alongside recognition of their rights (Christensen, 2004; Buckingham and De Block, 2007), but eliciting participation from young children in particular poses particular challenges (Prout and James, 1997). Research on fathers and fatherhood is still relatively new in the sociology of the family, as other contributions in this volume acknowledge (see also Dermott and Miller, 2015), and work that includes children's perspective as its primary focus or at all is relatively rare. In fact, researchers began to be interested in children's perspectives on parenting in cases of divorce and separation as long ago as the 1960s (see in particular Warshak and Santock, 1983), not least due to changes in the legal treatment of divorce cases, but children's perspectives on their everyday interactions with fathers is much less studied. Hence there appears to be a gap between the relatively abundant literature on the impact of fathering on child outcomes on the one hand, and research that elicits children's perspectives on fathering on the other. Investigating children's perspectives on fathering and fatherhood is therefore an important emerging and future area for research.

This chapter focuses on father–child interactions in early years and early childhood development, which has been the subject of intense policy interest over the past two decades (Daly, 2010; DfE, 2015), but where the challenges for researchers are heightened by the difficulties of eliciting views from very small children. Father involvement in children's social and educational development during the early years is found to have a significant impact on developmental outcomes (Sarkadi et al, 2008; Lamb, 2010; Lamb and Lewis, 2013; Roggmann et al, 2013). Children whose fathers are involved in their education 'benefit from higher academic achievement and social and emotional well-being'

(Morgan et al, 2009, p 168). Fathers are thought to encourage early years development through play and other action-based interactions that challenge children and expose them to the wider world (see Paquette, 2004). Fathers may also be more familiar with technologies that help prepare children for contemporary socialisation and education (Roggmann et al, 2013, pp 194-5). However, they are thought to be less directly involved in children's learning in formal educational settings, whether through less engagement with such institutions or through less presence in home-based learning because of less time spent at home with children. Thus fathers' observed behaviours stand in contrast with those of mothers, whose interactions with children are more often associated with care and routine 'housekeeping' tasks such as interactions with institutional settings (Lamb and Oppenheim, 1989).

Yet leading researchers such as Michael Lamb caution against overemphasising differences between mothers' and fathers' interactions with children (2010, p 3). Both mothers and fathers encourage exploration in play. Father sensitivity or responsiveness – talking, listening, teaching and encouraging children to learn – 'predicts children's socio-emotional, cognitive, and learning achievements just as sensitive mothering does' (Lamb, 2010, p 4). It is the interplay between different dimensions of father involvement that matters, along with the quality of the dyadic relationships within the family: 'fathers' influence children's development in embedded contexts of the father-child relationship, the mother–father relationship, paternal employment, culture and technology' (Roggmann et al, 2013, p 186). Researching these interactions and relationships therefore requires in-depth, contextually sensitive methods that allow for triangulation of multiple perspectives. In this chapter we draw on two small case studies to offer thoughts on how visual technologies can both reveal home-based interactions that might otherwise be hidden, and how methods aiming to situate those technologies in reflexive child-centred ethnographic projects can help to elucidate different perspectives.

The use of visual technologies in research on children and families

Since the 1990s, researchers from different social sciences have explored the reflexive use of video in ethnography, using video not simply to record data, but as a medium through which ethnographic knowledge is created (Pink, 2007). Researchers have begun to use visual technologies as a way of capturing experiences in the intimate sphere of the family and potentially overcoming difficulties such as small children's relative inability to convey emotions and experiences through use of language, particularly in an age when younger people relative to older generations develop expertise in the use of technologies from a young age and may enjoy using them, associating them with play as well as learning (Ofcom, 2013). Visual technology sources might include photographs, a whole array of web-based sources, tablets, digital camera recorders, mobile phones, indeed anything that incorporates that which we experience though the visual technology medium. The use of visual technologies does not constitute a research approach in itself but rather a means of data elicitation and collection; nevertheless their use lends itself particularly well to ethnographic approaches to research in which the technologies may 'stand in for' the participant researcher (Silverstone et al, 1991).

In addition, research using these technologies has often taken an epistemological stance based on the idea of co-production and participatory research (participatory video or PV). These approaches not only take account of the multiple perspectives of participants but explicitly go beyond consideration of the possible source of the data 'to include the ways in which the researcher works with the source and the data it might yield' (Pole, 2004, p 4; see also Pink, 2007), that is, they require a position of reflexivity that depends on the researcher's capacity to make sense of the interface between people and the image (Grint and Woolgar, 1997). Despite the most scrupulous adherence to ethical guidelines and norms, communication within a research project on families is always subject to power relationships, within the family and between members of the family and researchers. Without being able to exclude those power relationships, a reflexive approach to research may help to recognise them and find ways to mitigate them.

This body of research is located within childhood studies and the sociology of childhood (for example, James et al, 1998) 'in which children are recognised and valued as competent social actors with knowledges about their social world' (Lomax et al, 2013, p 232). As these authors highlight and discuss, such research raises a number of potentially challenging and even 'troubling' methodological questions, beginning with understandings of competence and knowledge. First, children's material family circumstances play a large part in determining their social world and their knowledge of it. Second, assumptions about children's competence may overlook the reality of power relationships within the family and beyond. Third, visual technologies raise serious ethical questions about confidentiality and consent, and children's capacity to act as informed participants in the full sense of the term. Fourth, and related to all these points, researchers themselves are part of the research process and outputs in ways that are not always easy to gauge or analyse (Lomax et al, 2013, pp 232-3).

The wider (but still relatively small) literature on the use of visual technologies as a tool in researching the domestic environment focuses on the opportunities and limits of the technologies themselves. As Buckingham and colleagues point out (2010, p 7; also referring to Stebbins, 2007), video recorders in their many forms are at once extremely easy to access and use in their everyday ubiquity, and so casually used as to be 'intermittent, spontaneous, even haphazard, rather than being a committed and regular practice'. This observation indicates the potential limits of the data yielded both in terms of quantity and quality, and therefore of the value of visual technologies as ethnographic observation tools. Thus, the 'home mode' (Chalfen, 1987) of data production using these technologies may allow greater access to the intimate sphere of father–child interactions than has hitherto been possible using techniques relying on either researcher observation or more strenuous methods of recording experiences such as diaries. At the same time, it may also be bounded by existing knowledge and practices of domestic video production, as well as by the conscious or unconscious choices exerted by children. Moreover, how do we, as researchers viewing and analysing the material produced, distinguish between 'fooling around' (Buckingham et al, 2010, p 8) and activities worthy of inclusion of the 'final cut', that is, how do we gauge and analyse the scholarly (or other) value of the footage that is produced?

Lomax and colleagues' (2013) project and their analysis of their data highlight the way in which children through their film-making activity perform their identities through talk and action. In our work we also aimed to construct the project in a way that allowed the children to produce and perform their identities through their choice of activities. Buckingham and colleagues (2010) remark on the difficulties faced as researchers in deciding whether to view 'raw' footage or to produce edited versions themselves for the purpose of academic analysis and discussion; in this respect they point to the tensions between the output as 'text' for analysis and the output as expression by the video maker. This tension will, of course, play itself out in various ways, depending on the way the research project is conceived and constructed, and the way the participants themselves conceive and construct their participation and output.

'Me and my dad': using visual technologies to explore a 'child's eye view' of fathers and fathering

In this chapter, we identify a number of key methodological challenges that have arisen in the research using visual technologies to capture children's perspectives on their relationship with their father, and discuss them with reference to our own small-scale projects conducted in 2012 and then 2014-15, and in particular to the later pilot project based on just one family.

In the first study, we evaluated an initiative taken by a local authority to encourage schools, nurseries and early years settings to hold an event to involve fathers. The initiative was conceived as a way of encouraging fathers to overcome the multiple constraints restricting their contact with their children's schooling (not just paid employment, but also unfamiliarity) and challenging assumptions on the part of teachers and mothers about fathers' readiness to become more involved. We employed a film maker to record the activities at a 'Fathers' Friday' event in one school, a large urban site comprising both an infants' (ages four to seven) and a primary (ages seven to 11) school under the same name and management structure. As well as responding to the perspectives of the local authority and the school, primarily aimed at reaching the maximum number of fathers (and other significant male caregivers) and finding ways to sustain their contact with the institutional setting, our project was therefore also informed from the beginning by the viewpoint of a professional film maker who framed it as a 'storyboard' (see Chawla-Duggan and Milner, 2016). Along with this multi-stakeholder perspective, we sought to elicit the views of fathers who participated in the event (chiefly through questionnaire responses as well as direct questions to camera on the day) and input from schoolchildren themselves.

In order to gather children's views on Fathers' Friday, we set up a drop-in 'video room' in a classroom, modelled on the idea of video booths seen on popular television shows. Cameras were staffed by volunteer schoolchildren who were members of a film club (mainly in the age range eight to 10). With the support of the teacher who ran the club, we set up cameras and trained the children in their use, and then left them to organise the filming themselves. However, as researchers, we directed the process by setting two questions for the camera operators to use as a guide: 'What does Fathers' Friday mean to you?' and 'What is a good dad?' The reason for setting these questions, as well as focusing on questions that were of interest to us as researchers and project evaluators, was to be able to gather useable material for the film, in line with the storyboard approach. The data gathered in this way was often amusing, touching and affectionate, capturing moments of easy intimacy between children and fathers, and was used in our film, which in turn was employed by the school and the local authority as marketing tools for further such events.[1] Nevertheless, the camera operators themselves independently used the opportunity to film each other and muse on the event and the nature of the father–child relationship, as well as on the task they had been given; as the children were left entirely to their own devices to run the video room, we did not see this as researchers until we viewed the film footage.

As researchers, we viewed the resulting footage not just for the purposes of the film but for own research interests in the changing nature of fathering and fatherhood. We coded the material manually (taking note of both verbal and non-verbal communication) using a broadly grounded approach, that is, using the terms generated by the children themselves, and then sorting those terms according to the types of father involvement used in the fatherhood literature. As noted above, particularly for the youngest children, several prompts were necessary to elicit views, sometimes from the older camera operator, sometimes from the father who was usually present with the child. The children's perspective was therefore constrained by adult framing and the need for a dyadic (father–child) narrative. Despite these limitations, children usually offered several views unprompted, even if they had begun by waiting for prompts or cues from their father or the camera operator, and the data generated held some surprises for us as researchers, in light of the assumptions derived from existing literature.

Thus, for example, we found that children frequently used a language of affective care and nurturing when talking about their father, as with this five-year-old girl:

Girl: "Well they [dads] look after you."
Older child: "Why do they look after you?"
Girl: "'Cos we love them."

Both boys and girls also referred to play:

"They're important because they're there for you a lot of the time and they're really fun" (girl); "Help me play my Star Wars games" (boy).

Several children also spoke, unprompted, about the role of fathers in household routine: "They tell you to brush your teeth"; "When you go to sleep they can say good night to you"; "They tell you to mend your bike if you break it"; "They make you breakfast." The child interviewers in this case reflected often on father absence and sometimes directly prompted answers about it: "It's sad when people don't have fathers because they're missing out on so much fun." Fathers, on the other hand, appeared to put greater importance on educational activities, probably because they were aware of the relatively novel experience of being in school: "read you stories". The use of visual technologies in this project may be seen as an adjunct rather than an alternative methods of eliciting children's views such as interviews on everyday life events (see, for example, Hedegaard et al, 2012), but had the added advantage that our presence as researchers was less intrusive, we were able to generate additional input from expert (child) participants, and the activity itself became 'fun', thus putting participants at ease.

In our second (pilot) project,[2] we sought to capture what goes on in a home-based learning environment. In the first project, father involvement (in school-based or school-related activities) had been sought by the local authority and education providers not as an end in itself, but as a means of building bridges between the school and home. It has been found that such bridges are necessary because parental involvement, that is, contact between school and parents, is not in itself likely to have an impact on children's educational development (Carpentieri et al, 2011); rather, it is parental engagement in learning both at school and, especially, at home that influences pupil achievement (Desforges and Abouchaar, 2003). Mothers tend to be significantly more involved than fathers in the home learning environment, not least because they spend more time in child-related, home-based activities. However, studies indicate that the quality of fathers' involvement that is more important than the quantity of time they spend with their children (Goldman, 2005). There is some evidence that fathers spend considerably less time than mothers on home-based learning but that a greater number of fathers than is commonly assumed take part in such activities. Partly this is because of the low participation rate of fathers, compared with mothers, in formal child literacy programmes (Clark, 2009; Morgan et al, 2009). These findings suggest that more information is required about how parents interact in the home learning environment.

In this pilot project, we sought to recruit families in one smaller school, within the same local authority area but in a predominantly rural location, to take part in filming father–child interactions. We gave no instructions to the family regarding their choice of what to film other than the general theme of 'activities with my dad', and we wanted the children to be in control of the choice of activities and the recording itself. In order to gain insight into the home learning environment, our project intended to include as participants children from a very young age group, that is, early years as defined in current government policy. We set out to recruit families with at least one child in reception class (aged four to five) and a slightly older sibling (age range six to 10); one of the aims was precisely to test levels of competence in handling the camera equipment at these ages. The ages of the child participants therefore strongly inform the way we present these methodological challenges and the way we sought to tackle them.

In line with the epistemological stance outlined in the previous section, when eliciting and analysing visual data, in looking and reflecting we constantly asked ourselves 'What does it tell us about the children's experiences of being with dad in the context of home and family life?' We were also interested in the process of children making their stories, in particular, 'How do they learn to use the visual technology and how do they create meaningful representations?' This reflexive approach involved a complex process of discussion with the participants and other key stakeholders at each stage, including watching the film footage together and discussing what was going on and why activities had been chosen for filming, with all discussions being filmed and transcribed; we also made lengthy field observation notes throughout.

A second major feature of this particular project is therefore the way we sought explicitly to build in multiple perspectives, including that of education providers at the children's school, but principally those of the children and their parents, and our own perspective as researchers. The data yielded therefore included, as well as the video footage generated by the children, video recordings of our meetings with the family and teachers. In addition, one end-of-project interview (audio-recorded) was conducted with the father in order to elicit his views on the project itself (in which he had participated as the subject of his children's videos) and more generally about his perspectives on family life. Finally, the project outputs also included our own written field notes at various stages of the project, including meetings between ourselves to discuss the data, and with key project stakeholders, namely a freelance film maker employed by us to help edit the footage, and an early years director at the local authority who was a key gatekeeper in the early stages of the project and had a particular policy interest in measures to support fathers. The project therefore included both 'talk' and 'action', and sought to integrate reflection and dialogue at all stages.

The following sections of this chapter highlight the main methodological challenges and also reflections on the findings they generated, in line with insights from existing research using visual technologies, as sketched out previously.

Access and recruitment

Initially our intention was to pilot the project by recruiting three families to film over a holiday period, so that the father would be more present during the filming. Information was sent out via the school and we arranged to be present in the school at pick-up time to answer questions and give information about the project. In the event, only one family volunteered to take part from that school, so at the time of writing all observations below relate to this one family. The family consisted of a mother and father; the mother was not in paid employment at the time of filming, although she took up a full-time job several months later, while the father's job entailed long hours away from home and driving long distances. It is intended that the pilot will continue at other schools in the local authority and beyond.

Several reasons have been identified for the difficulties of recruitment, in discussions with the school and the family. First, our research design narrowed the potential pool of participants: in the school in question, only 10 families corresponded to our profile of having one sibling in reception class and another aged at least two years older. This, combined with the considerable demands the study would make on participants' time, meant we could only expect a small number of volunteers. Second, we anticipated the need to overcome barriers of distrust about the intrusiveness of the project, exacerbated by the use of cameras rather than conventional 'talk' methods. We sought to overcome those barriers by working collaboratively with the school, and in this case the head teacher was a strong supporter of the project, but such concerns seem inevitable where no prior relationship exists between the school and the researchers such that familiarity can build trust. Aligning the project more closely to school activities or obtaining sponsorship from a trusted third party could possibly help to improve recruitment in future projects using similar methods. Finally, it was suggested to us that the timing of the participation request, just before Christmas and therefore at a busy time for schools and families, had discouraged parents from taking part in the project; it may be useful therefore to pilot filming at other times, for example during the summer vacation.

Despite the obvious limitations of drawing conclusions from the findings of such a small project, the filming yielded a considerable quantity of rich data: hours of film footage consisting of many short extracts and three very long extracts; four hours of videoed discussion meetings; six hours of videoed meetings between the researchers and various stakeholders external to the family; an audio-recorded meeting with the father lasting over an hour; transcripts and coded notes of these recordings; and a book of field notes. There is thus a trade-off between the quantity of participants and quantity of data in terms of project management.

Ethics

Any work involving contact with young children requires strict adherence to professional guidelines for ethical conduct, and full compliance with legal disclosure requirements.[3] The need for an ethical approach to research underlies all aspects of the research process, from initial access to all contacts with research participants to data generation and analysis, and decisions about publication of data. A reflexive approach that takes full account of ethical dimensions of research helps to make researchers constantly aware of the sensitivities and the need to listen to any concerns of children or their parents. As parents ourselves, we as lead researchers were also highly aware of the need to adopt a protective approach to the use of images of children, which is paramount and takes precedence over any research-motivated decisions about the generation or use of data.

The issue of full and informed consent is central to these concerns. Children, particularly very young children, are not necessarily in a position to give fully informed consent. For this reason, parental control over research processes is essential, and all parts of the research process must be discussed with them in advance and consent received. In the context of schools and early years settings, head teachers or centre heads are necessary intermediaries in the negotiation of consent. Thus, for example, full written information about the school filming in the first project outlined earlier, the Fathers' Friday initiative, was sent to parents in advance and the head teacher made herself available to talk to any parents with concerns. Filming could only take place with the assurance that no child could be filmed without the written consent of parents or guardians; moreover, the choice of footage extracts and stills was explicitly subject to approval by the head teacher based on parental consent. No data could be published until the full consent process had been finalised.

In addition to parental consent, the 1989 United Nations Convention on the Rights of the Child stipulates that children under the age of 16 have the right to express views on all matters that affect them. In accordance with this convention, even very young children may be able to give assent, if not consent, when those matters are explained clearly to them. This places researchers in a position of responsibility to ensure that their actions are always fully set out and subject to discussion and questioning by participants. In this sense, it may make sense to refer to consent not as informed, but as 'provisional' and 'negotiated' (see Flewitt, 2005).

In the second project, carried out in a home setting, similar procedures applied, but a more thorough dialogic approach took place throughout in order to ensure not only that parents gave full consent but also that as far as possible the children were involved all discussions and given the opportunity to participate on the basis of clear explanations. This meant, for example, that when we as researchers explained what we wanted to do and why, all participants (except sometimes the father who was absent due to work commitments) were present, and we sought to verify that all had understood. The children and their parents had full control over the images, which they presented to the researchers. We ensured that they knew that they could delete any images they did not wish to include, at any stage. This included, for example, a small selection of images that the children had filmed. When we subsequently viewed the footage together, it was clear that these images caused them some embarrassment, so we deleted them immediately.

It was also important to explain to all participants that they themselves could not film others without their consent; so, for example, it was decided collectively (by the mother and children, in discussion with the researchers) that it would be best not to take the camera on a visit to grandparents over the Christmas holiday. Such decisions necessarily restrict the scope of research findings (potentially excluding important social and familial interactions outside the nuclear family), but this loss can be mitigated by other complementary methods such as interviews in order to shed light on those wider family relationships and activities (which were an important part of family life for our participants in this case).

Technology: using the cameras

One of the aims of the pilot project was to test which form of camera children preferred to use. It has been observed in other studies that compact portable technologies have advantages over fixed cameras as children may feel more in control of the content with the former and more at ease in expressing themselves, although picture and sound quality may sometimes suffer (Flewitt, 2005). We offered three types of video recorder and left examples of each for all three children to use: a telephone recorder, a small hand-held video recorder that could also be used as a static camera, and several action cameras of the type that can be worn on a headband or attached to clothing, and that is increasingly commonly used in everyday lives. At our initial session, when we introduced all the equipment and explained how to use it, the children were immediately drawn to the mobile telephones and began spontaneously to film objects in the room and around the house. The hand-held recorder, which we had also found complex to use at first, was declared too difficult and left to one side, and although the boy (one of the younger children) put on an action camera he soon abandoned it.

When we returned to pick up the equipment after the Christmas holidays, we found that most of the footage had been filmed on the camcorder, which had been used both statically and portably. Using a static camera allowed all the children to participate in activities with their father: in this case, it was used in this way for more static activities, in particular reading, and some rough and tumble. Hand-held, it provided more opportunity for creative filming by the older daughter, who often provided a narrative to accompany the footage: thus, an introduction to the family and the house; an enquiry into the father's mechanical/DIY activities in the garage/shed; and mealtimes. The father confirmed that while the camcorder had initially proved difficult to use, the children soon worked out not just how to switch it on and off, but also how to film long, sweeping and close-up shots; the only problem had been that it was not always easy to delete material, limiting editorial choice. The action cameras were used for two long films showing a bicycle ride (which we had been told by the mother was the principal father–child activity at weekends) and a walk through fields to an adventure playground. The quality of images and sound for all three types of equipment was very good, although movement sometimes meant that images were out of shot.

Asked about whether he had found the cameras intrusive, the father said that he had not experienced discomfort with the filming as "the children didn't go mad", and the family had got used to cameras being there, but he confirmed that he had preferred the less direct presence of the action cameras. Both parents had exercised some control by setting limits, for example defining some spaces within the house (largely bedrooms and bathroom) as out of bounds. We noticed also that at several points when being filmed the father had asked children to switch off the camera: "That's enough now." He explained this to researchers:

Father:	"Yeah, I think I thought … just 'not now' [laughs]….
	It is hard, when you get home from work, it is that hour, I get home at seven o'clock, and they're generally, well maybe a bit later now they're getting a bit older, you know, that is like the witching hour, so it's like, and then filming as well, and it's like …"
Researcher:	"Too much?"
Father:	"It's like hang on, do what you've got to do, and then…. It'd be different, like if I was home at like ten past five, but that's just how we are, we want our evening, so we concentrate on getting 'em into bed. And it's, job done, and then we can relax."

The interviews confirmed that the family had not found filming to be intrusive as they felt in control, but it may have interfered with their ability to direct household routine, which was particularly important in the context of a strong family (couple-negotiated) norm about the use of the father's quality time.

Age of children

The pilot project was intended to test whether children as young as four are sufficiently expert users of technologies such as mobile phones and tablets to be able to act as reliable research participants generating information about everyday family life. To a limited extent, this was proved to be true, but principally when guided by an older sibling. The father in his interview confirmed that in general terms the camera techniques themselves posed few problems even for the younger children:

"They always have done videos. Bits and pieces. And taking photographs of themselves, they love seeing themselves on the screen, don't they. Get the camera out, and they can just see themselves on the telly, and they think that's great."

He also reflected at some length about the children's age, in relation to the individual development and temperament of each child. In particular, he noted that the younger twins had struggled, not with the technology as such but with the notion of creating a filmic narrative, although he felt that during the six months between filming and our interview they had changed in their interests and their attentiveness:

> "Well they were four then, they were just a bit too young. Like another year, and they'd be really into it. Almost now, being a bit more grown-up, and they'd be able to understand it a bit more. Well, Rosie would, I don't know if you'd get much out of Michael.[4] But no, it's just nice to see how they've changed, you know."

The older daughter, who turned seven during the time of the filming, proved to be particularly adept not just at using the technologies but at taking a creative directorial approach to film making. Ultimately it was she who provided the 'family' narrative about father–child interactions. Although the mother and the father held a strong and cohesive set of values and norms about family life that determined the day-to-day organisation of family activities and their routine division of labour, the (just) seven-year-old eldest sibling framed those activities, deciding on the selection of activities in the filming and taking editorial control over the footage. The father saw this as reflecting the child's individual interests: "Yeah, she is keen on making films, whether it was to do with that, she's always been keen to do things with her phone and make videos, she's always done that, it's interesting." When the teachers (both of whom had taught the elder daughter) saw edited footage, they interpreted her direction of the film as a sign of her strong affection for her father, which he also acknowledged: "[She's] always been a bit of a daddy's girl, being the first, I think, you know, she had a lot of my attention, and she plays on that a bit sometimes with her sister." On the other hand, the younger sister, who of the twins was more drawn to the cameras and to our discussions about the films than her brother, and who, teachers confirmed, was more outgoing in class than her twin sibling, remained withdrawn from many of the more physical activities filmed. The father confirmed this pattern and interpreted it as the girl's own development path in relation to that of her siblings. Conversely, the twin brother, whose attention was easily distracted during our meetings and who showed little interest in the cameras initially, led many of the filmed activities not just in outdoor play but also in many home-based games.

Classifying, analysing and publishing the data

One of the key ideas explored here is whether visual technologies help to elucidate home-based interactions that might otherwise remain hidden. Earlier research into the home learning environment using film crews has found that learning activities, such as counting, take place much more frequently than teachers assume (see, for example, Griffiths, 2006). We found similarly that when we showed edited footage of the children's activities with their father to teachers, the latter showed surprise at the amount of learning-based interactions; for them, the father was largely absent from the children's education because he was rarely able to drop off or pick up from school, unlike the mother who carried out this task routinely and was also exceptionally active in the life of the school. In fact, the children's selection of activities, coupled with maternal gatekeeping, may have led to significant under-recording of home-based learning in this case: for example, we discovered only by chance in conversation with the mother that the father regularly worked with the elder daughter on maths homework, and it was never alluded to in any of the recording.

As researchers, we were therefore wary of generating labels for activities that the children had chosen, and spent a good deal of time discussing those categories not only with the children and the mother and then in a later stage of the project the father, but also between ourselves. Our labels for the activities may therefore also be seen as 'provisional' and 'negotiated', and to be investigated further in future research, rather than categorically fixed. As a result of those discussions, we divided the footage into five main activities: Lego building and play; reading; rough-and-tumble/tickling; and outdoor play; and a fifth category that caused us the most discussion as we could not decide whether to classify it as routine household/nurturing or authority-based rule giving. The father in his interview described the latter category as: "Trying to … calmly. Trying to keep them in line…. So they know they're loved". He also explained, however, that as an active family involved in many out-of-school activities it was necessary to avoid "fractious" behaviour and for parents to take it in turns to "play good cop, bad cop". He explained that, as his wife "bore the brunt of it" while he was at work, his duty was to help her maintain overall control of family time when he was at home.

Of these activities, the one most obviously linked to formal education was reading, and in this instance the book used was one that had also been read recently at school by the two youngest children (and previously by the older sibling). Interestingly, this was also the activity that caused the most difference of perspective between researchers and stakeholders: for example, the film maker found this activity most difficult to frame in a way attractive to external viewing. The teachers found in this footage extract an indication that the father was not familiar with reading activities as he had not approached it in the way they would have done in class and paid little attention to the written text itself, focusing on the characters and the sound effects; however, we as researchers saw in the footage evidence of a good deal of expert direction of the reading by the father, beneath an apparently chaotic approach that included the younger boy leaving the room to fetch a prop made at school, and affectionate involvement of all three siblings.

Finally, we found, as have previous studies, that the need to obtain as full consent as possible and to be sensitive to any potential external or future misuse of or participants' embarrassment at use of the images limited our ability to use film footage in publications resulting from the study (see Buckingham, 2009). Beyond the basic principle of consent in all research involving human participants, the use of images in the digital age is subject to very limited guidelines and very little societal consensus, given (currently) widespread image sharing, including images of children, and a sense of constant flux in behavioural norms (Flewitt, 2005). However, working from the principle that it is better not to publish, even with consent, if there is any doubt at all, has advantages: it forces us as researchers to use only material that has a pressing intellectual value unobtainable by other means, and to ensure that we comply fully with our own values. This means that 'our primary obligation is always to the people we study, not to our project or to a larger discipline' (Denzin, 1989, p 83), in other words to reflect responsibly and collaboratively on our professional practice.

Conclusion

The use of visual technologies creates a rich corpus of recordings and transcriptions that we supplemented in our projects with other materials such as interviews, recordings of meetings with the family and with other research stakeholders to discuss the film footage, and our own field notes. Such work is extremely time-consuming, which necessarily induces a trade-off between richness of data and clarity of narrative (or other concerns such as aesthetic view, depending on output), as researchers are 'drawn into the systematic complexities of the briefest of social situations' (Ochs et al, 2006, p 390). Nevertheless, we have sought to show here that visual technologies can offer a glimpse into everyday fathering that may not otherwise be available to researchers, particularly when dealing with young children. In particular, they offer us insights into the dynamics of dyadic, triadic and multiple parenting relationships between parents and different children, between siblings, and within the couple.

Of course, we do not suggest here that visual technologies offer better insights than other methods that continue to be used to capture everyday interactions within the family such as longitudinal studies (for example, Belsky et al, 1984), ethnographic and other research based on interviews and diaries. Rather, they take their place alongside those other methods and may indeed usefully be combined with them. We have suggested here ways in which a reflexive approach to the use of visual technologies can help to reveal additional layers of understanding that one method alone could not have provided. For example, the children's choice of activities and sequences sometimes required explanation from the children, with prompting and further information from the mother or father, in order for the researcher to be able to understand.

By designing research to elicit multiple perspectives on the home as a learning environment, we also identified a gap between educationalists' and fathers' approaches to learning activities that existing literature has indicated may be explained by the relative lack of mutual contact and knowledge. Since schools tend to see mothers rather than fathers, and fathers readily admit their lack of familiarity with the school environment, teachers may underestimate fathers' involvement and competence as enablers of their children's educational development. Finding ways to build bridges between the home and school may therefore be a fruitful avenue for policy and for research.

Notes

[1] See www.bath.ac.uk/ipr/policy-briefs/fathers-friday.html.

[2] Both projects were supported by the University of Bath's public engagement funds.

[3] See 'The research ethics guidebook. A resource for social scientists', available at www.ethicsguidebook.ac.uk/research-with-children-105. This resource brings together guidelines of the UK research councils and provides links to further reading and resources.

[4] Names have been changed.

References

Belsky, J., Robbins, E. and Gamble, W. (1984) 'The determinants of parental competence: towards a contextual theory', in M. Lewis and L. Rosenblum (eds) *Beyond the dyad*, New York: Plenum Press, pp 251-279.

Buckingham, D. (2009) '"Creative" visual methods in media research: possibilities, problems and proposals', *Media Culture Society*, 31(4): 633-652.

Buckingham, D. and De Block, L. (2007) *Global children, global media: migration, media and childhood*, Basingstoke: Palgrave.

Buckingham, D., Willett, R. and Pini, M. (2010) *Home truths? Video production and domestic life*, Ann Arbor, MI: University of Michigan Press.

Carpentieri, J., Fairfax-Cholmeley, K., Litster, J. and Vorhaus, J. (2011) *Family literacy in Europe: Using parental support initiatives to enhance early literary development*, London: Institute of Education.

Chalfen, R. (1987) *Snapshot versions of life*, Bowling Green, OH: Bowling Green State University Press.

Chawla-Duggan, R. and Milner, S. (2016) 'Father involvement in young children's care and education: exploring boundaries and starting conversations', *Cambridge Journal of Education*, 46 (4): 473-489.

Christensen, P. (2004) 'Children's participation in ethnographic research: issues of power and representation', *Children and Society*, 18(2): 165-176.

Clark, C. (2009) *Why fathers matter to their children's literacy*, London: National Literacy Trust.

Daly, M. (2010) 'Shifts in family policy under New Labour', *Journal of European Social Policy*, 20(5): 433-443.

Denzin, N. K. (1989) *The research act: a theoretical introduction to sociological methods*, London: Prentice Hall.

Dermott, E. and Miller, T. (2015) 'More than the sum of its parts? Contemporary fatherhood in policy, practice and discourse', *Journal of Families, Relationships and Societies*, 4(2): 183-95.

Desforges, C. and Abouchaar, A. (2003) *The impact of parental involvement, parental support and family education on pupil achievement and adjustment: A literature review*, London: DfES Publications.

DfE (Department for Education) (2015) *2010 to 2015 government policy: Children and early years*, London: DfE.

Flewitt, R. (2005) 'Conducting research with young children: some ethical considerations', *Early Child Development and Care*, 175(6): 153-165.

Goldman, R. (2005) *Fathers' involvement in their children's education*, London: National Family and Parenting Institute.

Griffiths, R. (2006) 'Young children counting at home', *Proceedings of the British Society for Research into Learning Mathematics*, 26(3): 13-18.

Grint, K. and Woolgar, S. (1997) *The machine at work: Technology, work and organisation*, Cambridge: Polity Press.

Hedegaard, M., Aronsson, K., Højholt and Ulvik, O.S. (eds) (2012) *Children, childhood, and everyday life: children's perspective*, Charlotte, NC: Information Age Publishing.

James, A., Jenks, C. and Prout, A. (1998) *Theorising childhood*, Cambridge: Polity Press.

Lamb, M.E. (2010) 'How do fathers influence children's development? Let me count the ways', in M.E. Lamb (ed) *The role of the father in child development* (5th edn), New York, NY: Wiley, pp 1-26.

Lamb, M.E. and Lewis, C. (2013) 'Father-child relationships', in C.S. Tamis-LeMonda and N. Cabrera (eds) *Handbook of father involvement: Multidisciplinary perspectives*, New York, NY/London: Routledge, pp 119-162.

Lamb, M.E. and Oppenheim, R. (1989) 'Fatherhood and father-child relationships: five years of research', in S.H. Cath, A.R. Gurwitt and L. Gunsberg (eds) *Fathers and their families*, Hillsdale, NJ: The Analytic Press, pp 11-26.

Lomax, H., Fink, J., Singh, N. and High, C. (2013) 'The politics of performance: methodological challenges of researching children's experience of childhood through the lens of participatory video', *International Journal of Social Research Methodology*, 14(3): 231-43.

Morgan, A., Nutbrown, C. and Hannon, P. (2009) 'Fathers' involvement in young children's literacy development: implications for family literacy programmes', *British Educational Research Journal*, 35(2): 167-185.

Ochs, E., Graesch, A.P., Mittmann, A., Bradbury, T. and Repetti, R. (2006) 'Video ethnography and ethnoarchaelogical tracking', in M. Pitt-Catsouphes, E. Kossek, and E. Erns (eds) *The work and family handbook: Multi-disciplinary perspectives, methods, and approaches*, Mahwah, NJ/London: Lawrence Erlbaum, pp 387-410.

Ofcom (2013) *Children and parents: media use and attitudes*, London: Ofcom.

Paquette, D. (2004) 'Theorizing the father-child relationship: mechanisms and developmental outcomes', *Human Development*, 47(4): 193-219.

Pink, S. (2007) *Doing visual ethnography: Images, media and representation in research* (3rd edition), London: Sage.

Pole, C. (ed.) (2004) *Seeing is believing? Approaches to visual research: studies in qualitative methodology*, Volume 7, Oxford: Elsevier.

Prout, A. and James, A. (1997) 'A new paradigm for the sociology of childhood? Provenance, promise and problems' in A. James and A. Prout (eds) *Constructing and reconstructing childhood* (2nd edition), London: Falmer Press, pp 7-31.

Roggmann, L.A., Bradley, R.H. and Raikes, H.H. (2013) 'Fathers in family contexts', in C.S. Tamis-LeMonda and N. Cabrera (eds) *Handbook of father involvement: Multidisciplinary perspectives*, New York, NY/London: Routledge, pp 186-201.

Sarkadi, A., Kristiansson, R., Oberkleid, F. and Bremberg, S. (2008) 'Fathers' involvement and children's development outcomes: a systematic review of longitudinal studies', *Acta Pediatrica*, 97: 153-158.

Silverstone, R., Hirsch, E. and Morley, D. (1991) 'Listening to a long conversation: an ethnographic approach to the study of information and communication technologies in the home', *Cultural Studies*, 5(2): 204-227.

Stebbins, R. (2007) *Serious leisure*, New Brunswick, NJ: Transaction.

Warshak, R.A. and Santock, J.W. (1983) 'The impact of divorce in father-custody and mother-custody homes: the child's perspective', *New Directions for Child and Adolescent Development*, 19: 29-46.

EIGHT

Interviewing young fathers: managing ethical risks

Carmen Lau-Clayton

Introduction

Given the rising scholarly interest concerning the lived experience of young fatherhood, it would be worthwhile examining the ethical issues that arise when researchers work closely with such a population while applying qualitative longitudinal (QL) methods. In this chapter, the Following Young Fathers (FYF) project (2010-15), funded by the Economic and Social Research Council (ESRC), is used as a reflective case study to explore the use of QL interviews with a sample of 31 young fathers (defined as under the age of 25) and the potential research impact it had on the interviewer–interviewee relationship, and what efforts were made to overcome and minimise any potential transgressions. An introduction to the FYF study is followed by a discussion of the conduct of the interviews and the implications this had on relations between the participants and the researchers. The chapter goes on to give examples of the various mechanisms employed to reduce the blurring of boundaries between both parties and how effective these strategies were in hindsight. By sharing such an account, this chapter hopes to stimulate and contribute towards the existing and ongoing debates concerning QL research and ethical practice with young parents found elsewhere.

Ethical conduct is a fundamental principle in any type of research; it is not confined to the data collection stage only and nor should it be seen as an afterthought. At the beginning of a project, researchers need to consider appropriate protocol and assess, and minimise, potential risks and harm in the design and successful completion of the study. During the fieldwork period, researchers should consider the safety of both participants and themselves, and the complexities of the fieldwork encounter, and uphold the integrity and transparency of the research. Towards the end of an investigation, researchers should maintain their ethical duties when leaving the field and during dissemination of the findings, and contemplate the possible impact that results may have on various audiences, including the sample themselves, while ensuring that data reuse and archiving procedures are completed to a high standard if applicable (ESRC, 2015). Ethical considerations throughout the lifecycle of a project allows for good practice among researchers and as the social sciences become increasingly intersectoral (for example, spanning government, academia and the voluntary sector), interdisciplinary and international, with an increased concern in litigation issues within contemporary society, ethical awareness and appropriate conduct cannot be overlooked (SRA, 2003). Although each academic discipline and professional body may have its own set of ethical recommendations, a number of core values concerning researchers' obligations to participants, sponsors/funders, society, their subject and their colleagues can be identified (SPA, 2009), with key principles such as anonymity, beneficence, non-maleficence, confidentiality and integrity consistently highlighted (AREC, 2013).

The consideration of ethics is particularly sensitive when using QL methods because of the prolonged period of contact with participants over time and the nature of the researcher–researched relationship that can form from such approaches (Neale, 2013). QL approaches seek to understand change as it happens, and how and why it happens in the socio-cultural context, thus enabling an understanding of complex issues, transitions and impacts within an individual's life (Neale, 2012). Although QL research is seen as a distinct methodological paradigm, it comprises a variety of approaches, concepts and project designs (Thomson and McLeod, 2015), but the key facet of data generation here is iterative. In other words, QL approaches draw on what has gone on before to understand the changes and contours of an individual's story told over time (McLeod and Thomson, 2009). Given the characteristics of QL enquires, the relationship between the investigator and participant is built on mutual understanding, reciprocal trust and collaboration, and such feelings may be heightened, leading to increased risks and vulnerabilities during the research encounter for both young fathers and researchers. Given the complexities and in-depth nature of QL approaches and the significance of ethical practice, it is clearly important to explore such issues. We discuss such matters after the introduction to the FYF project, before moving on to the writer's reflections.

Introducing the FYF study: a brief synopsis

The FYF study, based at the University of Leeds, was funded by the ESRC (grant number J022993/1) and aimed to investigate the lived experience of young fatherhood and service support needs. Qualitative semi-structured interviews were the principle method of investigation and such approaches have been argued to emphasise notions of situated knowledge and subjective understanding (Neale, 2012). Furthermore, QL methods have the ability to engage with change as it unfolds, linking macro-level processes or events to the lives and circumstances of individuals, particularly during times of social transformation (Neale, 2012). Using qualitative interviews to give young people a voice was especially important in the study, as societal attitudes often marginalise and discriminate against young fathers (Lau-Clayton, 2015). Qualitative interviewing is said to be powerful tool in eliciting and generating data that is concerned with individuals' interpretations of knowledge and meaning, allowing participants to tell their own stories, on their own terms and using their own words, an approach that appeals to young people in particular (Silverman, 2011). Repeating interviews over time enables a good level of trust and rapport to be built up between the researcher and participants, and provides opportunities to revisit, extend and clarify interviewees' accounts and interpretations, an approach that has been argued to elicit high-quality data (Vincent, 2012).

FYF tracked 35 young fathers over a period of two to four years and consisted of a linked baseline study and follow-up project (2010-15; full details can be found in Neale et al, 2015). The study first emerged from an established Timescapes project called Young Lives and Times (an ESRC initiative – see www.timescapes.leeds.ac.uk/research/young-lives-times.html), which explored young people's experiences of personal and family life with a focus on their future values and aspirations. In 2010, a sub-sample of young fathers were recruited into the study, which was set up in consultation with a team of teenage pregnancy co-ordinators, leading to the development of a local partnership with an educational service provider and a specialist learning mentor who supported school-aged young fathers up until the age of 19. As a result of this collaboration, 11 fathers were recruited through, and had received support from, the learning mentor, and through personal contacts we also contacted one young father who had had no formal support. The 12 young men were interviewed between December 2010 and May 2012 via three waves of data collection that were approximately nine months apart. Some fathers also participated in a small focus group at the beginning of the fieldwork stage.

In 2012, further funding was successfully sought from the ESRC for a follow-up study and we continued to follow the original 12 fathers from the baseline sample and recruited a further 19 fathers to interview, six of whom were referred through the key practitioner as before. Two waves of interviews were conducted between December 2012 and April 2014, and were typically spaced between two and six months apart. In sum, the whole study involved 31 young men who were tracked longitudinally, but there were also four 'one-off' interviews conducted to gain a particular insight into selected service providers such as a local children centre, a secure residential unit and a youth offending service (amounting to 35 participants in total). In total, 28 participants were recruited via professional referrals, five through advertisements in further and higher educational settings, and two through personal contacts. Three female researchers were involved in the data collection process; the author undertook all the longitudinal interviews with the exception of one participant in this group and the remaining one-off interviews were conducted by the research fellow and research assistant. Group interviews were jointly conducted by the research team. In total, data was gathered from six focus groups and 89 QL interviews.

Each interview wave focused on a particular topic (for example, identities as fathers, grandparents, socioeconomic circumstances, relationships with the mother of the child, and relationship education) and consisted of a set of core questions with regard to continuity and change for the young men and individualised questions relating to the young father's circumstances. At every interview encounter, young fathers were also invited to complete activities such as timelines, self-portraits and relationship maps, which acted as helpful ice-breakers, and enabled further data to be collected and considered in subsequent

Table 8.1: Recruitment pathways

	Learning mentor service	Other professional referrals	Further education	Higher education	Personal contacts
Baseline study	11				1
Follow-up study	6	6	1	4	2
One-off interviews		4			
Total number of fathers	17	10	1	4	3

interviews; these proved to be very useful as prompts and reminders of important life events and experiences for the sample (Hanna and Lau-Clayton, 2012).

At the first interview, the majority of young fathers were in the 16-22 age bracket; 11 were school age, nine in their mid- to late teens and 11 were in their early to mid-twenties. Young men were aged 13-24 at the time of the first conception (18 were school age, the rest aged 17-24); five were expectant fathers, 20 had one child and six had two or more children (two of the fathers had twins). Fifteen young men were in a relationship with the mother of the child at the time of the first interview and 16 were separated. By the end of the study, 19 young men (almost two thirds) were no longer with the baby's mother. There were 11 co-habiting couples, two of which were married, one of which was separated. One father was not in a relationship with the young woman at the point of conception. All of the pregnancies except two were unplanned, although these unborn babies were by no means unwanted after the young men's initial period of adjustment to the news. Young fathers' children were mostly under a year old (16 cases), one was over the age of six and the rest were aged between one and three years at the time of the first interview.

Interviewing process

The interviews, timelines, relational maps and self-portraits provided a great insight into the lives of young fathers and their support needs. A safe and non-judgemental environment was necessary to help draw out the participants' accounts (Sivell et al, 2015). The conditions to create such an atmosphere arguably began with the researcher's first encounter with the participants during the recruitment stage, most often by telephone call or text message, which introduced the purpose, aims and nature of the study, and, it was hoped, set the tone for the entire research process. As part of the communications, potential participants were reassured that the interviews were an informal opportunity for young fathers to speak about their experiences with a trained interviewer in a friendly and confidential manner at the university. As the nature of the research and the researcher's approach can affect a study's recruitment rates and success (Newington and Metcalfe, 2014), it was doubly important to present and explain the study in a suitable manner.

After the recruitment stage, young fathers were asked if they were willing to participate in a group and individual interview. For most, the preference was for the one-to-one format; there was a large degree of hesitancy about speaking in groups and a desire to avoid the sharing of life stories with direct peers (interestingly, this contrasts with writings that suggest that participants may prefer the neutrality of focus groups and find them less intimidating than one-to-one interviews – see O'Reiley, 2012). Regardless of the interviewing type, once informed consent had been obtained from the young men and the interviews began, the flexibility of the QL method helped to create a respectful and comfortable environment for participants in which to share their accounts in a flexible and mostly organic manner. Key to this process was the research team's experience with QL research, thoughtful questioning, perceptive probing and interpersonal skills, all of which helped to put the participants at further ease during the interviews. Given that a number of young fathers had expressed difficult encounters with adults and authority figures in schools, the police service or social care settings, it was extremely important to reassure participants that the researchers were not there to judge or criticise them, as this could have created defensive behaviours and have a negative impact on the interviewing process. As one interviewee stated:

> "I liked the fact that you asked really open questions, I think it was really quite inviting. And you didn't stick to like a strict kind of set of questions. Like you were obviously listening to me and you obviously acknowledged what I was saying, and, you know, you responded to me, like as a person what I was saying not just a machine. So, you know, it was really good." ('Zane'[1], aged 20, wave 2)

The interactions between researchers and participants were crucial in the data-gathering process (Sanjari et al, 2014), and it is through the researcher's facilitative interaction that a conversational space is created, defined by Owens (2006) as an arena where respondents can share their narration of stories, including those of a sensitive nature. Crucial to this is the establishment of trust and rapport between the researcher and interviewee to help develop and maintain an open, non-judgemental and honest dialogue that arguably elicits a richer set of materials. As one participant commented,

> "Yeah it's been good to be able to talk about things to someone who I can trust." ('Iman', aged 17, wave 2)

The reciprocal exchange was often viewed by the participants as akin to a regular conversation and the perceived neutrality of the researcher also helped to provide more nuanced and detailed accounts (Yates, 2013), as the following comment shows.

> "I enjoyed having someone to talk to who's away from my friends and someone who I can actually express my thoughts to without having to worry about it going back to anyone else.... If you knew my circle of friends, everything gets twisted and turned around. It's like Chinese whispers." ('Darren', aged 24, wave 5)

Often the interviews explored private and sensitive issues around each of the main topics explored per interview wave, such as upbringing and childhood experiences, feelings about pregnancy and abortion choices, and fragile relationships with the mother of the child. Many of the young fathers also raised personal issues and anxieties, and would disclose mental health concerns that had not been discussed elsewhere, even with those closest to them, such as partners, family and friends.

> "It's really nice to actually talk about it and get it off my chest. It's nice to talk to someone that's neutral. 'Cause obviously when I talk to my friends they're gonna have an opinion about you ... I'm not really good at talking, you know, expressing my feelings to people or anything like that because I'm scared of upsetting people. So it's been nice to get it off my, you know, talk about it here, yeah." ('Jock', aged 21, wave 2)

Having the opportunity to speak openly and frankly to someone seemed to alleviate a degree of stress for those affected by it and helped to instigate a clearer way of thinking for fathers during and after the discussion. As Hughes (2012) identified, qualitative interviews often act as a catharsis, and allow self-acknowledgment, sense of purpose, self-awareness, empowerment and healing to emerge. As many young fathers were the first in their peer group to have a child, or had little formal or informal support, the ability to discuss their feelings and thoughts in an open manner with another person was welcomed. The study provided some participants with the first opportunity to speak about fatherhood in a meaningful manner since becoming a parent. As one participant put it:

> "I've enjoyed it, like coming and talking about things. 'Cause you don't get chance to. It just feels good to like

speak about it, get it all out of the way. I feel more relaxed and better than I did before." ('Simon', aged 16, wave 3)

All the young fathers suggested that their involvement in the research study was enjoyable and they had felt comfortable being interviewed in a respectful, non-intrusive manner with the rare opportunity to discuss their viewpoints and opinions at length. But for those undergoing difficulties at the time of the interview, the rawness of experiences such as separation from the mother of the child or losing contact with children meant that these young men could become quite emotional. Nevertheless, as one participant commented, the opportunity to discuss their experiences at the time of the interview, and to have a voice throughout the duration of the study, was a strong factor in their openness and continuation of the project:

> "I'm talking about things that are not good, not fun, but if it'll help some other person down the line then yeah.... It [research] could lead to something in a few years." ('Jason', aged 24, wave 5)

The ability to look back on their accounts and activities was met with an overwhelmingly positive response by all the young men and it acted as a motivator for the fathers, providing some degree of validation for their decisions and past and present behaviours. Their final interviews enabled an appreciation of how things had turned out as they reflected on the process. As young fathers are often known as a 'hard-to-reach' and 'hard-to-keep' sample, the ability to track such a group for two to four years was a very positive result for the study; the practitioners who helped to facilitate the interviews were key to this process, particularly the learning mentor. Actions that helped in this regard included introducing the idea of the research to the young men before contact was made by the research team, escorting fathers to the university for their first interviews to help put them at ease about setting foot on a university campus (some had never been to a university before), accompanying participants to some of the initial interviews and taking part in focus groups. One father, reflecting on his participation in the study, stated:

> "It's been nice actually seeing that [past interviews] and being able to compare myself now to the way I was then and thinking I'm much more, much happier and much more content with my life." ('Ben', age 21, wave 2)

Although the young men's ability to speak in an open manner was welcomed in terms of data accumulation, the sharing of private life stories and the level of disclosure to the researcher had the potential to transfer the role of the researcher from an interviewer to a close acquaintance. As Caven (2012) suggested, narrators are inclined to feel close to someone who has listened to them in an understanding fashion, and may begin to think of the interviewer as a friend or 'agony aunt'. Such feelings could be further compounded when young fathers lacked appropriate support outlets in their day-to-day lives, which could increase the interviewee's positive feelings towards the researcher. As 'Adam' (aged 16, wave 3) suggested:

> "Whatever I need to talk about I can just talk about. I mean you're not a stranger but you are a stranger. So I can just say whatever really…. It feels like you actually listen. I don't know if you are listening but it does feel like you're listening. So I like it better. It's better than talking to a counsellor, let's put it that way."

It was acknowledged early on that any interpretation of the interviewer as a friend or as an adviser could be detrimental to interviewees' long-term support plans. For example, if young fathers became overly reliant on the interview encounters to 'let off steam' and only confided in the researcher, they may not have utilised the help available to them through family, friends or professional agencies. In order to minimise the possibility of participants becoming overly reliant on the research team and to avoid any blurring of professional boundaries, several mechanisms were employed to remind participants of the purpose of the research and the role of the interviewer. This included the choice of the research site, interview protocol, consistency in research approach and the act of reflexivity by the researcher. Each of these aspects is explored in turn in the following section.

Research considerations

From the outset, the research location was thoroughly considered as it is well established that different interview settings can not only affect the power relations between the interviewer and interviewee, but can also influence the participant's response and engagement during the meeting (Denscombe, 2014). As Edwards and Holland (2013, p 46) suggest:

Positions in hierarchies of gender, class, age, ethnicity and other dimensions are not just aspects of multiple identities of individuals (or groups) but are experienced, created and enacted in *places*. (Original emphasis)

After careful thought and deliberation, the university setting was chosen as the most appropriate site, as it provided a clear and visual indicator to the participants that the meetings were not an informal get-together occurring by chance or between friends, but instead were arranged to serve a purpose for the research team (to investigate young fatherhood) and the participants (to share their experiences of young fatherhood). The use of university meeting rooms in busy occupied parts of the building provided further reminders to both parties. Such a choice proved to be quite effective, as young fathers (many of whom had never been to a university before) were often quite inquisitive about the university and the experience of higher education, thus reminding them of their surroundings and the purpose of the interviews. Young fathers are also known to lack a stable abode, often 'sofa surfing', for example, or living in hostels (Neale and Ladlow, 2015) and so the use of the university setting was a practical decision, and one that may have saved embarrassment on the participants' part as many came from disadvantaged backgrounds and circumstances and may not have wanted the researcher to know about their living arrangements. Furthermore, the instability of young fathers' residency status posed ethical issues for the safety of the female researchers in the study, as women conducting research on their own are generally considered more vulnerable than lone male researchers and home visits can be more problematic (Becker et al, 2012); as such, the use of the university campus served to alleviate some potential risks.

It is worth noting that the 'hard-to-reach' nature of the sample (Fatherhood Institute, 2013) meant that communicating and contacting young fathers was often very difficult, and as a result social conventions regarding the acceptable hours of contact were not always maintained. The main method for arranging interviews was via mobile phone text messages as only a small minority of fathers had or used an email account, and young fathers were known to send text messages outside office hours regarding confirmation of meetings or asking general questions. Being aware that contact with the participants could be infrequent and difficult, the researcher responded, within reason, to out-of-hours requests to arrange, confirm or rearrange interviews. Young fathers were known to change their plans with the researcher at the last minute, change their mobile phone number without warning, lose their mobile phone, or have no credit to reply to the researcher's original telephone messages, so any contact that the young men initiated required a swift response to retain sample numbers and interest. Such conditions are not ideal, and as Hemmerman (2010) suggested, setting and maintaining ethical boundaries are heightened when working with hard-to-reach and vulnerable participants. With such considerations in mind, the researcher was very careful with the wording and formatting of replies to ensure that professional boundaries remained intact. This included the use of Standard English in text messages (not text speech), references to the research project or the university during the conversation, and a formal thank you and signing off at the end of each reply. Although there may have been several text messages as part of the exchange when arranging and organising an interview meeting, the researcher was highly mindful of the less-than-ideal conditions for such communications and felt that the formality of the messages helped to safeguard against any potential transgression in the research relationship by being responsive yet professional.

Managing participants' expectations is a key responsibility for researchers and this includes explaining clearly the nature of participants' involvement and what they should expect during the process of participation (Eide and Kahn, 2008). The period before the interview formally began was seen as a key opportunity to ensure that the nature of the research was clearly understood and overtly clarified by the researcher. This included thanking participants for their time and help with the research before the interview began, obtaining consent or ongoing consent for the interviews, seeking permission to record the discussion, outlining the interview topics and providing the interviewee with the chance to ask questions or to withdraw from the study. This protocol was followed at every interview to reinforce the message (Durand and Chantler, 2014). During the interview, visual clues such as the dictaphone on the table and the visibility of the interview guides acted as reminders about the nature of the meeting, and extreme care was taken over the level of formality and familiarity displayed by the researcher at all times. For example, the researcher's attitude towards the participants was friendly but not overly friendly or familiar, thus creating a degree of professional distance before, during and after an interview. At the end of each discussion, participants were again thanked for their participation and informed of the next phase of the project, provided with estimated time frames for further meetings, updated with any dissemination plans and provided with a gift voucher as a token of thanks for their involvement and time. Although such practices may seem to be common sense, researchers are obligated to indicate the professional nature of the interviewer and interviewee's relationship (Ritchie and Lewis, 2013), and ensuring a consistent approach was one way to achieve this goal. At the same time, the protocol followed provided a level of familiarity and reassurance for the young fathers in relation to both parties' interview conduct and what to expect from the research encounter. Reflecting on this protocol, one participant made the following observation:

> "To start off with it were a bit strange if you know what I mean. But then once you get used to it, yeah, it's easy. It was mostly talking about myself, you know, sitting in a room and talking about myself." ('Darren', aged 24, wave 5)

Despite participants' perceptions that the researcher held a neutral stance during the research meeting as mentioned earlier, it is well recognised within the literature that qualitative researchers are, by virtue of being human, 'emotionally engaged participants who are sharing an experience with the interviewee (Edwards and Holland, 2013, p 84) and the phrase 'researcher as instrument' is often used to refer to the researcher as an active respondent in the research process (Pezalla et al, 2012). As such, researchers should acknowledge how they influence the research and how their interactions with participants may lead to a renegotiation of meanings, understanding and practices (Edwards and Holland, 2013). Mason (2002) argues that researchers need to do more than 'listening beyond' (to retain a critical awareness of what is being said); they also need to 'understand beyond', that is, to be aware of how the social and cultural factors that both parties bring to the encounter can affect what happens in the interview and thereafter. Researchers should therefore be reflexive in their studies, understanding that the act of engaging in research actually affects the process being studied (Mason, 2006), and should recognise that knowledge is generated and shaped through the interactions between those who are involved within the research. Such a practice is common within qualitative research and examples within FYF include the use of a research diary, debriefs with colleagues after interviews and regular team meetings, alongside ongoing research training, which were all vital in the reflexive journey and retained the integrity of the researcher–researched relationship.

When engaging and speaking to young fathers over a period of time, the level of personal involvement between the researcher and the participants inevitably increases, and may feel more relaxed, not only with the interviewing process but also with the interviewer. Clearly, the management of these relationships requires careful consideration, and one suggestion by Patrick (2012) is to avoid regular forms of contact on which the participant might come to rely. The FYF adhered to this through the systematic organisation and conduct of the interviews, and clarity of roles. Keeping young fathers up to date with the timescale of FYF and the potential end date of the project ensured that participants understood that contact with the researcher would also cease when the research ended. The ending of a piece of research needs to be treated with care, especially given the vulnerable nature of the research group and the depths of the accounts shared within the interviewer. Rupp and Taylor (2011) point out that some participants may feel betrayed, exploited and disappointed when a project ends, so it is necessary to be mindful of such issues, and how these feelings can be prevented. By drawing on and reminding participants of the professional nature of the interviews during any communication and the status of the research relationship at various points of the FYF study, it was hoped that there would be no traumatic after-effects once the study had ended. As David and Sutton (2010) have commented, one has to consider the after-effects of leaving the field and to take care that no one is harmed by or is worse off as a result of the research.

The ability to leave the field with good relationships and with the participants' wellbeing intact (especially when researching young and vulnerable groups such as young fathers) is particularly pertinent for longitudinal studies, as researchers may wish to return to their original sample in the future. In the final interview wave, young fathers were specifically asked about their research involvement and the methods used. All felt highly positive about their participation and were incentivised by the possibility that their accounts would be used to help improve academic, political and societal knowledge of young fatherhood and contribute towards better service provision in general. At the end of the study, participants were updated with the study's progress and dissemination routes (achieved or planned), and they were sent copies of a number of varied outputs from the study where further information could be sought. Although such a gesture was essentially a token of thanks and appreciation for the young fathers' involvement in the study, it also served as a final reminder of the extent of the researcher–researched relationship and provided an ending to this association in a respectful and considerate manner.

Conclusion

The interview can be seen as a social and learning event for the participant and researcher; each field relationship is unique, and can be seen to unfold in its own way. Arguably, ethical considerations with regard to the researcher–participant relationship are further magnified in QL research, as high levels of trust and rapport are built and established over the life course of a study and there are long periods of contact between the researchers and respondents. However, through careful planning of a study, reflexivity by researchers and transparent communication and consultation with participants about the nature and expectations of their involvement, ethical standards are upheld and the boundaries around the research relationships are clarified and remain unobscured. It is hoped that the reflections provided here on the participant–researcher relationship have offered some insight into the potential difficulties that may arise when researching vulnerable populations such as young fathers, and that the mechanisms employed to help overcome ethical risks will be used as an aid for reflection and best practice for other investigators in the future.

Note

[1] Names have been changed.

References

AREC (Association of Research Ethics Committees) (2013) 'A framework of policies and procedures for university research ethics committees', available at http://arec.org.uk/wp-content/uploads/Framework-of-policies-and-procedures.pdf.

Becker, S., Bryman, A. and Ferguson, H. (2012) *Understanding research for social policy and social work: Themes, methods and approaches* (2nd edn), Bristol: Policy Press.

Caven (2012) 'Agony aunt, hostage, intruder or friend? The multiple personas of the interviewer during fieldwork', *Intangible Capital*, 8(3): 548-563.

David, M. and Sutton, C. (2010) *Social research*, London: Sage Publications.

Denscombe, M. (2014) *The good research guide*, Maidenhead: Open University Press.

Durand, M.A. and Chantler, T. (2014) *Principles of social research*, Maidenhead: Open University Press.

Edwards, R. and Holland, J. (2013) *What is qualitative interviewing?*, London: Bloomsbury Academic.

Eide, P. and Kahn, D. (2008) 'Ethical issues in the qualitative researcher–participant relationship', *Nursing Ethics*, 15(2): 99-207.

ESRC (Economic Social Research Council) (2015) 'ESRC framework for research ethics', available at www.esrc.ac.uk/files/funding/guidance-for-applicants/esrc-framework-for-research-ethics-2015.

Fatherhood Institute (2013) *Fatherhood Institute research summary: Young fathers*, Marlborough: Fatherhood Institute.

Hanna, E. and Lau-Clayton, C. (2012) *Capturing time in qualitative longitudinal field enquiry: Timelines, relational maps and future accounts*, Timescapes Methods Guide Series, Leeds: University of Leeds.

Hemmerman, L. (2010) 'Researching the hard to reach and the hard to keep: notes from the field on longitudinal sample maintenance', in F. Shirani and S. Weller (eds) *Conducting qualitative longitudinal research: fieldwork experiences*, Timescapes Working Paper Series No. 2, Leeds: University of Leeds, available at www.timescapes.leeds.ac.uk.

Hughes, J. (2012) *Sage internet research methods*, London: Sage Publications.

Lau-Clayton, C. (2015) *Young fatherhood: Sharing care with the mother of the child*, Leeds: University of Leeds.

Mason, J. (2002) *Qualitative researching* (2nd edn), London: Sage Publications.

Mason, J. (2006) 'Mixing methods in a qualitatively driven way', *Qualitative Research*, 6(1): 9-25.

McLeod, J. and Thomson, R. (2009) *Researching social change*, London: Sage Publications.

Neale, B. (2012) 'Qualitative longitudinal research: an introduction to the Timescapes methods guides series', available at www.timescapes.leeds.ac.uk/assets/files/methods-guides/timescapes-methods-guides-introduction.pdf.

Neale, B. (2013) 'Adding time into the mix: stakeholder ethics in qualitative longitudinal', *Methodological Innovations Online*, 8(2): 6-20.

Neale, B. and Ladlow, L. (2015) *Finding a place to parent?*, Leeds: University of Leeds.

Neale, B., Lau-Clayton, C., Davies, L. and Ladlow, L. (2015) *Researching the lives of young fathers: The following young fathers study and data-set*, Leeds: University of Leeds.

Newington, L. and Metcalfe, A. (2014) 'Factors influencing recruitment to research: qualitative study of the experiences and perceptions of research teams', *BioMed Central Medical Research Methodology*, 14(10): 1-11.

O'Reiley, K. (2012) *Ethnographic methods* (2nd edn), London: Routledge.

Owens, E. (2006) 'Conversational space and participant shame in interviewing', *Qualitative Inquiry*, 12(6): 1160-1179.

Patrick, R. (2012) *Recruiting and sustaining sample populations over time: Possibilities and challenges*, Timescapes Methods Guide Series, Leeds, University of Leeds.

Pezalla, A.E., Pettigrew, J. and Miller-Day, M. (2012) 'Researching the researcher-as-instrument: an exercise in interviewer self-reflexivity', *Qualitative Research*, 12(2): 165-185.

Ritchie, J. and Lewis, J. (2013) *Qualitative research practice*, London: Sage Publications.

Rupp, L.J. and Taylor, V. (2011) 'Going back and giving back: the ethics of staying in the field', *Qualitative Sociology*, 34(3): 483-497.

Sanjari, M., Bahrammenzhad, F., Fomani, F.K. and Shoghi, M. (2014) 'Ethical challenges of researchers in qualitative studies: the necessity to develop a specific guideline', *Journal of Medical Ethics and History of Medicine*, 7(14): 1-6.

Silverman, D. (2011) *Qualitative research*, London: Sage Publications.

Sivell, S., Prout, H., Hopewell-Kelly, N., Baillie, J., Bryne, A., Edwards, M., Harrop, E. and Sampson, C. (2015) 'Considerations and recommendations for conducting qualitative research interviews with palliative and end-of-life care patients in the home setting: a consensus paper', *BMJ Supportive & Palliative Care*, 0: 1-7.

SPA (Social Policy Association) (2009) 'Social Policy Association guidelines on research ethics', available at www.social-policy.org.uk/downloads/SPA_code_ethics_jan09.pdf.

SRA (Social Research Association) (2003) 'Ethical guidelines', available at http://the-sra.org.uk/wp-content/uploads/ethics03.pdf.

Thomson, R. and McLeod, J. (2015) 'New frontiers in qualitative longitudinal research: an agenda for research', *International Journal of Social Research Methodology*, 18(3): 243-250.

Vincent, K.A. (2012) 'The advantages of repeat interviews in a study with pregnant schoolgirls and schoolgirl mothers: piecing together the jigsaw', *International Journal of Research & Method in Education*, DOI: 10.1080/1743727X.2012.705276.

Yates M. (2013) 'Before, during, and after: identity and the social construction of knowledge in qualitative research interviews', *Hydra: Interdisciplinary Journal of Social Sciences*, 1(1): 31-41.

NINE

Engaging fathers with family support services: using conversation analysis

Jon Symonds

Introduction

Working with fathers represents a classic tension in social work practice. On the one hand, social work is predicated on the basis that parents, including fathers, have the capacity for growth and to improve their own and their children's lives. On the other hand, social workers are required to identify when a parent presents a risk to the child and should no longer be caring for them. Given that most social work continues to be with mothers, fathers represent a practical dilemma for social workers in terms of their presence or absence in a child's life, the quality of that involvement, and the potential for them to be positively engaged with change. Although it is now well established that practitioners should 'engage' fathers with child welfare services, their continued invisibility to services represents a challenge to researchers interested in improving the situation. This chapter considers how conversation analysis can be used to understand professional practice as it happens and the circumstances in which fathers are made more or less visible in the interaction.

Fathers and family support

Social work has historically had an uneasy relationship with fathers. Tasked with safeguarding the welfare of children, social workers have to make decisions about the capacity of the adults in the house to meet the child's needs. When parents have separated, and because children are more likely to live with their mother, this frequently involves assessing the capacity of, and the risks presented by other men in the child's life, such as step-fathers and mothers' new partners. The risks of not doing so can lead to tragic consequences and the history of social work is marked by a series of high-profile child deaths, including those of Maria Colwell, Jasmine Beckford and Peter Connelly, all of whom were killed by new male partners in their mothers' lives. The importance of identifying and understanding the presence of men in the lives of children has continued to resonate in reviews of other child deaths since then (Brandon et al, 2009).

Gathering information about the men in a child's life is therefore important when conducting statutory investigations of risks to children. Even when there is no immediate threat to a child's life, harsh parenting behaviour exacted by fathers has negative consequences for children in their future relationships with peers (Allen et al, 2002) or displaying problematic behaviour (Lamb and Lewis, 2010). Conversely, cases where fathers have withdrawn from family life through paternal depression have been correlated with externalising behaviours in children (Cummings et al, 2008). Given that social workers come into contact with families when there are concerns about the child's welfare, the involvement of the father in the child's life may be characterised by workers as absent, of no use, irrelevant, or harmful (Scourfield, 2003).

However, this bleak picture is set against four decades of research that demonstrates the benefits to children's development brought about when fathers are positively involved (Lamb, 1976, 2010), outcomes that include a higher cognitive ability (Sarkadi et al, 2008), better mental health (Welsh et al, 2004) and reduced likelihood of being in trouble with the police (Flouri and Buchanan, 2002). Pleck (2010) characterised positive paternal involvement as caring directly for children, playing with them, responding warmly to them, providing emotional support, and setting limits (and consequences) for their behaviour. When there are concerns about a father's capacity to care for his child, working with him to make improvements in each of these areas therefore offers a practical means of improving his contribution to the child's life.

This work is often conducted by family support services where practitioners work directly with parents to improve their family relationships and parenting skills, as well as monitoring information about the family that is assessed in terms of risk (Quinton, 2004). For both reasons, it is important to understand the position of the father in family support services so that he can be supported to make a positive contribution to his child's life and any risks that he may present become known and shared with child protection workers.

Despite this, child welfare services have long been recognised as failing to engage effectively with fathers both in family support services (Ferguson and Hogan, 2004; Featherstone, 2003) and in child protection services (Farmer and Owen, 1998; Baynes and Holland, 2012). An illustration of this is the number of fathers who attend parenting programmes, which has remained consistently low over the last three decades. In 1982, a study of parenting programmes by Budd and O'Brien found that fathers represented less than 15% of participants on parenting programmes (cited in Bagner and Eyberg, 2003) and in a large-scale evaluation of parenting programmes for parents of 8- to 13-year-olds, Lindsay and colleagues (2008) found that fathers represented just 12% of participants. In a subsequent evaluation of a large-scale national trial of parenting programmes, the same team found that only 9% of the 2,956 participants were fathers, despite there being a particular effort to recruit them (Lindsay et al, 2014). As a result, significant numbers of men are not engaging with parenting services and opportunities to promote the wellbeing of their children are being missed.

Explanations for the non-involvement of fathers in family support services cluster around three positions, in which the key agents are the fathers, the mothers, or practitioners. Each of these appeals to the notion of gender as an organising principle, for example, that there are intrinsic properties of men and women that govern their approach to parenting and services, or that the attitudes that practitioners hold towards gender inform the development and delivery of services. I now consider each position briefly.

The first position holds men responsible. Addis and Mahalik (2003) argued that men are less likely to seek help for problems they are facing because this is viewed as a sign of weakness and therefore a threat to their self-concept of masculinity. As parenting and childcare are still commonly viewed as predominantly female tasks, a willingness to seek help in this area may compound the perceived threat to a masculine identity. Further to simply not seeking help, some fathers, it is argued, actively avoid services. Fathers interviewed by Bayley and colleagues (2009) embodied this threatened self-identity by speaking of their fears of being 'dictated to' by staff and a similar concern was raised by fathers interviewed by Butt (2009) who avoided parenting programmes because they thought they would be 'told what to do' by staff. As a consequence, this position has fathers taking active measures to remain 'invisible' to services and withdraw from contact with workers.

A second position explains the lack of fathers' involvement with services by locating responsibility in the actions of the mother. By concealing information about the father (or male partner) from the practitioner, it is argued that the mother acts as a 'gatekeeper' to practitioners' access to information about the father (or other men involved in the child's life). This is illustrated in the findings of some studies of family support services where some mothers who participated felt that parenting (and therefore parenting services) were their 'territory' (Ferguson and Hogan, 2004) and that some of the support mothers derived from children's centres came from it being a female space (Ghate et al, 2000). Other studies have argued that mothers might conceal the identity of a male partner because they were in unauthorised receipt of state benefits or because the knowledge of a partner's violence might result in the children being taken into care (Dominelli et al, 2010). The notion of the 'maternal gatekeeper' is drawn from psychological and sociological studies of the family (see Allen and Hawkins, 1999; Walker and McGraw, 2000; Schoppe-Sullivan et al, 2008) that has identified maternal gatekeeping behaviours such as mothers moderating the father's access to opportunities for childcare, play or responsibilities. However, this term has been adopted in the professional literature which positions the mother as the 'gatekeeper to the family' (Glynn and Dale, 2015) through whom the practitioner has to negotiate access to other members of the family. The adoption of this position in social work is problematic, given that it locates the problem with the mother who becomes the focus of intervention and is then held responsible for the safety of the family, even when it may be the violence of the father that is creating the risk (Farmer and Owen, 1998; Featherstone and Peckover, 2007).

A third position holds that practitioners fail to engage fathers through their own embodied and interactional practices. Ghate and colleagues (2000) found that the absence of fathers in publicity materials in a children's centre and the lack of male staff there produced a 'feminised' environment in which fathers did not feel welcome. When practitioners work directly with families, they have been found to make the mother the focus of the work and involve the father less often, sometimes for reasons of perceived absence in the family, or for the perceived threat they represent (Ferguson and Hogan, 2004).

The three positions considered here each focus separately on fathers, mothers and practitioners and have identified numerous factors associated with the lack of fathers engaged by family support services. It is commonly recognised that these three components do not exist in isolation; rather, they interact with each other, but it is much rarer to collect data of those interactions to examine how these encounters are negotiated in practice. One reason for this is that most evidence on the topic is based on self-reported data in which participants have a stake in the research process and produce a representation of practice that reflects, in part, their identity, for example as a professional practitioner. Roulston (2014) has illustrated how this occurs in her analysis of key events taken from qualitative research interviews. The complexity of interactional events during practice encounters also makes it impossible for anyone to recall the exact sequences and details of what was said and what difference it made to the outcome (Silverman, 2011).

If we are to understand a practice phenomenon such as engaging fathers, having access to direct recordings of practice enables researchers to analyse whether and how different theories about engaging fathers are apparent in any particular encounter. Such an empirically derived standpoint requires an approach to analysing recorded data in a methodologically robust manner and having been developed over recent decades, conversation analysis offers a means of achieving this at the intersection of linguistics and sociology as discussed below.

Using conversation analysis

Researchers using conversation analysis collect data by making recordings of interactions as they are occurring in their natural environment and without them being provoked by the researcher (ten Have, 2007). Detailed transcriptions are then made and analysed for evidence of how participants navigate their way through sequences of interaction to achieve particular outcomes.

Conversation analysis starts from the principle that speakers use talk to achieve social action. It draws on the work of speech act theorists who have investigated how people 'do things with words' such as marking the moment of marriage with 'I pronounce you man and wife' (Austin, 1962) or by formulating different ways to make a complaint (Searle, 1969). Where speech act theorists used 'ideal' examples of utterances because of the perceived 'messiness' of actual interaction, one of the insights of conversation analysts is that speakers coordinate their talk in very fine detail to achieve an orderly progression of talk (Sacks, 1984). It has also been used to show how our intuitive, or theory-driven understandings of talk may be mistaken. For example, influential studies of interaction in the 1970s found that men were more likely than women to interrupt others in conversation and this was treated as evidence of the reproduction of patriarchal power in ordinary settings (discussed in Speer and Stokoe, 2011). Subsequent analysis by Schegloff (1993) showed that examples of interruptions identified in the original research were not treated as such by the participants of those conversations. When this more endogenous analysis was taken into account in further analysis of the original dataset, the differences based on gender fell away. The importance of identifying phenomena that can be shown to be relevant to the participants themselves is therefore an important consideration in conversation analytic work.

Treating interaction as a resource through which to pursue action has enabled conversation analysts to examine how people retain anonymity during calls to a suicide helpline (Sacks, 1967), how people manage compliments (Pomerantz, 1984), and how politicians elicit applause during political speeches (Atkinson, 1984). The approach has also been applied to professional practice, such as handling calls to emergency services (Whalen et al, 1988), exploring patients' concerns in medical settings (Heritage et al, 2007) and recruiting neighbours in conflict to mediation services (Stokoe, 2013). In the context of the current chapter, it also affords the possibility of enhancing our understanding of how fathers might 'avoid' contact with, or how practitioners might 'recruit' them to, a family support service. As well as the linguistic content of interaction, conversation analysts recognise that people deploy resources such as intonation, silence and other paralinguistic features to achieve actions, and these features are carefully incorporated into transcriptions following a system developed by Jefferson (2004).

Once the transcripts have been prepared, and in conjunction with repeated listening to the recordings, features of interest are identified and subjected to further analysis that interrogates the action that is being pursued, the sequential position in which it has been produced and how it is treated in the next turn of talk. In the current study, the focus was on occasions when fathers were spoken about, with a view to identifying utterances that contributed to their involvement with the service. Having identified instances of talk that were relevant to the ongoing involvement of the father, comparisons were made with those in other calls across the dataset for evidence of regularities in interactions and outcomes. In this way, conversation analysis offers a way to make empirically justified investigations into the links between specific interactional practices and outcomes in applied fields such as the recruitment of fathers to family support services.

The study

The findings presented here are drawn from a doctoral study funded by the Economic and Social Research Council and set in three local authorities (Symonds, 2015). In the previous decade, the UK government had been concerned to provide more support to families and to address the perceived rise in antisocial behaviour among young people by delivering structured parenting programmes (Home Office, 2006). Parenting programmes are usually designed to support parents' competencies in building relationships managing the behaviour of their children and are commonly delivered in weekly sessions of group discussion, filmed examples and tasks to practise at home (Webster-Stratton, 2005).

Three family support services took part in the study, selected because they offered, and received referrals for, group-based parenting programmes. Although each service differed in how it delivered its service (one service encouraged parents to go to an information session before deciding whether to do a group-based programme), the standard practice on receipt of a referral was that practitioners would phone the referred parent to introduce and make arrangements for the service. Recordings were made of all those initial telephone conversations to provide the basis for comparisons across the calls during analysis.

Six practitioners made audio recordings of their initial conversations with parents. All practitioners were female and had between four and 19 years' experience in the field. One was a qualified social worker. Although practitioners had already had time to consider their consent to take part in the study, parents were being recorded before they were aware of the study. In order to manage this sensitivity, practitioners informed parents about the study shortly after they had introduced themselves and asked them if they would consent to the recording continuing (if the parent did not consent, the practitioner stopped the recording and the recording was deleted). Because the parent had not had time to consider their consent at the beginning of the call, practitioners were required to check consent again at the end of the call after the parent was aware of what the content of the conversation had been.

Recordings were attempted with 51 parents. In only four instances did parents decline to be recorded, but another 16 recordings had to be discounted for reasons such as failure to fully insert the lead into the microphone socket of the recorder, forgetting to ask for consent, or not being able to confirm consent again at the end of the call. Of the 31 recordings available for analysis, three were excluded because the call did not proceed to an arrangement for other reasons (such as the parent already doing a parenting programme). This resulted in a dataset of 28 recordings in which the conversation proceeded to making an arrangement for the service. In 25 calls, the main parent spoken to was the mother, from which five fathers were recruited. In the three other calls, the main parent spoken to was the father, from which one mother was recruited.

The focus of the analysis was to identify how fathers were talked about in these calls. However, it soon became apparent that not all relevant males were fathers and there were references in the calls to the mother's partner and the child's grandfather as well as to birth fathers. This range of 'social' types of fatherhood is well recognised and supports Collier and Sheldon's (2008) contention that fatherhood is 'fragmenting'. Although it was safe to assume that the referred parent had a direct relationship with the child and was resident at home, the status of the other parent was often unclear. References to 'father' were entirely absent from the data with other terms used, such as 'dad', 'step-dad', 'husband', 'hubby', 'partner' or 'wife'. These terms sometimes implied, but did not always establish, the individual's relationship to the child or their status in the home and because these people were not present in the conversation, it became an interactional problem that was rarely resolved. There was evidence in some calls that the practitioner already had knowledge of the name of the father, but would wait for the mother to introduce his name into the conversation. Although the mother sometimes referred to him by his relationship in the family, such as 'his dad', or 'my husband', she might not name him, and this absence of his name became a problem when the practitioner sought to include him in the service. The pattern was the same when it came to mother's details in the calls to fathers, and this contrasting data was used to investigate whether the differences in outcome could be associated with gender or with the presence or absence of the other parent in the conversation. The analysis focused on the ways that practitioners and referred parents spoke about other carers in ways that were associated with an agreement by the end of the call that the other carer would be included in future arrangements. In the remainder of this chapter, I consider extracts of data that illustrate three moments that occurred in calls where there were opportunities for practitioners to negotiate the involvement of fathers in family support services.

Fathers 'slipping away'

The first opportunity for practitioners to recruit fathers is if the father answers the phone. At that moment, he is not aware who is calling and, in two examples from the data, passed the practitioner to his wife. In the following extracts, 'Par' denotes the parent and 'Wor' denotes the worker. All names have been anonymised with fictional alternatives.

Extract 1:

Yvonne and Mick

```
01          [ring]
02  Par:    Ha:llo?
03          (0.3)
```

```
04  Wor:    Hello is ↑that ↑Mick?
05          (2.0)
06  Par:    Y-yeah it's Mick yeah.
07  Wor:    °Hello° Mick, uh my name's
Yvonne, I'm
08          ringing from: (name of service),
.hh um, I've
09          had a referral for you:, .hh from
(name of
10          service)? Samantha ↑Beattie?
11          (0.6)
12  Wor:    Um: mt (0.3) suggesting that you,
might,
13          (0.3) like some help around
parenting.
14          (1.3)
15  Par:    .Hhhh ah right, i- gu- I'd d
right ah hhh.
16  Wor:    HHo(hh).
17  Par:    =So =oh yeah, yu- you got me
confu(h)sed now
18          [so   I]
19  Wor:    [Sorry,]
20  Par:    I go' t it's, no it's so much
going on >it's
21          alright u[m,<]
22  Wor:             [↑Oh]h:, o[kay.]
23  Par:                       [U h,] mk c:
i:h, .hh (0.5) the best
24          way for me to deal with thi:s,
25  Wor:    [°°Yeah°°]
26  Par:    [  I f  ] I give you to my wife,
cos I don't
27          wanna (0.3) um (.) mess it up if
you see what
28          I me[an]?
29  Wor:        [Th]at's absolutely ↑fi:ne,
yes: no
30          pro[blem at all.]
```

```
31   Par:        [O  h          o]kay,
32               (0.3)
33   Wor:     Lo[vely.]
34   Par:        [U(hh)] a(h)'r(h)'t.
35               (0.4)
36   Wor:     Thank [you.]
37   Par:            [Ta. ]
38               (6.1)
39   Par2:    Hello?
```

One of the advantages of having the recording of the actual encounter is that the analysis can reveal how things develop from the very beginning of an interaction. After Mick has answered the call in line 2, Yvonne greets him, but as she uses his name in line 4, she also reveals herself to have prior knowledge about him (presumably from the referral information). There follows a relatively long gap of two seconds, which indicates that Mick might have some trouble with how to respond and this is evident when he confirms his identity in line 6 by his repeated 'y' sound. Nevertheless, Yvonne continues to introduce herself and explain her warrant for the call, that she has received a referral. Stivers and Rossano (2010) have shown how a rising intonation at the end of a speaker's turn can be used to pursue a response from the next speaker and Yvonne ends her turn there, providing a slot for Mick to show his recognition of the referral and therefore endorse Yvonne's call. Instead, though, he does not respond, and 0.6 seconds pass before Yvonne treats her current explanation as not adequate enough for Mick to have recognised the situation. With some evidence of her own sense of delicacy about the emerging difficulties in the interaction (Yvonne hesitates at the start of line 12 and pauses mid-turn), she explicitly names the reason for the referral, which is that Mick 'might like some help around parenting' (lines 12-13).

Up until this point, Mick has made minimal contributions to the conversation, but although they have been marked with some caution, they have been coherent in their production. Once the topic of parenting support is mentioned, he allows another 1.3 seconds to elapse before embarking on a long, troubled turn that is characterised by a marked shift in understanding ('ah right' in line 14), false starts, an appeal to being 'confused' (line 17) and an account of there being 'so much going on' (line 20). Eventually, Mick suggests that the 'best way' (lines 23-24) to proceed is for him to hand Yvonne to his wife so that he doesn't 'mess it up' (line 27). Having extracted himself from the conversation, his wife, Tracey, picks up the receiver and Yvonne continues the call with her.

What is of note in this extract is that Yvonne makes no mention of Mick's wife, either by name or by designation, until he refers to her in line 26. His account for doing so directly contrasts his own capacity to 'mess it up' (the 'it' referring to a conversation about parenting support) with that of his wife, who is to be understood as more competent in this matter. He achieves this by invoking gender as the grounds for avoiding the conversation (his wife is competent in matters of parenting, but he may mess it up) and provides evidence of how a father might avoid a service at the first available opportunity. Appealing to gender-based notions of competency in parenting is also deployed by the father in the second extract, which follows a similar pattern.

Extract 2:

Kelly and Tim

```
01          (ring)
02  Ans:    Hello. Your call cannot be taken
at the
03          moment, so please leave your
message, after
04          the tone. ((bee:p)).
05          (0.4)
06  Wor:    Mt .hhhhh hi, um, my name's Kelly
Teater and
07          I work with Gladys Smith at (name
of
08          service). You've been referred
for some
09          parenting support so:,
10  Par:    =Hello,
11          (0.4)
12  Wor:    ↑Oh he↑llo:!
13  Par:    Hello:, hhh.
14  Wor:    [Y- ]
15  Par:    [The] answering 'chine g'n (.)
before I got
16          to the phone.
```

```
17  Wor:    ↑Oh::h, okay um, who am I talking
to?
18  Par:    Mister Lumbard
19          (0.4)
20  Wor:    Megan?
21          (0.3)
22  Par:    No:, Tim=
23  Wor:    =Tim, oh I apologi:se, Mister
Lumbard. Tk
24          calling you Megan, .hhhh Hi.
25  Par:    H[ello,]
26  Wor:     [U m ,]
27          (0.5)
28  Wor:    Yeah, as I said, >my name's<
Kelly and um,
29          you've been working with Gladys:.
.Hhhhh,
30          (0.8)
31  Wor:    Yeah?
32  Par:    I'll pass you to my wife cos she
probably
33          know more.
34  Wor:    =She knows exactly what I'm
talking about
35          [does] she?
36  Par:    [Yes,]
37  Wor:    Brilliant. Okay, thanks Tim,
38          (2.9)
39  Par2:   Hello?
```

In this call, Tim has picked up the phone part way through Kelly leaving a message on the answer machine just at the point at which she mentioned the referral for parenting support. After some confusion about establishing his identity, Kelly returns to the purpose of the call in line 28 by introducing herself in relation to 'Gladys', whom she introduces as somebody who has been working with Tim. On the completion of Gladys' name, Kelly takes a breath and pauses, leaving time for Tim to mark his recognition of Gladys' name and therefore the implication that he is a relevant person who has been involved in the work. However, much as with Mick in the first extract, Tim withholds any sign of recognition and after 0.8 seconds have elapsed, Kelly pursues his recognition more directly with 'Yeah?' in line 31. Even at this point, Tim ignores the opportunity to mark his knowledge of Gladys and instead declares that he will hand Kelly on to his 'wife' 'cos she probably knows more' (lines 32–33). This has direct parallels with Mick's reason in extract 1 and appeals to a gendered notion of his wife being more knowledgeable (and therefore more capable) in this matter. Tim is also successful in extricating himself from the call and his wife, Mary, takes the rest of the call.

In both extracts, men displayed interactional strategies to avoid being any more involved in the service interaction. They appealed to categorical associations of gender in passing the practitioner on to their wives, who were associated with greater knowledge and ability in relation to the call. To this extent, their avoidance of the service was successful. Although these might both be characterised as fathers avoiding services, they had answered the phone and identified themselves. This information provided resources that practitioners were able to return to use later in the call, and which will be returned to in more detail later in this chapter.

Mothers gatekeeping fathers' involvement

The next two examples are taken from other calls when practitioners enquire about a partner being involved in the service. In these extracts, the parent acknowledges the presence of a partner, but responds by giving a reason why he might not be able to be involved in the service. There are no examples from the conversation analytic literature of how gatekeeping behaviour gets achieved based on recordings of actual situations, but the following offer a glimpse into gatekeeping situations that practitioners and parents might find themselves in.

Extract 3:

Mel and Poppy

```
01  Wor:    Ok 'n if you've got a partner uhm
(0.3)
02          they're they're welcome to come
along as
03          we:ll
04          (0.3)
05  Par:    Ooh at'd be good as well yeah
lovel- I know
```

```
06          he w- 'e's a train driver so he
does some
07          awkward shifts but yeah I'm
definitely
08          interested in .hhh in doing some
more
09          cours:s: see if I can .hhh >I
don't know make
10          myself< a better parent 'oo knows
11          (0.3)
12  Par:    [Hhhh]
13  Wor:    [Yeah] totally
```

In this call, the practitioner (Mel) has made an offer for Poppy's 'partner' to 'come along' (line 2) to the programme. This offer is designed to propose a low degree of certainty on the likely acceptance of the offer, with the conditional 'if' making the offer contingent on whether Poppy has got a partner (which Mel has not yet established). Second, if this condition is met, the offer is one of the partner being 'welcome' (but not a requirement) and Poppy is positioned as somebody who is entitled to speak on his behalf. When Poppy starts to respond in line 5, she does so with a mark of surprise, 'Ooh' and an appreciation 'at'd be good'. However, she then goes on to calibrate this by introducing a reason why her partner might not be able to be involved in the programme because he is a train driver and does 'awkward shifts' (line 7). By prioritising her partner's work over his involvement in a parenting programme, Poppy deploys categorical associations of gender to support her position that he might not be able to attend. Having downplayed his possible involvement, though, Poppy apparently realises that this less enthusiastic presentation might reflect on her own commitment to the service and she makes the point that she remains committed to making herself a 'better parent' (line 10). Whether intentionally or not, Poppy has not revealed any other information about her partner or suggested that Mel could speak to him directly, maintaining her position as the point of contact for the service. She has already established a reason for his potential non-involvement with the service and presented herself as a responsible and willing participant. This is treated as unremarkable by Mel and the possibility of his involvement is left unresolved. The call ended with no further exploration of the topic and the practitioner having no contact details or arrangements to follow up the matter of the partner being involved in the service. These actions are consistent with findings in studies of maternal gatekeeping where the mother is the point of access to the family and moderates the involvement of the father. However, this interactional sequence was also evident in a call to one of the fathers, during which the practitioner used the same approach to involve his partner in the parenting programme with a similar lack of success.

Extract 4:

Mel and Raf

```
01  Wor:    Alri:ght, yeah an' it's the
taste:r (.) next
02          wednesday >and we'll book you a
place on
03          that< and you're welcome to bring
your
04          partner alo:ng bu' uh:m: you
might have
05          childcare [pr(h)oblems.]
06  Par:              [No    well   ] she
won't be able to
07          cos she'll have the young
08          'un:[s        won't    she:.     ]
09  Wor:        [Sh:e'll have the young 'un]
s. Yeah yeah,
```

In this call, the offer is made in the same format as the previous extract, by extending a 'welcome' to a partner. The decision is also made contingent on the parent on the phone rather than making it an expectation of the service. In fact, Mel pre-empts a reason for the partner not being able to attend because of childcare 'problems' (earlier in the call, she had referred to the father as having 'quite a big family'). Raf begins his turn before Mel has finished to confirm both that his partner will not be attending and that this is because of childcare. The use of the tag question 'won't she' in line 8 marks the issue of childcare as a barrier that Mel should already have known would prevent her from attending and therefore that the suggestion was inapposite. Much as was the case with Poppy in the earlier extract, the referred parent did not disclose any other details about the partner and treated himself as entitled to manage her availability without consulting her or suggesting any subsequent contact between her and the practitioner. The similarities with Poppy suggest that the interactions of both Poppy and Raf result in a phenomenon that might be described as gatekeeping.

However, the evidence in these two extracts challenges the notion that gatekeeping access to the family is a gendered phenomenon, associated only with mothers. It was apparent in the call to Raf as well, with a very similar interactional structure. This is not to say that gender was irrelevant to these sequences. Poppy and Raf both drew on gendered categories of activity to support their claims of unavailability. In Poppy's case, her partner's employment was treated by both speakers as reasonable grounds for his absence, reproducing the trope of the man as provider to the family. In contrast, Raf drew on the notion of the mother's responsibilities for childcare as justification for her non-involvement in the parenting programme. Within a conversation analytic framework, gender is treated as a resource that participants use to pursue and achieve certain actions rather than a topic through which to explain phenomena such as gatekeeping. An alternative explanation for the gatekeeping in these extracts is that it is an interactional accomplishment achieved by the combined actions of both the practitioner and referred parent. It is the absence of the other parent from the conversation that is more consistent than their gender.

As was described earlier in the chapter, the issue of gatekeeping has been critiqued in relation to the social work because it locates responsibility for action with the gatekeeper and the consequences for mothers has been that they have been held accountable for risks for which they are not responsible. To hold Poppy and Raf responsible for not facilitating access to their partners ignores the responsibilities of practitioners for how they might manage the interaction in ways that promote the involvement of other carers in more positive ways. Examples of how this might be achieved will be considered in the final two extracts in the next section.

Recruiting other carers

When it came to securing agreement that the other carer should be involved in the service, practitioners were successful in just six of the 28 calls. When practitioners were successful, there were three features that appeared in systematic ways across the data. First, practitioners had said the name of the other carer earlier in the conversation. Second, they had established that the other carer had an ongoing relationship in the family (either with the referred parent as a spouse or partner, or with the child). If these two were established, the opportunity arose for the practitioner to ask about their involvement in the service by including their name in the question and designing the question to prefer a 'yes' response (see Raymond, 2003 on the design of these questions). This format is illustrated in the following two extracts:

Extract 5:

Briony and Kate

```
01  Wor:   Would your (.) partner Paul like t'
>come
02         along< >to it< as we:ll?
03  Par:   U:hm (0.7) yeah yeah,
04  Wor:   =(Sh'll I?)
05         (0.2)
06  ?      .Hh
07  Par:   Yeah.
```

Earlier in this call, Kate had already expressed reluctance about the service and the speakers had also established that her partner, Paul, had been omitted from the referral. Nevertheless, Briony's question in line 1 makes specific reference to Kate's relationship with Paul, as well as his name, and anticipates that she is likely to accept. Despite some initial hesitancy on Kate's part, she agrees in line 3 and goes on to confirm this when Briony seeks to clarify the commitment afterwards.

Knowledge of the other carer was obtained in different ways in the calls, but one was when they had picked up the phone and slipped away, as with Mick and Tim in extracts 1 and 2. By establishing their name and presence in the family, practitioners were able to use these resources later in the call when trying to recruit them. The following extract comes from the call where Tim had passed the practitioner to his 'wife' because she would 'know more'. By establishing these details, however, the practitioner was able to draw on them when attempting to recruit him to the service later in the call.

Extract 8:

Kelly and Tim

```
01  Wor:   Lovely okay s:o .hhh and will Tim
be there
02         as well?
03         (0.2)
04  Par:   yes::.
```

When these details about fathers (and other carers) were established and the question was designed in this way, practitioners were successful in securing agreement that they would be involved in the service. Conversely, when these details were not established before asking about their involvement, practitioners were much less successful in involving fathers. The fact that this pattern was consistent across the whole dataset suggests that there are some practitioner actions that can be effective whether they are speaking to either the mother or the father.

Using conversation analysis to research fathers

The instances examined in this chapter reveal some of the practical difficulties that practitioners have to manage when recruiting fathers to family support services. When a father is evidently avoiding a service, practitioners face dilemmas as to whether they should pursue him or let him pass the telephone to his wife on the grounds that she would know more than him about parenting support. Similarly, when practitioners are faced with situations where parents present their partner as being unavailable to the service, what resources are available to address these potential barriers in the moment of their production? These dilemmas represent problems in engaging fathers that have long been recognised by scholars across the social sciences. The contribution that conversation analysis can make to this field is to understand how participants address the practical management of these problems based on an empirical analysis of data from what actually happened in the encounter. Some examples of how this is done have been included in this chapter.

Schegloff (1997) argued that conversation analysts should derive findings based on categories that the participants themselves are demonstrably oriented towards rather than those derived by the analyst. This has been described as 'methodological severity' by Hammersley (2008), but means that the insights from participants' own use of categories can be used to evaluate categories such as 'engaging fathers' or 'maternal gatekeeping' for utility. Conversation analysis is necessarily detailed in its procedures, but offers a route by which these explanations of professional encounters can be considered alongside a methodologically robust account of the actual interactions as they were produced in the moment. Although the instances in this chapter represent a tiny proportion of all the interactions that occur across family support services, it opens the prospect of building further collections of recordings to develop and refine existing explanations. One example that has been considered in this chapter is the status of a partner's 'awkward shifts'. The analyst can never fully 'know' whether this is the case or not and whether those shifts will prove an insurmountable barrier to his involvement with the service. What can be shown, though, is that these shifts became a relevant topic at the moment the mother was convincing the practitioner of the father's unavailability. By basing data on the recordings of actual encounters and analysing each utterance in the sequential context of its environment, conversation analysis offers a means by which the relationships between people can be empirically investigated, what Heritage (1984) has described as 'the architecture of subjectivity'. For researchers of fatherhood and of the services that work with them, this offers interesting topics of inquiry for how best to work with fathers and improve the welfare of their children as a result.

References

Addis, M. and Mahalik, J. (2003) 'Men, masculinity and the contexts of help seeking', *American Psychologist*, 58(1): 5-14.

Allen, J., Hauser, S., O'Connor, T. and Bell, K. (2002) 'Prediction of peer-rated adult hostility from autonomy struggles in adolescent-family interactions', *Development and Psychopathology*, 14(1): 123-137.

Allen, S. and Hawkins, A.J. (1999) 'Maternal gatekeeping: mothers' beliefs and behaviors that inhibit greater father involvement in family work', *Journal of Marriage and Family*, 61(1): 199-212.

Atkinson, M. (1984) *Our masters' voices: The language and body language of politics*, London: Routledge.

Austin, J. (1962) *How to do things with words*, Oxford: Clarenden Press.

Bagner, D. and Eyberg, S. (2003) 'Father involvement in parent training: when does it matter?', *Journal of Clinical Child and Adolescent Psychology*, 32(4): 599-605.

Bayley, J., Wallace, L. and Choudhry, K. (2009) 'Fathers and parenting programmes: barriers and best practice', *Community Practitioner*, 82(4): 28-31.

Baynes, P. and Holland, S. (2012) 'Social work with violent men: a child protection file study in an English local authority', *Child Abuse Review*, 21(1): 53-65.

Brandon, M., Bailey, S., Belderson, P., Gardner, R., Sidebotham, P., Dodsworth, J., Warren, C. and Black, J. (2009) *Understanding serious case reviews and their impact: A biennial analysis of serious case reviews 2005-07*, Norwich: University of East Anglia.

Butt, J. (2009) *Reaching parents: Improving take-up of parenting programmes*, London: Social Care Institute of Excellence.

Collier, R. and Sheldon, S. (2008) *Fragmenting fatherhood: A socio-legal study*, Oxford: Hart.

Cummings, E.M., Schermerhorn, A., Keller, P. and Davies, P. (2008) 'Parental depressive symptoms, children's representations of family relationships, and child adjustment', *Social Development*, 17(2): 278-305.

Dominelli, L., Strega, S., Walmsley, C., Callahan, M. and Brown, L. (2010) '"Here's my story": fathers of "looked after" children recount their experiences in the Canadian child welfare system', *British Journal of Social Work*, 41(2): 351-367.

Farmer, E. and Owen, M. (1998) 'Gender and the child protection process', *British Journal of Social Work*, 28(1): 545-564.

Featherstone, B. (2003) *Family life and family support: A feminist analysis*, Basingstoke: Palgrave Macmillan.

Featherstone, B. and Peckover, S. (2007) 'Letting them get away with it: fathers, domestic violence and child welfare', *Critical Social Policy*, 27(2): 181-202.

Ferguson, H. and Hogan, F. (2004) *Strengthening families through fathers: Developing policy and practice in relation to vulnerable fathers and their families*, Waterford: Centre for Social and Family Research.

Flouri, E. and Buchanan, A. (2002) 'Father involvement in childhood and trouble with the police in adolescence: findings from the 1958 British cohort', *Journal of Interpersonal Violence*, 17(6): 689-701.

Ghate, D., Shaw, C. and Hazel, N. (2000) *Fathers and family centres: Engaging fathers in preventive services*, York: Joseph Rowntree Foundation.

Glynn, L. and Dale, M. (2015) 'Engaging dads: enhancing support for fathers through parenting programmes', *Aotearoa New Zealand Social Work*, 27(1&2): 59-72.

Hammersley, M. (2008) *Questioning qualitative inquiry: Critical essays*, London: Sage Publications.

Heritage, J. (1984) *Garfinkel and ethnomethodology*, Cambridge: Polity Press.

Heritage, J., Robinson, J., Elliott, M., Beckett, M. and Wilkes, M. (2007) 'Reducing patients' unmet concerns in primary care: the difference one word can make', *Journal of General Internal Medicine*, 22(10): 1429-1433.

Home Office (2006) *The Respect agenda*, London: Home Office.

Jefferson, G. (2004) 'Glossary of transcript symbols with an introduction', in G. Lerner (ed) *Conversation analysis: Studies from the first generation*, Amsterdam: John Benjamins, pp 13-35.

Lamb, M. (ed) (1976) *The role of the father in child development*, New York, NY: Wiley.

Lamb, M. (ed) (2010) *The role of the father in child development* (5th edn), Hoboken, NJ: John Wiley & Sons.

Lamb, M. and Lewis, C. (2010) 'The development and significance of father-child relationships in two-parent families', in M. Lamb (ed) *The role of the father in child development* (5th edn), Hoboken, NJ: John Wiley & Sons, pp 94-154.

Lindsay, G., Cullen, M.-A., Cullen, S., Totsika, V., Bakopouli, I., Goodlad, S., Brind, R., Pickering, E., Bryson, C., Purdon, S., Conlon, G. and Mantovani, I. (2014) *CANparent trial evaluation: Final report*, London: DfE.

Lindsay, G., Davies, H., Band, S., Cullen, M.-A., Cullen, S., Strand, S., Hasluck, C., Evans, R. and Stewart-Brown, S. (2008) *Parenting early intervention pathfinder evaluation*, London: DCSF.

Pleck, J. (2010) 'Paternal involvement: revised conceptualization and theoretical linkages with child outcomes', in M. Lamb (ed) *The role of the father in child development* (5th edn), Hoboken, NJ: John Wiley & Sons, pp 58-94.

Pomerantz, A. (1984) 'Agreeing and disagreeing with assessments: some features of preferred/dispreferred turn shapes', in J. Heritage and J.M. Atklinson (eds) *Structures of social action: Studies in conversation analysis*, Cambridge: Cambridge University Press, pp 57-102.

Quinton, D. (2004) *Supporting parents: Messages from research*, London: Jessica Kingsley.

Raymond, G. (2003) 'Grammar and social organization: yes/no interrogatives and the structure of responding', *American Sociological Review*, 68(6): 939-967.

Roulston, K. (2014) 'Interactional problems in research interviews', *Qualitative Research*, 14(3): 277-293.

Sacks, H. (1967) 'The search for help: no one to turn to', in E. Schneidman (ed) *Essays in self-destruction*, New York, NY: Science House, pp 203-223.

Sacks, H. (1984) 'Notes on methodology', in J.M. Atkinson and J. Heritage (eds) *Structures of social action: Studies in conversation analysis*, Cambridge: Cambridge University Press, pp 21-8.

Sarkadi, A., Kristiansson, R., Oberklaid, F. and Bremberg, S. (2008) 'Fathers' involvement and children's developmental outcomes: a systematic review of longitudinal studies', *Acta Paediatrica*, 97(2): 153-158.

Schegloff, E. (1993) 'Reflections on quantification in the study of conversation', *Research on Language and Social Interaction*, 26(1): 99-128.

Schegloff, E.A. (1997) 'Whose Text? Whose Context?', *Discourse & Society*, 8(2): 165-187.

Schoppe-Sullivan, S., Brown, G., Cannon, E., Mangelsdorf, S. and Sokolowski, M. (2008) 'Maternal gatekeeping, coparenting quality, and fathering behavior in families with infants', *Journal of Family Psychology*, 22(3): 389-398.

Scourfield, J. (2003) *Gender and child protection*, Basingstoke: Palgrave Macmillan.

Searle, J. (1969) *Speech acts*, Cambridge: Cambridge University Press, pp 1-29.

Silverman, D. (ed) (2011) *Qualitative research* (3rd edn), London: Sage Publications.

Speer, S. and Stokoe, E. (2011) 'An introduction to conversation and gender', in S. Speer and E. Stokoe (eds) *Conversation and gender*, Cambridge: Cambridge University Press.

Stivers, T. and Rossano, F. (2010) 'Mobilizing response', *Research on Language and Social Interaction*, 43(1): 3-31.

Stokoe, E. (2013) 'Overcoming barriers to mediation in intake calls to services: research-based strategies for mediators', *Negotiation Journal*, 29(3): 289-314.

Symonds, J. (2015) '"Have you got a partner as well?" Engaging fathers and other carers with parenting services: a study using conversation analysis', Unpublished thesis, University of Bristol.

ten Have, P. (2007) *Doing conversation analysis: A practical guide*, London: Sage Publications.

Walker, A. and McGraw, L. (2000) 'Who is responsible for responsible fathering?', *Journal of Marriage and Family*, 62(2): 563-569.

Webster-Stratton, C. (2005) *The incredible years: A trouble-shooting guide for parents aged 2-8*, Seattle, WA: Incredible Years.

Welsh, E., Buchanan, A., Flouri, E. and Lewis, J. (2004) *'Involved fathering' and child well-being*, London: National Children's Bureau.

Whalen, J., Zimmerman, D. and Whalen, M. (1988) 'When words fail: a single case analysis', *Social Problems*, 35(4): 335-359.

TEN

Mixing methods in fatherhood research: studying social change in family life

Allan Westerling

Introduction

This chapter reflects on the ways in which mixing methods allow empirical exploration of the impact of social change on family life and how this process opens up fathering and fatherhood as research themes. Forming the basis of this analysis is a Danish research project called Families and Social Networks in the Modern Welfare State (FAMOSTAT), which studies the consequences of ongoing modernisation for family life. A presentation of the research design and analytical approach illustrates how fathers and fatherhood emerged as an important research theme by focusing on everyday family life primarily from a social psychological perspective. Working with multiple methods facilitates a genuinely exploratory approach that unleashes both empirical sensitivity and theoretical creativity. Mixing methods, however, is neither easy nor straightforward as a research strategy due to the epistemological dilemmas and theoretical challenges that are not easily resolved, yet this messiness and ambiguity must be tolerated in order to allow an open exploration of changing social phenomena such as fatherhood.

Divided into three major sections, this chapter begins with a presentation of the theoretical background and main focus, which is the impact of modernisation on family life in a Scandinavian welfare context, namely Denmark. We conceptualise modernisation as processes of individualisation and detraditionalisation and aim to investigate these processes empirically. The next section presents our mixed-method study and begins by briefly introducing mixed methods as the framework of our analytical approach. This section also contains a description of the empirical design, sampling strategies and data generation methods. The study comprises quantitative survey data (n=1,003) from computer-assisted telephone interviews and qualitative interview data from face-to-face interviews. Next, the comprehensive analytical process, which employed survey and interview data, is accounted for to explain how the exploratory approach that results from using mixed methods led to the emergence of fathering and fatherhood as a research theme. So vast was the amount of data generated that only a fraction of it is presented here. The third section discusses the benefits and challenges of mixing of methods. The central argument presented is that establishing a dialogue between qualitative and quantitative data provides greater empirical insight and enables in-depth theoretical analysis, which demonstrates that a social psychological approach to everyday life facilitates the coherence of the work. Taking this approach was neither simple nor neat nor straightforward, but its challenges and numerous paradoxes nonetheless allowed us to arrive at new insights on fathers and family life.

Background

FAMOSTAT's purpose is to study the consequences of ongoing modernisation on family life in the Scandinavian welfare state. Although a highly politicised battleground, constantly changing and proliferating with many stakeholders, the Scandinavian welfare state is *universalistic* (Esping-Andersen, 1997). As such, it is characterised by a comprehensive redistribution of services, with entitlements primarily based on rights rather than means testing. The Danish welfare state provides universal, state-sponsored, high-quality childcare from an early age as well as healthcare, employs health nurses and general practitioners and runs hospitals, in addition to furnishing a comprehensive system of social services and care for sick, disabled and elderly people. In this respect the state supplies services, care and education for both parents and children. A comprehensive parental leave scheme offering paid parental leave available to both parents for up to one year with a relatively high degree of compensation (and full pay in some instances) is yet another policy measure that reflects how the universal welfare state provides a supportive framework for families. Some scholars use the term woman-friendly (Borchorst and Siim, 2008) to describe this set-up and emphasise how it alleviates the burden of care for families compared with policies in other welfare states. Rights and privileges in the universal welfare model are first and foremost *individual* rights and privileges. Economic entitlements and provisions are based not on the recipient's family status but primarily on the labour market or position in the education system. In this sense, the universalistic welfare model promotes an unmediated relationship between the individuals and the state, thus supporting individual autonomy and gender equality, making citizens less dependent on family relations for care and provisions than in other welfare regimes.

Beck and Beck-Gernsheim (2002) refer to this as individualisation or institutionalised individualism, arguing that the process of individualisation puts the individual at the fore of social life, that is, the self becomes a point of reference for one's orientation in life. Processes of individualisation are understood as both drivers – and results – of modernisation and social change. The consequences for family life involve both potential democratisation (cf. Giddens, 1992) and destabilising social relations, as well as the erosion of solidarity and communality. Another key concept is detraditionalisation (Beck et al, 1994), which emphasises the breaking up of the standard biography and conventional, cultural frameworks of orientation. This does not mean that traditions disappear; rather, it implies that they become objects of choice and scrutiny. The welfare state and its institutions are part and parcel of the processes of modernisation that transform the conditions for family life and the family as an institution. Analysis of the historic transformations and development of the Scandinavian welfare states (Arvidson et al, 1994) supports this argumentation. Dencik (1997), however, also contends that the consequences of modernisation for the social orientation of modern individuals should be studied empirically. This is the aim of FAMOSTAT.

Informed by theories of individualisation, detraditionalisation and the concept of reflexive modernisation (Beck et al, 1994, 2003), the FAMOSTAT project focuses on what happens when conventional forms of family life are called into question and lose institutional support. This process is understood as highly ambivalent and by no means progressive and straightforward. The family practices of the past do not evaporate into thin air overnight; in fact, historical cultural frameworks of interpretation are continually invoked. Gender inequality related to work, income, household and education decreases (although at different paces) but does not, by any means, disappear. Traditional and conventional norms nonetheless lose their authoritative status; they are not merely reproduced without potentially being contradicted or scrutinised. Beck-Gernsheim (2002) argues that there is no room in the conventional categories of sociology for the new forms of family life emerging on the social scene. She calls for a reinvention of the concepts and theories of family studies as modern families reinvent themselves. FAMOSTAT addresses this call by focusing on the relationship between individuality and 'we-ness' in family life.

Focusing on individuality and we-ness means that 'the family' is conceptualised as social interactions and relations, not as an entity or unit, and implies a knowledge interest in what family members do together and what they mean to each other. When collecting data, this interest translates into concrete interview questions about who the participants share their life with, that is, who they are connected to in both practical and emotional ways; who they care for; and who they coordinate their daily activities with. This approach translates into questions about who the participants argue and fight with, who they lean on for support and who they ask for help. Who makes them happy, angry and sad? By asking and analysing questions of this nature, we hope to learn more about who they feel a sense of belonging with, or who they feel entrapped by, or both. All this and more is within our area of interest as we approach modern family life to investigate the relationship between individual family members and the communal 'we' of families, that is, the individuality and we-ness of family life. These questions alone do not pinpoint fathers as a category or fathering as a social practice, yet they allow for the inclusion and exploration of such themes.

The broad focus of FAMOSTAT makes it possible to move away from the functionalistic heritage of family sociology and allow an orientation towards social actions, practices and doings to guide the way, resulting in the abandonment of family concepts that imply unity and coherence in favour of an emphasis on everyday practices and social relations. This also means taking a social psychological approach inscribed in traditions of thought developed by Simmel (1908), who discusses the relationship between the individual and the social, emphasising interdependency and the ongoing process of co-constitution. Simmel (1908, p 27) argues that the individual is always part of the social but also always outside the social, as the two mutually co-constitute one another, *in statu nascendi*. According to Swedish social psychologist Johan Asplund (1983), Simmel's thinking reflects the historic period of industrialisation and modernisation, when the relationship between the individual and the social became problematic, that is, when this relationship presented itself as unstable, was undergoing change and could not be taken for granted, demonstrating that it constantly required work and reworking. Asplund (1983) identifies social psychology in the cross-section between sociology and psychology, oriented towards the relationship between individuals and society. It is not society, as such, nor the individuals in themselves, but the relationship between the two that constitutes the object of social psychology. From this perspective, studying social relationships means studying the relationship between the individual and the social. This does not mean that people or societies are excluded from the focus of the study, or that they are reinterpreted as relationships. The social psychological perspective is an inclusive one. Studying families and family life includes the study of general societal processes as well as the individual members' experiences and actions. It comprises the study of general structural patterns as well as individual psychological dynamics. Moreover, it includes the study of social relationships in everyday life, of daily practices and of the mundane activities of family life.

Theories of everyday life comprise three key facets: time, space and modality (Felski, 2000). A main feature of time is **repetition**; in other words, the rhythm of everyday life that revolves around cycles of recurring events that occur at more or less fixed intervals. Getting up at the same time, going to work at the same time, having dinner at the same time – doing the same things day after day – are easily identifiable features of everyday life in many households and families. Furthermore, the spatial ordering of everyday life is anchored in a sense of **home**. Felski refers to Agnes Heller when she contends that we experience space in circles of increasing proximity or distance from the experiencing self, asserting that home lies at the centre of these circles. Felski also identifies **habit** as the mode of everyday life, arguing that habits rule everyday life because they go unnoticed. Unless a specific problem emerges to demand our attention, we rarely pause to reflect on the mundane, ritualised practices that much of our everyday life revolves around.

Danish cultural sociologist Birthe Bech-Jørgensen (1988) emphasises in her discussion of everyday life face-to-face relations, where human beings construct themselves and each other by negotiating historical and cultural norms and values, traditions and social institutions. Doing so entails an analytical focus on interpersonal social practices. According to Bech-Jørgensen, the world is interpreted and becomes meaningful through social interaction, with the aforementioned practices constituting everyday life. At the same time, everyday life is made up of material structures and social contexts that are, in a sense, independent of each individual and yet constitute the conditions for individual existence. The structure of the material world can be understood as one of collective meaning that serves to frame and recreate norms and needs, one that connects the individual's practices with each other.

The concept of everyday life that informs the research design of FAMOSTAT refers not merely to activities and events isolated from general cultural and societal structures, but in fact comprises both micro interaction and macro structures, transgressing the dichotomy between actor and structure from a dual perspective on the actor/structure. Everyday life is thus both the actions and interactions of individuals, as well as the collective patterns and structured frameworks that can be identified as both a condition for – and a result of – these actions and interactions.

With this concept of everyday life, the FAMOSTAT project aims to empirically study the consequences of ongoing modernisation for family life. With this aim follows a methodological dilemma that can be phrased as a question: How can the consequences of social change be studied when we are not entirely sure what these consequences are and what it is we are looking for? By looking at it from a social psychological perspective, this dilemma is amplified by the inclusive approach outlined earlier since the study of families *ideally* should include both societal patterns and individual experiences. The keyword here is 'ideally' since the social psychological approach the project employs is by no means dogmatic. On the contrary, it is downright frivolous in its orientation towards the fields of study from which it gets inspiration, which entails a pragmatic approach that sometimes borders on eclecticism (Dencik, 2005). The subsequent sections of this chapter describe how the research objective is pursued using a mixed-method approach that includes data and an analysis of both structural dimensions of society and individual actors' experiences. Moreover, it is argued that mixing these levels of analysis allows fatherhood to become the focus of the study.

Mixing methods and FAMOSTAT

Mixed method is a broad term that refers to various aspects of the research process. Generally, it is used to identify a community of research as alternative to the qualitative and quantitative domains. Advocates of this approach argue against maintaining a sharp division between qualitative and quantitative research and support combining and integrating the two methods (Teddlie and Tashakkori, 2010). Bergman (2008) talks about the straw men of the divide between qualitative and quantitative methods and calls for a reconceptualisation of the domains by rethinking the division of labour between them. Sometimes the term multiple method is used synonymously with mixed method but may also refer to approaches that consider the mixing of methods as more than just the combination of qualitative and quantitative approaches, where the inclusion of various qualitative approaches is an option that does not draw on quantitative methods, or vice versa (Fielding, 2009). Some advocates of mixing methods suggest abandoning the discussion on quantitative and qualitative research altogether since they are both interpretative approaches to empirical studies. Henningsen and Søndergaard (2000) argue for substituting the distinction between quantitative and qualitative research with another one, suggesting that a line be drawn between experimental and empirical research instead. Empirical research should then be understood as studies that engage with people's worlds of experience and investigate these experiences and their settings based on people's own perspectives and interpretations. In contrast to these approaches stands experimental research, which studies people in laboratory settings, isolating them from their daily context in an attempt to control variables and stimuli and the object of study. While this chapter is not involved in the production of division and demarcation as such, it aligns with Henningsen and Søndergaard in considering multiple methods as relevant and applicable in empirical research.

Brannen (2005) argues that we should differentiate between the phases of the research process in which mixing methods is involved since it is of importance whether methods are mixed during the design phase, during the fieldwork or during the analytical phase. She states that, 'Data collected from different methods cannot be simply added together to produce a unitary or rounded reality' (2005, p 176). Data may corroborate and produce the same results, but the findings derived from different methods may also contradict each other. Moreover, Brannen (2005, p 176) mentions elaborations and complementarity as possible outcomes of using multiple methods.

The FAMOSTAT[1] project is mixed in several aspects in that it draws on two types of data – quantitative survey data and qualitative interview data – and it utilises these two types of data in an analytical strategy that is both elaborative and complementary.

The survey

The survey data was collected from computer-assisted telephone interviews with a representative sample from the 1968 cohort. The focus of the project is adults 25 to 45 years of age. At the time of the original data collection process, the participants were 35 years old. Moreover, according to existing statistics from Statistics Denmark, the 1968 cohort exhibits the evenly distributed observations of different family forms (Qvist, 2003), comprising a relatively high number of single people, as well as cohabiting couples and reconstituted families. The 1978 cohort (25 years old in 2003) had a relatively high number of single people and a correspondingly low number of reconstituted families, whereas the 1958 cohort (45 years old in 2003) exhibited the reverse pattern. Since the resources allocated to survey data collection were limited, the 1968 cohort was selected in an effort to ensure the largest degree of variation on the family forms represented and a high degree of statistical representativity. A randomised sample of 1,600 people (1.9% of the cohort population) born in 1968, living in Denmark in 2003, were selected and 1,414 of them were contacted, of which 1,003 agreed to participate in the survey. This randomised sampling approach did not discriminate between the respondents' marital status or household affiliation. Rather, we treated the respondents as individuals and used the survey questionnaire to uncover the household structure and social networks in which the respondents live and participate.

The telephone interview followed a standardised interview format comprising approximately 148 questions (adapted to the household structure and familial network of the individual respondent). The first part of the questionnaire focused on the household structure, with the questions about the identity of members of the respondents' households (with categories such as spouse, romantic partner, children – including step-children – parents, siblings, kin, relatives, friends, co-workers and so on) and how often the other members were part of the household. The second part of the questionnaire focused on the daily life, enquiring about who the respondents interact with and what these interactions relate to. The third part of the interview focused on the frequency of contact between the respondent and the same wide variety of categories used to identify members of the household. The final part of the questionnaire focused on the emotions and experiences of the respondents related to the activities and actors in the respondent's household and social network. There was quite a large number of detailed and, at times, personal questions. The interview lasted 30 to 45 minutes. Despite the considerable effort respondents were expected to make during the telephone interview, 98.6% of them agreed to be included in a panel for further studies (Westerling, 2008). SPSS Statistics software was used for the data from the telephone interview, which comprised over 1,000 items for each respondent.

From survey data to qualitative interviews

Initial analysis of the survey data showed that in 2003, 1.8% of the respondents lived in households that consisted of more than one adult other than a partner. This means that over 98% of the respondents were either single (with or without children) or had a partner (with or without children). The minority of respondents living in extended households were excluded from the statistical analysis since the number of observations rendered this kind of analysis irrelevant. As a result, the qualitative interviews only included respondents living as single or with a romantic partner. Informed by Beck-Gernsheim's (2002) argument, Budgeon and Roseneil (2004) suggest that family research focus on people living on the cutting edge of social life and study novel tendencies and new forms of togetherness and living arrangements in order to gain insight into the consequences of modernisation for family life. Others (Bäck-Wiklund, 2003), in accordance with Beck-Gernsheim, argue that conventional forms of cohabitation and family relations should also be included in such research strategies in order to learn about the changes taking place in modern family life. FAMOSTAT uses its broad base of respondents to study the consequences of modernisation for family life among people exhibiting more conventional lifestyles than the ones of interest to Budgeon and Roseneil (2004). For this reason, the survey data was used to generate a strategic sub-sample using two dimensions: whether or not the respondent lived with a partner, and whether or not the respondent had children in the household. This generates four categories of household as shown in Table 10.1.

Table 10.1: Household categories in FAMOSTAT

	Has a partner	No partner
Has children	Couple with children	Single with children
No children	Couple	Single

The two 'single' categories were further divided into two sub-categories based on whether the respondent had a romantic partner that he or she did not live with. The category 'couple with children' was further divided into three sub-categories based on whether at least one of the children in the household had parents outside the household, creating the list of eight different types of household, as follows:

- single: respondent lives alone, no children;
- single with children: respondent lives alone, has at least one child;
- LAT (living-apart-together): respondent lives alone but has a romantic partner, no children;
- LAT with children: respondent lives alone but has a romantic partner and at least one child;

- couple: respondent lives with partner, no children in the household;
- nuclear couple: respondent lives with partner, has children in the household, no children in the household have parents other than the couple (and none of the partners in the household has children with anyone other than their current partner);
- network couple: respondent live with partner, has children in the household, all the children in the household have a parent outside the couple;
- all-inclusive couple: respondent lives with partner, has children in the household, some of the children in the household have parents outside the couple, other children in the household do not have other parents. (Westerling, 2008)

The various types of household can be differentiated even further based on other criteria, such as age of the youngest child, same-sex partnership, the ethnic, religious and cultural background of the adults, and so on. Rather than generating yet another sub-category, we used the eight types of household as a sample filter to ensure a balanced diversity in the qualitative sample. Using SPSS, four respondents, two men and two women, from each category (n=32), living not more than 50 km from where the research was being conducted (for logistical reasons), were selected.

Face-to-face interviews

Face-to-face, semi-structured interviews were set up with 15 of the respondents who were able to participate in the qualitative interviews within the period of qualitative data collection. The primary criterion for inclusion in the sub-sample was thus the willingness and ability to meet. The interviews, with the exception of one, took place in the homes of the informants.

The interview approach applied considers the interviewee as an informant (Spradley, 1979), emphasising the person as someone who has knowledge, experience and insight into his or her own life. An important task for the interviewer was to aid the process of reflection during the interview. In this sense, the interview is a constructed situation in which the participants 'are as much constructive practitioners of experiential information as they are repositories or excavators of experiential knowledge' (Gubrium and Holstein, 2012, p 32).

Semi-structured, the interviews followed the path the interviewer and the informant jointly embarked on during the interview. The point of departure, however, was the everyday life of the informants and the social actors involved in it. Using an ordinary day and its activities as the framework, the activities and the people involved in them were explored, allowing informants to elaborate on their experiences of everyday life in a narrative format, which is the guiding principle behind the type of interview selected. The informant and the interviewer jointly explored the meaning of the events and the people. The interviewer served as an interested audience, guiding the informant towards topics and themes relevant to the FAMOSTAT study of family life while still permitting the informant to act as the narrator. Themes of particular interest were the relationship between the individual and the communal aspects of family life as informants presented themselves in relation to, for example, managing time, parenting issues, career choices, household chores, holidays, celebrations, the household budget, and so on. We were interested in the narratives where the relationship between 'I' and 'we' was described in detail or problematised. During the interview, we encouraged informants to reflect on their experiences and to elaborate the meaning related to the themes when they emerged in the narratives of everyday family life. All the interviews were transcribed verbatim and saved as text files.

In this fashion, the computer-assisted telephone interviews and the face-to-face interviews differed in central ways. Most significantly, the former treated the person being interviewed as a respondent, whereas the latter viewed him or her as an informant. In the questionnaire-based interview, the respondents were only allowed to give a limited number of answers, with no opportunity provided to further describe or change the circumstances of the interview. The agency of the informant is critical, on the other hand, to the success of semi-structured interviews, which encourage detailed accounts. Because of these differences, rather than despite them, mixing methods aids in the empirical study of the overall research question.

Analysing the data

First step: moving beyond the family

Studying the consequences of ongoing modernisation for family life without knowing exactly what to look for calls for an exploratory approach. The first step involved analysing the extent to which individualisation and detraditionalisation translated into living alone or living in non-traditional family forms. In this case, the nuclear family represents a traditional definition of family, which is delineated as two partners living together with at least one child. In order for the family nucleus to be 'intact' in the literal sense of the word, both the partners must be the parents of all the children in the household and neither of the parents must have children with a partner other than the one they are currently living with. An analysis of the survey data applying this restrictive and exclusionary definition of the nuclear family showed that 59% of all the respondents (n=1,003) lived in a nuclear family (Westerling, 2008).

This result could indicate the erosion of the nuclear family since 41% of all respondents appeared not to live this way. When the different types of household described in the previous section are introduced, however, another pattern emerges. Table 10.2 shows the distribution of the respondents across the eight different types of household sub-category.

Table 10.2: Distribution of respondents across different types of household

Single	7.7%
Single with children	3.2%
LAT	2.1%
LAT with children	3.8%
Couple	11.4%
Nuclear couple	58.7%
Network couple	5.5%
All-inclusive couple	7.6%

This analysis clearly shows that the nuclear family was the most dominant type of household in the 1968 cohort in 2003. If we observe the other types of household, individuals who are single with no children and couples with no children account for 19.1%, or 7.7% and 11.4%, respectively, of the respondents. These respondents could potentially still move into the nuclear family category, which means that only 22.2% of the respondents (including the 2.1% LAT without children) can be defined as having 'moved beyond' the nuclear family. This analysis defines a cohabiting couple with step-children as a non-nuclear family, which makes sense from a demographic perspective but may introduce a demarcation between network couple and nuclear couple that does not reflect the family dynamics and social interactions of everyday life. This becomes clear when we take a closer look at households with children.

Across the different types of household, 77.6% of the respondents live a life shared with children, either their own or their partner's children, or in some cases both. In 97.6% of these households, including single with children, LAT with children, nuclear couple, network couple and all-inclusive couple, the respondents report that at least some of the children are part of the household daily or almost daily (Westerling, 2008, p 113). This indicates that living with step-children may be no different from living with children who are not step-children when considering the everyday practices and routines of the household. Children appear to be part of the everyday life of the family. The main point, however, is that we do not know if the household typology derived from the survey data adequately reflects distinctions and differences in the everyday practices and relationships of family life. To study these practices and relationships (which means studying the relationship between individuality and we-ness in family life), we must focus more directly on the interactions of everyday life. In other words, we need to take another analytical step to study these practices and to learn more about everyday family life with children. To this end, we draw on the qualitative data.

The second step: interactions and relations in family life

The next analytical step involves the qualitative data, which is derived from interviews rich with complexities of everyday life. Making sense of a large amount of narrative material is a daunting task. Even though the framework of the interviews is the activities, actions and actors of everyday life, they each unfold and proliferate heterogeneously. For example, one interview focused on conflicts with a partner, post-divorce, and vacations and holidays, while another focused on the ongoing negotiations of relationships between step-parents and step-children. As such, both interviews are about life in the network family but still might be entirely different from each other in their structure and content. This is, however, not a fault of qualitative interviewing but exactly the reason why such research methods are employed: to capture the complex qualities of the informants' experiences. For this reason, this type of interview does not adhere to a standardised format, making the analysis time-consuming and iterative. For the sake of illustrating how methods can be mixed, which is the purpose of this chapter, we now focus on the relationship between informants and children.

The initial review of the interview transcripts involved identifying activities with children, looking for what is done with the children, which situations are talked about and who is involved. We then identified narratives about children. Next, we looked for the positions children took in these narratives by asking what kinds of agency are ascribed to them, how the actions and motives of the children are interpreted, and what can (and should) the children do?

Through such readings, we both condensed the stories or elaborated on or reinterpreted the accounts initially produced during the interviews.

Certain themes and patterns emerged across the interviews. In one story, Esben, who was both a residential, biological father and a step-father, in addition to being a non-residential father, talked about the ways in which he had decided to change his confrontational approach to his step-son in a conflict about allowance and household chores. Esben accounted for his irritation, bordering on rage, regarding what he considered to be his step-son's unappreciative participation in the household chores. The boy simply did not do the least of what was asked of him, yet expected an allowance and privileges. According to Esben, this was both inappropriate and intolerable, but he decided to let it pass – or rather, to let his step-son's biological mother (Esben's partner) confront the boy. Esben decided not to engage in a conflict, even though he clearly felt he had the moral high ground and parental authority, in order to respect his partner's position as the primary parent in the household.

In another interview, a mother recounts the negotiations between her former husband and herself regarding their children's attendance at different family gatherings. These negotiations were not without the potential for conflict, but the parents mediated these conflicts in accordance with the children's preferences. In yet another interview a step-father described his acceptance of his step-daughter's strategic use of 'dad' when she addressed him. He willingly accommodated her changing practices while being mindful of her emotional struggles with her new step-mother in her biological father's household.

We can reinterpret such accounts as narratives of reflexive adaptation and the negotiation of parental practices. These practices are related not only to children but also to the other parents (including step-parents). Yet, they are always also about the children and the narrators' relation to the child. Through these narratives, we begin to see the contours of a subject position for children that includes an intentionality that adults must respect. These narratives and this emerging subject position can be understood in light of both individualisation and detraditionalisation. Respecting the individual integrity of the children in the family instead of exercising some traditional version of parental (or paternal) authority seems to be a feature in these narratives and connected with the child's position as an individual in his or her own right. These positions are most clearly identified in the interviews with parents in network families or all-inclusive families. One likely reason for this is that these families have more experience with negotiation positions and practices than nuclear families do. Another reason is that the relationship between parent and child is not taken for granted in families with step-children in the same way as it is in nuclear families. The parent–child relationship is almost always naturalised and simply assumed as existing regardless of what parents, children or other people do in the latter type of family constellation. This becomes quite clear in an interview with another father, Anton, which shows the opposite case. Anton lives and a nuclear family but in his narrative, the relationship between him (as a father) and his (biological) infant son is not assumed as pre-existing but has to be worked at to be established.

Fathering and fatherhood: the next analytical steps

Anton has decided to take a large part of the parental leave available to parents because his partner would like to finish her graduate degree. A relatively equal distribution of the parental leave is the preferred option. Anton is looking forward to taking time off from paid work, but not without reservations. He is not quite sure how he will be able to relate to his first child, who is three months old at the time of the interview. Anton reflects on his approach and evaluates his motives for engaging in interactions with his son.

> "It is not an emotional but an intellectual motivation. When the intellectual part is over then the other [emotional] part will come.... It's a challenge for me ... to have to engage in a relationship with him. It's a challenge, but I think it's enriching. That's how I feel so far. It's not a bad thing; it's a good thing."

This account of the child's position as someone whose individual integrity must be respected is identified but not clearly marked. Interestingly, Anton is able to take on the position of someone who is not naturally connected to his (biological) offspring. This is where the emergence of fatherhood as a research theme becomes clear.

If we had interviewed Anton's partner, she would not have been able to speak from a similar position without much more work needing to be done for the audience (the interviewer) to recognise her actions as morally legitimate mothering. This becomes clear when conducting an analytical exercise of letting Anton's partner, the mother, repeat Anton's words verbatim: "It's a challenge for me to relate emotionally to my child". In fact, none of the mothers interviewed said anything to this effect. At this point in our analysis, fathers, fatherhood and fathering begin to emerge as a relevant and interesting analytical focus. An analysis of the interviews from this perspective clearly shows that mothers also experience challenges in their relationship to children. It is not only fathers who face challenges, but not all fathers talk about them. It appears, however, that fathers have a much easier time articulating these kinds of experiences. They seem to have a more marginal position in the parent–child relationship than mothers. Why?

One way of addressing this question is to revisit the quantitative material for further analysis. With fatherhood and fathering as a key focus, we can study how men and fathers take up positions that are distinctly different from those of women and mothers. Analysing the quantitative material allows us to confirm whether what we are identifying through the qualitative analysis is coincidental or whether it is representative of more general patterns and trends.

It goes beyond the purpose of illustration to adequately present the results from our analysis here. The overall picture, however, is a complex pattern of involvement that, in some central aspect, reflects symmetry and equality between men and women, while in others shows a more unequal and somewhat traditionalistic pattern of gender behaviour and involvement (Westerling, 2008). The positions taken up by fathers during interviews are related to more general patterns of everyday family life, where fathers are further removed from care practices and intimate child relations than mothers, even though fathers are also highly involved in the daily care practices of family life. These results led to a further exploration of the interview transcripts that involved a sharper focus on interaction during the interview and the positions from which fathers accounted for and narrated their everyday lives.

The concepts of position and positioning, originally developed within a discursive analytical framework (Davies are Harré, 1990), are central to our analytical strategy as a means to study the negotiation of identities and subjectivities that also includes cultural frameworks and ongoing social interaction. Later developments on position and positioning focus much more on interactive analysis in a discourse analytical framework (Harré and van Lagenhove, 1999; Harré and Moghaddam, 2003), but the conceptual framework certainly lends itself generously to the kind of analysis exemplified in this chapter. In accordance with Brannen (2005), the analytical strategy is elaborative and corroborative in the sense that the qualitative data is used to elaborate on the positions identified using the quantitative data, with the qualitative data being used as the basis and framework of the narrative analysis. The next step in the analysis nevertheless also used quantitative data to explore the fathers' positions in family life and to identify the ambiguity and complexity in the effort to bolster and expand the qualitative analysis. The analysis explored the relationship between the social positions in everyday life and the practices these positions enable while simultaneously understanding these practices as conditions for ongoing negotiation of fathering identities and subjectivities (Westerling, 2008, 2010). This is a dialectic approach that grew out of mixing methods, cross-fertilised by the social psychological perspective and the concept of everyday life. This approach allows us to begin understanding fathers' involvement as complex and ambiguous, as driven by individual motives and actions but at the same time enabled through specific cultural and institutional conditions. We are able to understand fathers' reflexive adaptation to their children's needs and preferences as both an articulation of individualisation, in the sense that it is oriented towards respect for the children as individuals, but also as a process by which men negotiate their positions as fathers in the practices of everyday life. The orientation of fathers towards intimacy in the parent–child relation (Westerling, 2015) can thus be seen not only as a driver of detraditionalisation and individualisation but also as a result of it.

Conclusion: social psychology of everyday life

We did not set out to study fathering and fatherhood from the beginning, but this theme emerged when we mixed methods to examine the consequences of modernisation for family life. Mixing methods led to an exploratory analytical approach that allowed us to develop our theoretical and conceptual understanding of the phenomena we had set out to investigate without pre-conceptualising it. We developed our theoretical understanding of the modern family from everyday life in dialogue with our empirical data. Everyday life experiences, understandings and practices became points of departure for analysis. The patterns identified through analysis and the subject positions negotiated in these patterns represent both the results of our studies and a gateway to these studies. Reflexive fathering represents both an answer to the question of what modernisation means for family life and a point of entry for understanding modern family life. The open, decentred approach of our study made it possible to sidestep classic sociological concepts of the family. Our point of departure was a concept of everyday family life that made us attentive to various practices and interactions, putting focus on the intersubjective dynamics involved. This approach represents the social psychology of everyday life. As such, our empirical study of family life and of fathering contributes to the development of this approach.

It is important to stress that this approach is *one* way of mixing method, not *the* way. Mixed-method research is a broad church, which is probably as it ought to be, since the object of research is not to align with any kind of methodological dogma, but to research, investigate, explore and learn. To this end, we need a flexible framework, especially when studying complex, multifaceted phenomena such as families and everyday life. To sum up, our mixed-method approach offers three key benefits, which of course also comprise certain challenges.

First, mixing methods allowed us to study the consequences of social change without knowing exactly what to look for beforehand. By drawing on quantitative survey data and qualitative interview data, and by establishing dialogue between the two types of data, we were able to unlock the insights hidden in the data in an exploratory, iterative and non-linear way, moving back and forth between the different kinds of data. This flexibility was time-consuming and demanding, causing us to lose our way several times. More often than not, we felt we were going round in circles and when we finally arrived at insights and conclusions, we could not rid ourselves of the feeling that we could have taken an easier path. Using and drawing on different sources of data requires not only a dual skill set in the methods used but also the ability to translate and travel between methods. This realisation was a hard-earned lesson that does not necessarily correspond to the impact of the results produced.

Second, the challenge of translating and travelling between two different methodological domains was to a large degree managed with the help of positioning theory. This analytical approach helped build bridges and establish dialogue between the patterns identified by quantitative analysis, as did the discursive formations analysed using a narrative approach to the interview transcripts. Productive and stimulating, the dialogue was also based on the grammatical foundation of positioning theory, developed primarily based on a discursive psychological framework. As such, there is an inherent inclination to pursue the qualitative material, also due to the fact that the researchers' professional background is solidly planted in discursive psychology. Resisting this proclivity is a challenge in most, if not all, multiple-method research, which is why being mindful of and taking it into consideration to ensure coherence in the analysis is warranted. Finally, there is always room for improvement in this regard.

Third, the concept of everyday life and the theoretical framework it invoked provided crucial assistance in creating coherence in the design. By departing from a coherent concept of everyday life in our quantitative and qualitative methods, we were able to establish connections between the two sets of data from the research design phase and into the analysis and dissemination phase. This contributed significantly to the epistemological coherence of the research – and it is also the reason why the research project serves as a contribution to the social psychology of everyday life. Yet, the concept of everyday life is both flexible and slippery in that it comprises both intimate exchanges and relationships and institutionalised practices and broad cultural frameworks. This combination makes the balancing act tricky as epistemological alignment means walking a thin line that is not always visible and, when it is visible, it is difficult to follow. Slipping, sliding and falling are unavoidable and our study was no exception.

In conclusion, mixed-method research contributed to the messiness and non-linearity of the results, the challenges involved installing ambiguity and paradoxes at all levels of the research. But, as we hope to have illustrated, tolerating the paradoxes and working with the ambiguity allows us to reap the benefits of mixed-method research and to genuinely contribute new insights while also developing our approaches and theoretical understanding. FAMOSTAT led to the study of fatherhood, by mixing methods, via an exploration of we-ness in family life. This approach allowed us to study the consequences of modernisation for family life without specifying and narrowing the focus prior to embarking on our analysis, thus permitting us to develop our understanding and our concepts through the everyday life experiences and practices of the study participants. Significantly, the result was that fathering justifiably became a more salient aspect in the study of social change and family life, leading to highly pertinent insights into the consequences of modernisation for family life.

Note

[1] FAMOSTAT is an ongoing longitudinal panel study comprising two waves of quantitative data, one in 2003 and one in 2014, and two waves of qualitative data, one in 2004 and the other in 2017. This chapter only presents the first wave from 2003/2004 and treats it as a cross-sectional study, which is how it was originally designed.

References

Arvidson, H., Berntsson, L. and Dencik, L. (1994) *Modernisering och välfärd – om stat, individ och civilt samhälle i Sverige* [Modernisation and welfare – on state, individual and civil society in Sweden], Gothenburg: City University Press.

Asplund, J. (1983) *Tid, rum, individ och kollektiv* [Time, space, individual and communality], Stockholm: Liber Förlag.

Bäck-Wiklund, M. (2003) 'Familj och modernitet' [Family and modernity], in M. Bäck-Wiklund and T. Johansson (eds) *Nätverksfamiljen* [The network family], Stockholm: Natur och Kultur, pp 17–39.

Bech-Jørgensen, B. (1988) "Hvorfor gør de ikke noget?" [Why are they not doing anything?], in B. Bech-Jørgensen, C. Bloch, L. Højgaard, and B.L. Nautrup (eds) *Hverdagsliv, Kultur og Subjektivitet* [Everyday life, culture and subjectivity], Copenhagen: Akademisk Forlag, pp 68–123.

Beck-Gernsheim, E. (2002) *Reinventing the family. In search of new lifestyles*, Cambridge/Oxford: Polity Press/Blackwell.

Beck, U. and Beck-Gernsheim, E. (2002) *Individualization*, London: Sage Publications.

Beck, U., Bonss, W. and Lau, C. (2003) 'The theory of reflexive modernization. Problematic, hypotheses and research programme', *Theory, Culture & Society*, 20(2): 1-33.

Beck, U., Giddens, A. and Lash, S. (1994) *Reflexive modernization. Politics, tradition and aesthetics in the modern social order*, Cambridge: Polity Press.

Bergman, M. (2008) 'The straw men of the qualitative-quantitative divide and their influence on mixed methods research', in M. Bergman (ed) *Advances in mixed methods research: Theories and applications*, London: Sage Publications, pp 10-22.

Borchorst, A. and Siim, B. (2008) 'Woman-friendly policies and state feminism: theorizing Scandinavian gender equality', *Feminist Theory*, 9(2): 207-224.

Brannen, J. (2005) 'Mixing methods: the entry of qualitative and quantitative approaches into the research process', *International Journal of Social Research Methodology*, 8(3): 173-184.

Budgeon, S. and Roseneil, S. (2004) 'Editors' introduction: beyond the conventional family', *Current Sociology*, 52(2): 127-134.

Davies, B. and Harré, R. (1990) 'Positioning: the discursive production of selves', *Journal for the Theory of Social Behavior*, 20(1): 43-63.

Dencik, L. (1997) 'The position of families in the transformation of the modern Scandinavian welfare states', in L.A. Vaskovics (ed) *Familienleitbilder und Familienrealitäten* [Family models and family practices], Leverkusen: Verlag Leske + Budrich, pp 248-277.

Dencik, L. (2005) *Mennesket i postmoderniseringen – om barndom, familie og identiteter i opbrud* [The human being in postmodernisation – in childhood, family and identities under change], Værløse: Billesø & Baltzer.

Esping-Andersen, G. (1997) 'Welfare states at the end of the century: the impact of labour market, family and demographic change', in D.J. Johnston (ed) *Family, market and community. Equity and efficiency in social policy* (1st edn), Paris: OECD, pp 63-80.

Felski, R. (2000) *Doing time: Feminist theory and postmodern culture*, New York, NY: New York University Press.

Fielding, N.G. (2009) 'Going out on a limb: postmodernism and multiple method research', *Current Sociology*, 57: 427-447.

Giddens, A. (1992) *The transformation of intimacy: Sexuality, love and eroticism*, Cambridge/Oxford: Polity Press/Blackwell.

Gubrium, J.F. and Holstein, J.A. (2012) 'Narrative practice and the transformation of interview subjectivity', in J.F. Gubrium, J.A. Holstein, A.B. Marvasti and K.D. McKinney (eds) *The Sage handbook of interview research: The complexity of the craft* (2nd edn), Thousand Oaks, CA: Sage Publications, pp 27-44.

Harré, R. and Moghaddam, F. (2003) *The self and others: Positioning individuals and groups in personal, political, and cultural contexts*, Westport, CT: Praeger.

Harré, R. and van Lagenhove, L. (1999) *Positioning theory: Moral contexts of intentional action*, Oxford/Malden, MA: Blackwell.

Henningsen, I. and Søndergaard, D.M. (2000) 'Forskningstraditioner krydser deres spor. Kvalitative og kvantitative socio-kulturelle empiriske forskningsmetoder' [Traditions of research crossing their own tracks. Qualitative and quantitative socio-cultural empirical methods], *Kvinder, Køn og Forskning* [Women, Gender and Research], 9(4): 26-38.

Qvist, A. (2003) *Statistiske efterretninger: Befolkning og valg* [Statisical notes. Population and choice], Copenhagen: Statistics Denmark.

Simmel, G. (1908) *Soziologie. Untersuchungen über die Formen der Vergesellschaftung* [Sociology: Inquiries into the construction of social forms] (1st edn), Berlin: Duncker & Humblot Verlag.

Spradley, J.P. (1979) *The ethnographic interview*, Belmont, CA: Wadsworth, Thomson Learning.

Teddlie, C. and Tashakkori, A. (2010) 'Overview of contemporary issues in mixed methods research', in A. Tashakkori and C. Teddlie (eds) *Sage handbook of mixed methods in social & behavioral research*, Thousand Oaks, CA: Sage Publications, pp 1-44.

Westerling, A. (2008) *Individualisering, familie og fællesskab. En socialpsykologisk analyse af hverdagslivets sociale netværk i en refleksiv modernitet* [Individualisation, family and communality. A social psychological analysis of the social networks of everyday life in a reflexive modernity], Roskilde: Roskilde University.

Westerling, A. (2010) 'Everyday family life: Investigating the individual/ social in a radicalized modernity', in K. Karlsson and K. Ellergård (eds) *Proceedings of the Sustaining Everyday Life Conference*, Linköping: Linköping University Electronic Press, pp 137-149.

Westerling, A. (2015) 'Reflexive fatherhood in everyday life: the case of Denmark', *Families, Relationships and Societies*, 4(2): 209-223.

ELEVEN

Capturing the bigger picture with big data: opportunities for fatherhood researchers

Esther Dermott

Introduction

This volume contributes both to a better understanding of contemporary fathers and fatherhood, and of how to conduct social research. This chapter does so by considering the challenges and value of engaging with 'big data' for fatherhood researchers. It argues that the arrival of new forms of data presents genuinely exciting possibilities for tackling important questions that have been either inadequately addressed, or sidelined, in previous work. The discussion therefore contributes to setting the agenda for near-future empirical studies of fatherhood through assessing the potential of newly available methods and, by implication, the limitations of those currently used. To do so, it looks at the value for fatherhood research of three forms of data that are commonly lumped together as 'big': administrative data; large-scale textual data; and data produced through mobile applications. Necessarily, the question of methods cannot be divorced from that of substantive lines of enquiry. So, in setting researchers the challenge of pursuing the possibilities of big data, attention is directed to particular aspects of fatherhood that deserve academic scrutiny. There need not then be a 'crisis' in empirical sociology prompted by the arrival of big data as initially suggested by Savage and Burrows (2007), but there is a need to engage with data generated through technological innovations. The challenge of big data is more profound than proposing a shift to include different methods of data collection; it requires social scientists to rethink the questions about fathers and fatherhood we are able to answer and work with other disciplines to do so.

'Go large': studying fathers and fatherhood

Family sociology has been inventive in developing qualitative approaches, for example, adapting qualitative interviewing methods to include emotion maps (Gabb, 2008) or moving away from interviewer-led data with participant produced videos (Muir and Mason, 2012), as well using multiple methods within a single research project (for example, Eldén, 2012: Gabb and Fink, 2015). In other words, researchers are increasingly 'creative' about the methods that are used. However, thinking has been less imaginative when it comes to the possibilities offered by large-scale data. This matters, given that it has been widely claimed that computational social science is what is going to really challenge and change the social sciences in the 21st century (see, for example, Christakis 2012).

UK sociological research on fatherhood has tended to prioritise qualitative methods over quantitative. (This is reversed in North America where quantitative analysis of large-scale datasets is more commonplace; in European studies there is arguably a better balance between different methodological approaches.) The result has been a range of studies focusing on the experience of contemporary fatherhood, comprising the everyday practices of men with different socioeconomic characteristics. We know about the lives of young fathers, fathers with disabilities, gay fathers, fathers from different ethnic backgrounds, step-fathers, divorced fathers, unemployed fathers, stay-at-home dads, and so on. We also have detailed information about the forms of care and support that fathers provide: from engagement in educational activities, sport and leisure pursuits, and babycare, to communication, household work and financial provisioning. And there has also been significant attention paid to how men feel about their role as fathers. What is less prevalent is the wider landscape of fatherhood; precisely the perspective provided by large-scale quantitative data.

The value of large-scale analysis is the ability both to observe patterns across the population and describe correlations between elements of interest. In relation to fatherhood, one example of quantitative work is exploring the extent to which the cultural trope of the 'breadwinning father' exists in practice. We therefore have evidence of patterns of working among fathers such as the tendency to work on a full- or part-time basis; the number of average hours spent in paid work; comparisons between fathers and mothers, fathers and non-fathers; and comparisons between fathers based on age of children and broader socioeconomic characteristics that we know influence employment patterns, such as ethnicity, education and age (see, for example,

Dermott, 2006; Biggart and O'Brien, 2010; Smith Koslowski, 2011). Quantitative research also lets us examine new phenomena in more detail, such as the rise of stay-at-home dads. Large-scale data should mean that it is possible to explore how widespread this trend is and the general characteristics of these men – are they, for example, highly educated with high-earning female partners or men with training in manual occupations living in areas of high male unemployment? However, while this is the *potential* of quantitative data, what is captured is often not what we want to measure: see, for example, Adams' (2015) reflection on a quest to find accurate data on the number of stay-at-home dads in the UK. Quantitative data often prioritises the ability to replicate data over time, which means asking the same questions or measuring the same kinds of activities. This means that it has limited value in giving an accurate picture of social activities that do not fit into existing categories, such as fathers who are primary caregivers but also engaged in some paid work carried out on a self-employed basis. Similarly, Norman (2017) discusses how the idea of father involvement can be translated into measures that in turn can be incorporated into large-scale surveys. She argues that while Lamb's three-fold formulation of fathering involvement is the most useful for constructing measures, this will necessarily mean leaving out elements such as emotional engagement and financial provisioning that have also been assessed as significant.

The (real) challenge of big data

Savage and Burrows provocatively announced in 2007 that empirical social science would need to reinvent itself as, with the arrival of big data, existing methods of data collection were increasingly becoming outdated. The term 'big data' refers to data that is large both in quantity and scope, and which therefore makes gaining information about entire populations of interest a reality. Laney (2001) demarcated big data through the 'three Vs' of volume, velocity and variety: Kitchin and McArdle (2016) state that fundamentally 'Small data are slow and sampled. Big Data are quick and n = all" (p 8). On this basis, various forms of mobile communication, websites, social media, sensors, cameras, transactional data and administrative data fit the profile.

The main concern raised by Savage and Burrows in their frequently cited article is that the sheer scale of big data makes the default methods of sociologists (small-scale interviews and the social survey) redundant. The suggestion is that the ways sociologists[1] tend to conduct their research are not simply limited in terms of the information they can provide, but have been comprehensively usurped by the generation of huge banks of data. 'Big data' was therefore posited as presenting a serious dilemma for the discipline. In the current decade, however, more optimistic accounts suggest that while sociology will need to be open to risk taking and evolution in order to benefit from new technological developments in data collection, there is still a central role for the discipline to occupy in making sense of the proliferation of new data (Halford et al, 2013; Tinati et al, 2014). In other words, the mere existence of big data does not obviate the need for a 'sociological imagination' to develop research questions, analyse data, and contextualise findings. Nevertheless, the arrival of big data may still offer a significant challenge to the discipline if, as Savage and Burrows (2007) suggested, sociology refuses to shift from a taken-for-granted assumption of its own importance that ignores engagement with questions of methods in favour of 'synthetic sociology' (Burrows and Savage, 2014, p 2). The limited involvement of sociologists in particular, and social scientists in general, in academic work that draws on big data can be partly attributed to a scepticism that big data necessitates 'data-driven' research that is problematically 'theory-free', and produces statistical associations that stand outside of ideas and concepts that should be the central 'stuff' of social science thinking. Given these debates and developments, it seems worthwhile (and important) to reflect on the potential implications of this digital data-gathering revolution for the specific topic of this volume, fathers and fatherhood. The following discussion unpacks the notion of 'big data' and makes some suggestions as to how its various forms can potentially contribute to our knowledge of social characteristics, cultural representations and behaviours, and everyday experiences of men's parenting.

Characteristics of fathers

The classification of fathers into sub-groups according to standard social characteristics such as age, ethnicity, sexuality, disability and class has produced valuable awareness of fathers who were previously relatively ignored in qualitative empirical research (Dermott and Miller, 2015). This has been important in recognising heterogeneity within the group 'fathers', which has implications for understanding behaviour and experiences. Taking social characteristics seriously sheds light on the value of fatherhood status as a lens through which to examine men's lives. However, capturing fathers across the full range of social characteristics has more often been an aim than an achievement. Research has tended to foreground the experiences and views of the most culturally dominant group – white, heterosexual, middle-class fathers – despite frequent acknowledgements of the limitations of such work in capturing the diversity of contexts for fathering. This is, at least in part, a consequence of the relative ease of recruitment of fathers with these characteristics to research projects. It is a methodological truism that accessing relatively disadvantaged or marginalised groups is more difficult due to their social invisibility and therefore relatively advantaged fathers have been overrepresented in qualitative work. This empirical gap has been recognised and researchers often indicate a desire to counter the imbalance. Notably, work has been undertaken on young fathers (for a review, see Lau-Clayton, 2016), Asian fathers in the UK (Salway et al, 2009), disabled men's experience of fathering (Kilkey and Clarke, 2010) and the practices and views of migrant fathers (Kilkey et al, 2014), all of which prioritise capturing the experiences of fathers with particular social characteristics that have been previously understudied.

However, there is a risk that marginalised fathers whose experiences are increasingly gaining attention are those whose fathering is viewed as problematic or potentially problematic in some way. So incarcerated fathers, or men who do not live with their children, or fathers who have a learning difficulty, may be under the sociological microscope not just as a particular group but because there is a popular view that in some way their fathering is inadequate. Meanwhile elites who are outside of the norm because of their significant social advantages remain un- or understudied (or when the subject of attention may be lauded for their exceptional nature: cf. Kaufman's term 'superdads' [2013]). Further, even while research findings may challenge preconceptions (and in fact often tend to confirm continuities of fathering attitudes and practices that exist between the marginalised and the mainstream), the methodological starting point of researching 'other kinds' of fathers reproduces this way of thinking. The response might be that capturing a large range of social characteristics can be addressed through quantitative research with larger sample sizes. However, the same problems tend to persist. Even in large surveys, meaningful analysis of sub-groups becomes difficult when combinations of characteristics are examined.[2] And survey methods are bad at accessing the most marginalised in society and so certain groups of fathers will still end up being excluded, which is often given as a rationale for undertaking small qualitative studies of hard-to-reach groups.

So there is an ongoing problem with who gets included in discussions about the nature of fatherhood and how this forms our thinking on the subject. This could be partly rectified through an increase in the number of studies of fathers with different combinations of social characteristics that have been relatively ignored. Yet, in addition to having practical difficulties (time and expense), this answer also fails to address the problem of the reification of social characteristics. This has been a concern of sociologists for some time: how to study particular groups without asserting that those groupings are necessarily meaningful categorisations (see Fox and Jones, 2013 for a discussion in relation to ethnicity). A really significant advantage of big data is that the 'n = all' inclusion of the total population of interest means that sub-groups are captured but not reified. These forms of data collection and analysis can therefore move us away from an atomistic approach to studying fatherhood in which increasingly narrow combinations of characteristics address empiricist concerns over lacunae that are not necessarily conceptually enlightening but that 'fill a gap', and, at the same time, avoid the dilemma of having to decide which social characteristics are, *a priori*, most important for understanding contemporary fatherhood. Ruppert and colleagues (2013, p 35) argue that increasing levels of digital data – particularly data that is based on commercial transactions and administrative collections – offer something of a return to an observational knowledge economy based around visualisation and mapping, with increased 'granularity'. At any rate, the advantages presented by big data mean that inductive thinking can have a greater presence at the data-collection stage.

The form of big data that is perhaps most central to this type of analysis is administrative data. Administrative data is derived from administrative systems held by public agencies such as medical, income and tax, or educational records, rather than being collected overtly for research purposes. Connelly and colleagues (2016) suggest that this form of data has often not been included in discussions of big data, which have instead focused on the opportunities offered by new technologies such as social media. However, research funding in the UK directed towards big data has been focused on opportunities offered by administrative data, specifically the possibilities offered by linking datasets together.[3] The attraction is that administrative records can capture similar types of information to social surveys but in a more extensive and detailed form. So, health records offer a more complete picture of medical interventions, tax records provide more detailed information on income, and educational records capture more fully school records, than that which is available by asking individuals directly. 'Found' data can therefore be suitably 're-purposed' (Halford et al, 2013). In relation to fathers, analysis of this type could, for example, examine the income sources of fathers on benefits or the medical histories of men who have been diagnosed with postnatal depression. One limitation of administrative data is that usually only a small number of variables are captured so that complex sets of social characteristics cannot be addressed. This form of data can then provide information about narrowly defined questions, which may be directly related to an element of social policy (Connelly et al, 2016). A second limitation is that this type of data is not well suited to linking people relationally; as the individual is the focus of attention, the data is often weak or fails to capture at all social networks or family relationships.

Cultural representations of fatherhood

Web scraping (of social media, for example) and the digitisation of texts and visual data means that larger amounts of data is available than before, data that can now be analysed more efficiently and robustly using large computing power. Cultural representations of fathers or fatherhood do not always require a large body of data to be informative. The political language around one specific policy (see, for example, Klinth's historical assessment of Swedish parental leave campaigns [2008]) or a single high-profile advertising campaign may be worthy of analysis precisely because of their status as an exceptional standalone event or because they are conceptually interesting rather than representative. Nevertheless, it seems that researchers are often restricted in the scope of what they can analyse due to practical rather than intellectual constraints. Other forms of big data offer the potential to capture **representations** of fatherhood. The arrival of big data here may be significant primarily because of the way in which it can cast a wide net, rather than prompting a different kind of research question.

It has, of course, been possible to search the content of blogs or databases such as LexisNexis for terms used in newspaper articles for some time. But these were incomplete resources and this is now changing rapidly. As just one example, Hansard, the official transcript of all parliamentary business in the UK that goes back to the beginning of the 19th century, was (until recently) typed up and bound. It could be accessed by researchers, but only those who could visit London in person and had applied in advance to look at the records. Now, following a digitisation project, these records have been scanned and the individual pages are available online.[4] As digitisation incorporates increasing numbers of textual and visual documents and records, it will be possible for academic analyses of cultural representations of a particular moment to become increasingly comprehensive.

It seems clear that reducing the quantity of data generated for research purposes has, up to now, been necessary because of limited access to all relevant sources. Perhaps more importantly, researchers are also limited in their ability to manage and analyse large quantities of material with any degree of sophistication. Prividera and Howard (2015) – who were interested in popular depictions of military fathers – used three American news sites to search for two terms 'military fathers' and military dads' over a 15-year period. While the selection of particular news outlets, terms and time period was justified on theoretical grounds, and more pragmatically due to access to news resources, choices over sampling were also made based on the limited ability to analyse really large amounts of data. Similarly, an analysis by Adams and colleagues (2011) of fathers in bestselling children's picture books in the UK started with a decision to focus on those books that had sold the most copies in a single year, but even within this sample there had to be further random sampling to reduce the books to a number that could be coded using a labour-intensive method. Mass digitisation facilitates the availability of considerably more data (even if it does not tell us what to do with it). Forms of analysis that are conceptually quite simple, such as counting the frequency of a certain word or phrase or observing its location, will be improved most easily as greater computing power will allow for more complete statements. Bail (2014) notes that cultural sociologists have so far been negligent in taking full advantage of the reams of text-based data available, but offers an optimistic perspective on future potential. In relation to ideas of fatherhood, this form of analysis should result in more robust claims about, for example, the kinds of newspaper reports in which fathers are mentioned and comparisons between the contexts in which descriptions of mothers and fathers are placed. Rather than put researchers out of a job, as was envisaged by Savage and Burrows (2007) (who saw private companies taking on the role of data analysts), the public availability of much of this data will mean academic researchers have the opportunity to conduct their current research but on a bigger scale. Indeed, it may mean that less external resource is required to conduct academic study, and so the quality of research conducted outside of the remit of research councils and other funding bodies can expand.

This expansion of data has merits, but is rather lacking the spark of excitement often associated with the discourse of big data. Witness, as one example, the head of the Economic and Social Research Council in the UK prioritising its value for social science (Elliot, 2016). There is much more excitement about the ability to access representations of cultural phenomenon through new forms of data such as those produced by social media. Picture-sharing sites such as Instagram and 'full pipe' social media such as Twitter that are tagged can offer insights into how fathers are represented, for example in relation to particular activities (which images of father–child activities tend to be posted on public sites?); the terms associated with fatherhood and how this is related to fathers' portrayal (do Twitter feeds from stay-at-home dads emphasise particular elements of fathering?); or how geographical location affects descriptions of fatherhood (do fathers located in Sweden 'look' different to those living in the UK?).[5] Lupton and Thomas's work (Lupton, 2016) offers one example: discussing the content of pregnancy mobile applications (apps), it notes that those aimed at prospective fathers offer a strongly gender-stereotyped view of men and women's parenting roles, and target men through a 'joking' style that positions them as relatively uninterested in their baby unless engaged through entertainment. The value offered by these new forms of big data is that a broader picture of how ideas of contemporary intimate fatherhood are practised and reproduced can be captured.

Fathering behaviour and practices

Most exciting perhaps are the possibilities offered by data produced by mobile communications and the ability of apps to provide information about the activities and interactions of fathers; a new arena of consumption and 'born digital' data. Social science methods are relatively strong at finding out what individuals think they should do, and think they do, but are relatively weak at quantifying actual activities and capturing how interactions are performed. Osborne and Rose (1999) argue that the technology of opinion polls created 'opinionated people' who were self-reflexively engaged with devices and processes that encouraged individuals to describe and categorise themselves. This intensive farming of attitudes leads to less useful data; either because those who are willing to be opinionated to pollsters and related others are a decreasing group (and thus unrepresentative of the wider population) or because we have now been too well trained in how to respond to surveys so they fail to reflect what we actually think and do. Burrows and Savage (2014) note that social sciences that rely on accounts of actions are now confronted by data that can actually record complex interactions in the social world (p 3). This is the area where 'big data' can make the most significant difference, not just in the scale and reliability of the data that sociologists can access, but also in the kinds of questions we are able to address. Family sociologists through qualitative studies have often succeeded in capturing something of the nature of father–child interactions – the meaning attached to a particular action, its significance, or how it can be interpreted differently depending on context. But while these are often reflections on commonplace activities, such as giving a teenager a lift in a car or reading a story to a child, we have little information on how these are actually *done*. Research, for example, has detailed that fathers value the time spent transporting children to the houses of friends or activities as a short period during which conversations that build intimacy happen (Dermott, 2008). However, how these interactions play out is unknown. We do have evidence from technology such as wearable cameras about interactions between parents of babies, which has been used by psychologists to capture evidence about eye contact (Yoshida and Smith, 2008), but sociological research has tended to rely on the accounts of individuals reflecting after the fact in general terms. Conversation analysts and those using other linguistic approaches tend to be limited to the accounts of 'outsiders' with some degree of formal authority (see, for example, Carver, 2014 on legal advisers, and Chapter Nine in this volume on social workers). The 'private' sphere – what happens within family homes – is poorly captured. If visual and verbal interaction data was extended to capture a wider range of activities, for example using a camera mounted on a car dashboard, those working on psychosocial approaches to family lives and researchers who look at how conversations between family members reflect assumptions and expectations about their roles could benefit from the ability to draw on real-life and real-time data.

Negative aspects of father–child relationships are a significant gap in family research. Agony aunt columns in newspapers, and journalistic and first-author biographical accounts, as well as our own conversations with friends and family members, often focus on the difficulties of being a 'good' parent or child; from detailing the minutiae of an argument to debating the acceptability of a course of action. But, perhaps with the exception of differences of opinion between separated/divorced parents (see, for example, Westerling, 2016), less positive elements of family relationships, particular when they occur as part of everyday interactions, are not a substantial part of sociological literature on personal life.[6] Even when they are presented in accounts, they exist in an especially mediated form. The ability of technology to capture the ordinary and local, in a way perhaps previously only encountered on a much smaller scale through ethnographic methods, offers family researchers access to the kind of data they require to make interventions in debates about the nature and meaning of father involvement.

Some inventive ways of capturing the nature and extent of behaviours have been adopted. Doucet's early work on the 'household portrait' (1996) not only asked couples to report how tasks were allocated within the household between members, but also captured their discussion about who did what in order to explain their preferences, decision making and any differences of opinion. The growth of time-use studies in the 1980s and 1990s was a response to the (justified) suspicion that individuals' recall ability and a desire to align themselves with dominant social norms meant that other forms of survey were poor at capturing what people did. Time-use studies, instead of relying on retrospective accounts of what people do, ask participants to record activities as they occur (or shortly afterwards). The majority of large-scale multinational studies have developed a precoded form from which participants choose an activity in which they are engaged for every 15-minute slot throughout the day. The inclusion of secondary as well as primary activities allows for the fact of simultaneous involvement in more than one activity. This has been especially valuable in capturing some of the messiness of domestic life where many child-related tasks overlap or, as with 'taking responsibility', are difficult to capture within a specific activity. Until now, this approach has probably been the best available for capturing behaviours and for making cross-national comparisons, but there are still significant limitations. As with many detailed surveys, the demand placed on participants may be excessive, and so achieving a reliable and representative population is difficult. While more recent innovations such as using smart phone apps to input information have been trialled and could reduce the demands made of participants (Chatzitheochari et al, 2015), recruitment and retention is still challenging and time-consuming. Also, it is arguable that, as with other forms of large-scale survey collection, the reliance on precoded activities in order to reduce the demands on the participants and to compare changes over time means that such studies are better placed to capture static activities rather than new forms of activity or alterations to how an older activity is done. As one example, the way in which television is viewed in 2017 is likely to be significantly different from a decade earlier, given the current access to a range of additional technologies and social media. 'Watching television' as a category of activity is therefore unlikely to be able to capture the multitude of ways that viewing is mediated, scheduled, paused, interrupted and interspersed with other digital communication.

The ability to use digital technology could add significantly to knowledge about how we 'do' family in the private sphere. Wearable technology, such as smart watches, can measure a range of activities, for example how much time is spent sleeping or doing physical activity. In relation to finding out more about what fathers do, it would be possible to find out relatively easily information about the levels of sleep disturbance fathers experience in a baby's first six months (and compare it to those of mothers, and non-fathers or fathers of older children). One question posed in the introduction to this edited collection is whether the main focus of fatherhood researchers should be on men who 'own' the social characteristic of being a father or on sets of practices that are defined as 'doing' fathering. This example presents one way in which access to big data can offer knowledge of the former type. It can offer insights into groups of men who are fathers and allow for comparisons to be made based on parental status. Data generated through wearable technology could also include the monitoring of physical space, thereby giving a stronger empirical basis to the concept of co-presence in the home (which is often referred to in discussions about fathers and children). Likewise in relation to public space, the existence in popular discourse of Swedish 'latte pappas' who because of long periods of parental leave spend time having *fika* (a break for coffee and cake) (Tan, 2017) could be explored more empirically to examine the public visibility of fathers and young children. Following Watts (2007), the analysis of network data to locate individuals can avoid some of the problems of cognitive biases associated with self-reporting. Mapping movements and co-location then seems to offer significant opportunities for improving the extent of our knowledge about the everyday practices of fathers.

Conclusion: assumptions, dilemmas and possibilities

This is not the place for an extensive discussion of how sociologists should theorise developments in digital technologies in terms of surveillance, control and ownership of knowledge, except to acknowledge that there is academic work being done in this area and to assert that the 'newness' in this domain is an extension of pre-existing trends rather than a wholesale revolution. Following Ruppert and colleagues (2013, p 40), there is certainly a need for 'heterogeneous understanding of the digital', and while large changes have, and are continuing to take place, talk of epochal shifts is not necessarily helpful. Nevertheless, having presented an account so far that has focused on opportunities, it seems reasonable also to note some potential problems and how they might be addressed.

A key problem associated with transactional and administrative data is that of ownership and access. The fact that administrative and transactional data may be largely in the domain of private companies rather than held by public (or publicly funded) organisations could leave such data outside of obligations of transparency and out of the reach of academic analysis. Administrative data generated by government may be available to academics, albeit with some constraints. However, a key concern expressed by Savage and Burrows in their 2007 article was that the ability of social scientists to predict and explore social phenomena would be eclipsed by the ability of commercial companies to do so: data held by Amazon could say much more about consumption patterns of fathers-to-be, for example, than would be possible from a 'standard' social survey. As highlighted in the discussion above, numerous important research questions exist that do not rely on such databases, and so one response would be to shift focus away from topics where data will be owned by commercial enterprises.

However, for those who consider that a sociological mindset brings a different, and valuable, perspective to big data, it may be that instead cutting-edge research requires developing relations with non-academic partners who do not fit the profile of third sector, voluntary, not-for-profit organisations, with which social scientists have often felt most comfortable. This involves a recognition that, following Thrift (2005), some elements of social science research are part of a 'knowing capitalism', in which 'systematic gathering of information about customers, clients, employees and competitors become routine to corporate strategy' (Ruppert et al, 2013, p 33). While these forms of research alliance may be new for sociology, they are not substantially different from those that other disciplines regularly negotiate and to do so is not in itself antithetical to intellectual pursuits. Both these responses offer the potential to step back and think in bigger terms about the research questions we wish to address rather than merely what is possible through 'traditional' methods.

Big data cannot alone offer a solution to the conundrum of how best to capture the dynamic nature of fathering and how this is intertwined with other activities and social relationships. But the potential of big data to offer researchers information about behaviours and views, over time and location, can provide an exciting new source of data for the next generation of fatherhood researchers. The limitation of many methodological tools has been the inability to build in recognition of the dynamic nature of personal lives and the complex organisation of paid and unpaid labour that is associated with care. Big data should be a tool to better capture this complexity. Methodological innovation, accompanied by social science analysis, could then make real progress towards the ambition of extending typologies of male caregivers and providing a better evidence base for policy makers (Boyer et al, 2017). Offering the possibility of both more depth and breadth, big data could lead to a genuinely more comprehensive 'big picture' of contemporary fathers and fatherhood.

Notes

[1]   While the article refers broadly to social science, it is sociology and sociologists who are the main target.
[2]   This has been noted, for example, in relation to ethnicity, where booster samples are required to permit meaningful sub-group analysis even within an already large, representative survey (Dermott and Main, 2017).
[3]   The Administrative Data Liaison Service (https://adrn.ac.uk) was founded in 2013 as part of a £64-million Economic and Social Research Council initiative to support analysis of big data by enabling researchers in the UK to access administrative data held by government departments and associated bodies.
[4]   www.hansard-archive.parliament.uk
[5]   Lupton and colleagues (2016) provide a useful review of research related to parenting and digital media.
[6]   Another exception is Smart and colleagues' (2012) article on 'difficult friendships' drawn from the mass observation archive.

References

Adams, J. (2015) 'It's official; stay at home dads do not exist', available at 'http://dadbloguk.com/its-official-stay-at-home-dads-do-not-exist.

Adams, M., Walker, C. and O'Connell, P. (2011) 'Invisible or involved fathers? A content analysis of representations of parenting in young children's picturebooks in the UK', *Sex Roles*, 65(3-4): 259-270

Bail, C.A. (2014) 'The cultural environment: measuring culture with big data', *Theory and Society*, 43: 465-482.

Biggart, L. and O'Brien, M. (2010) 'UK fathers' long work hours: career stage or fatherhood?', *Fathering*, 8(3): 341-361.

Boyer, K., Dermott, E., James, A. and MacLeavy, J. (2017) 'Regendering care in the aftermath of recession?', *Dialogues in Human Geography*, 7(1): 56-73.

Burrows, R. and Savage, M. (2014) 'After the crisis? Big data and the methodological challenges of empirical sociology', *Big Data and Society*, April-June: 1-6.

Carver, N. (2014) 'Displaying genuineness: cultural translation in the drafting of marriage narratives for immigration applications and appeals', *Families, Relationships and Societies*, 3(2): 271-286.

Chatzitheochari, S., Fisher, K., Gilbert, E., Calderwood, L., Huskinson, T., Cleary, A. and Gershuny, J. (2015) *Measuring young people's time-use in the UK Millennium Cohort Study: A mixed-mode time diary approach*, CLS Working Paper 2015/05, London: Institute of Education.

Christakis, N.A. (2012) 'A new kind of science for the 21st century', available at www.edge.org/conversation/nicholas_a_christakis-a-new-kind-of-social-science-for-the-21st-century.

Connelly, R., Playford, C.J., Gayle, V. and Dibben, C. (2016) 'The role of administrative data in the big data revolution in social science research', *Social Science Research*, 59: 1-12.

Dermott, E. (2006) 'What's parenthood got to do with it? Men's hours of paid work', *British Journal of Sociology*, 57(4): 620-634.

Dermott, E. (2008) *Intimate fatherhood*, Basingstoke: Palgrave Macmillan.

Dermott, E. and Main, G. (eds) (2017) *Poverty and social exclusion in the UK: The nature and extent of the problem*, Bristol: Policy Press.

Dermott, E. and Miller, T. (2015) 'More than the sum of its parts? Contemporary fatherhood policy, practice and discourse', *Families, Relationships and Societies*, 4(2): 183-195.

Doucet, A. (1996) 'Encouraging voices: towards more creative methods for collecting data on gender and household labour', in L. Morris and E. Stina Lyon (eds) *Gender relations in the public and the private*, London: Macmillan, pp 156-175.

Eldén, S. (2012) 'Inviting the messy: drawing methods and children's voices', *Childhood*, 20(1): 66-81.

Elliot, J. (2016) 'Why is big data important and what are the challenges for social scientists', available at www.ncrm.ac.uk/news/show.php?article=5489.

Fox, J. and Jones, D. (2013) 'Migration, everyday life and the ethnicity bias', *Ethnicities*, 13(4): 385-400.

Gabb, J. (2008) *Researching intimacy in families*, Basingstoke: Palgrave Macmillan.

Gabb, J. and Fink, J. (2015) 'Telling moments and everyday experience: multiple methods research on couple relationships and personal lives', *Sociology*, 49(5): 970-987.

Halford, S., Pope, C. and Weal, M. (2013) 'Digital futures? Sociological challenges and opportunities in the emergent semantic web, *Sociology*, 47(1): 173-89.

Kilkey, M. and Clarke, H. (2010) 'Disabled men and fathering: opportunities and constraints', *Community, Work & Family*, 13(2): 127-146.

Kilkey, M., Plomien, A. and Perrons, D. (2014) 'Migrant men's fathering narratives, practices and projects in national and transnational spaces: recent Polish male migrants to London', International Migration, 52(1): 178-191.

Kitchin, R. and McArdle, G. (2016) 'What makes big data, big data? Exploring the ontological chacteristics of 26 datasets', *Big Data & Society*, 3: 1-10.

Klinth, R. (2008) 'The best of both worlds? Fatherhood and gender equality in Swedish paternity leave campaigns, 1976-2006' *Fathering*, 6(1): 20-38.

Laney, D. (2001) *3D data management: Controlling data volume, velocity and variety*, Meta Group Research Note 6, Stamford, CT: META Group.

Lau-Clayton, C. (2016) 'The lives of young fathers: a review of selected evidence', *Social Policy and Society*, 15(1): 129-140.

Lupton, D. (2016) 'Pregnancy apps and gender stereotypes', This Sociological Life blog, available at https://simplysociology.wordpress.com/2016/03/10/pregnancy-apps-and-gender-stereotypes.

Lupton, D., Pedersen, S. and Thomas, G.M. (2016) 'Parenting and digital media: from the early web to contemporary digital society', *Sociology Compass*, 10(8): 730-743.

Muir, S. and Mason, J. (2012) 'Capturing Christmas: the sensory potential of data from participant produced video', *Sociological Research Online*, 17(1), available at www.socresonline.org.uk/17/1/5.html

Norman, H. (2017) 'Paternal involvement in childcare: how can it be classified and what are the key influences', *Families, Relationships and Societies*, 6(1): 89-105.

Osborne, T. and Rose, N. (1999) 'Do the social sciences create phenomena? The example of public opinion research', *British Journal of Sociology*, 50(3): 367-396.

Prividera, L.C. and Howard, J.W. (2015) 'Soldiers and fathers: archetypal media representations of service, family, and parenting' in L. Tropp and J. Kelly (eds) *Deconstructing dads: Changing images of fathers in popular culture*, Lanham, MD: Lexington Books, pp 51-76.

Ruppert, E., Law, J. and Savage, M. (2013) 'Reassembling social science methods: the challenge of digital devices', *Theory, Culture & Society*, 30(4): 22-46.

Salway, S., Chowbey, P. and Clarke, L. (2009) *Parenting in modern Britain: Understanding the experiences of Asian fathers*, York: Joseph Rowntree Foundation.

Savage, M. and Burrows, R. (2007) 'The coming crisis of empirical sociology', *Sociology*, 41(5): 885-899.

Smart, C., Davies, K., Heaphy, B. and Mason, J. (2012) 'Difficult friendships and ontological security', *The Sociological Review*, 60(1): 91-109.

Smith Koslowski, A. (2011) 'Working fathers in Europe: earning and caring', *European Sociological Review*, 27(2): 230-245.

Tan, T-T. (2017) 'Changing practices on fatherhood in postmodern Sweden', *Journal of Literature and Art Studies*, 7(5): 608-620.

Thrift, N. (2005) *Knowing capitalism*, London: Sage Publications.

Tinati, R., Halford, S., Carr, L. and Pope, C. (2014) 'Big data: methodological challenges and approaches for sociological analysis', *Sociology*, 48(4): 663-681.

Watts, D.J. (2007) 'A twenty-first century science', *Nature*, 445: 489.

Westerling, A. (2016) 'Parenting together apart: parenthood and we-ness in everyday life', in A. Sparrman, A. Westerling, J. Lind and K. Ida Dannesbo (eds) *Doing good parenthood: Ideals and practices of parental involvement*, Basingstoke: Palgrave Macmillan, pp 127-136.

Yoshida, H. and Smith, L.B. (2008) 'What's in view for toddlers? Using a head camera to study visual experience', *Infancy*, 13(3): 229-248.

Index